COLLINS CHEERFUL COOKING

BUDGET RECIPES

© Wm. Collins Sons & Co. Ltd. 1973
First published 1973
ISBN 0 00 435269 6

Devised, edited and designed by Youé & Spooner Ltd.

Printed in Great Britain by Collins Clear-Type Press

The Publishers gratefully acknowledge
the help given by Allders of Croydon
in supplying china and hardware for
use in the colour pictures

COLLINS CHEERFUL COOKING

BUDGET RECIPES

CAROL WRIGHT

COLLINS
LONDON & GLASGOW

Useful weights and measures

WEIGHT EQUIVALENTS

Avoirdupois		Metric
1 ounce	=	28·35 grammes
1 pound	=	453·6 grammes
2·3 pounds	=	1 kilogram

LIQUID MEASUREMENTS

$\frac{1}{4}$ pint	=	1$\frac{1}{2}$ decilitres
$\frac{1}{2}$ pint	=	$\frac{1}{4}$ litre
scant 1 pint	=	$\frac{1}{2}$ litre
1$\frac{3}{4}$ pints	=	1 litre
1 gallon	=	4·5 litres

HANDY LIQUID MEASURES

1 pint	=	20 fluid ounces	=	32 tablespoons
$\frac{1}{2}$ pint	=	10 fluid ounces	=	16 tablespoons
$\frac{1}{4}$ pint	=	5 fluid ounces	=	8 tablespoons
$\frac{1}{8}$ pint	=	2$\frac{1}{2}$ fluid ounces	=	4 tablespoons
$\frac{1}{16}$ pint	=	1$\frac{1}{4}$ fluid ounces	=	2 tablespoons

HANDY SOLID MEASURES

			Approximate
Almonds, ground	1 oz.	=	3$\frac{3}{4}$ level tablespoons
Arrowroot	1 oz.	=	4 level tablespoons
Breadcrumbs fresh	1 oz.	=	7 level tablespoons
dried	1 oz.	=	3$\frac{1}{4}$ level tablespoons
Butter and Lard	1 oz.	=	2 level tablespoons
Cheese, grated	1 oz.	=	3$\frac{1}{2}$ level tablespoons
Chocolate, grated	1 oz.	=	3 level tablespoons
Cocoa	1 oz.	=	2$\frac{3}{4}$ level tablespoons
Desiccated Coconut	1 oz.	=	4$\frac{1}{2}$ tablespoons
Coffee—Instant	1 oz.	=	4 level tablespoons
Ground	1 oz.	=	4 tablespoons
Cornflour	1 oz.	=	2$\frac{1}{2}$ tablespoons
Custard powder	1 oz.	=	2$\frac{1}{2}$ tablespoons
Curry Powder and Spices	1 oz.	=	5 tablespoons
Flour	1 oz.	=	2 level tablespoons
Gelatine, powdered	1 oz.	=	2$\frac{1}{2}$ tablespoons
Rice, uncooked	1 oz.	=	1$\frac{1}{2}$ tablespoons
Sugar, caster and granulated	1 oz.	=	2 tablespoons
Icing sugar	1 oz.	=	2$\frac{1}{2}$ tablespoons
Syrup	1 oz.	=	1 tablespoon
Yeast, granulated	1 oz.	=	1 level tablespoon

AMERICAN MEASURES

16	fluid ounces	=	1 American pint
8	fluid ounces	=	1 American standard cup
0·50	fluid ounces	=	1 American tablespoon *(slightly smaller than British Standards Institute tablespoon)*
0·16	fluid ounces	=	1 American teaspoon

AUSTRALIAN MEASURES
(Cup, Spoon and Liquid Measures)

These are the measures in everyday use in the Australian family kitchen. The spoon measures listed below are from the ordinary household cutlery set.

CUP MEASURES

(Using the 8-liquid-ounce cup measure)

1 cup flour	4 oz.
1 cup sugar *(crystal or caster)*	8 oz.
1 cup icing sugar *(free from lumps)*	5 oz.
1 cup shortening *(butter, margarine, etc.)*	8 oz.
1 cup honey, golden syrup, treacle	10 oz.
1 cup brown sugar *(lightly packed)*	4 oz.
1 cup brown sugar *(tightly packed)*	5 oz.
1 cup soft breadcrumbs	2 oz.
1 cup dry breadcrumbs *(made from fresh breadcrumbs)*	3 oz.
1 cup packet dry breadcrumbs	4 oz.
1 cup rice *(uncooked)*	6 oz.
1 cup rice *(cooked)*	5 oz.
1 cup mixed fruit or individual fruit such as sultanas, etc.	4 oz.
1 cup grated cheese	4 oz.
1 cup nuts *(chopped)*	4 oz.
1 cup coconut	2$\frac{1}{2}$ oz.

SPOON MEASURES

	Level Tablespoon
1 oz. flour	2
1 oz. sugar *(crystal or caster)*	1$\frac{1}{2}$
1 oz. icing sugar *(free from lumps)*	2
1 oz. shortening	1
1 oz. honey	1
1 oz. gelatine	2
1 oz. cocoa	3
1 oz. cornflour	2$\frac{1}{2}$
1 oz. custard powder	2$\frac{1}{2}$

LIQUID MEASURES

(Using 8-liquid-ounce cup)

1 cup liquid	8 oz
2$\frac{1}{2}$ cups liquid	20 oz. (1 pint)
2 tablespoons liquid	1 oz.
1 gill liquid	5 oz. ($\frac{1}{4}$ pint)

Metric equivalents and oven temperatures are not listed here as they are included in all the recipes throughout the book.

When using the metric measures, in some cases it may be necessary to cut down the amount of liquid used. This is in order to achieve a balanced recipe and the correct consistency, as 1oz equals, in fact, 28·35gm.

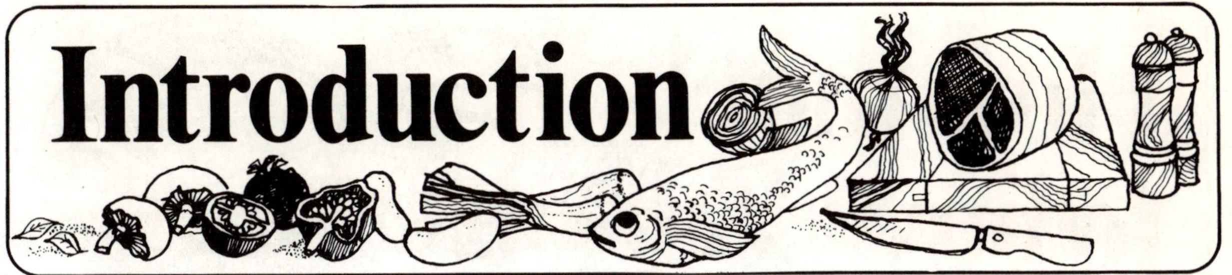

Introduction

Mrs Beeton was a cookery writer now noted for the prodigality of her 'take a dozen eggs'. In fact she was a careful cook with a resolute eye on her budget. She said: 'Frugality and economy are home virtues without which no household can prosper. We must always remember that it is a great merit in housekeeping to manage a little well'.

Managing a little well needs watchfulness in shopping, taking advantage of lower prices when seasonal gluts occur and using cheaper foods to substitute or stretch more expensive items. Use of vegetables is healthy and can make meat go further. The cook on a budget should learn the use of herbs and spices, sauces and flavourings, so that her dishes are always exciting if not costly. It's sense to build up a storecupboard of flavourings as you can afford them, and grow your own herbs even in a flower pot or window box.

Remember it is ideas not income that create a good table. Since the need of the budget cook is mainly variations on basic foods to give versatility to meals, I have arranged the recipes under the basic food types so that the reader can select ideas from the foods she can afford.

Budget cooking isn't managing on no money, it is shopping wisely and then being able to present foodstuffs in many different ways, avoiding too much stodge and repetition. Many of the recipes I have learnt through a love of entertaining and not always being able to afford lavish, luxurious foods. I hope this book will help cooks invite as many friends as they wish to impressive meals without worrying about cutting back for the rest of the week.

How much to buy

A basic rule of economical cookery is not to buy too much and serve too big a portion that will only be wasted. Sometimes frozen foods are in fact more economical than fresh items since there is no waste. But the housewife must relate this to seasonal price fluctuations in fresh goods and whether she can afford the time to prepare fresh foods correctly.

MEAT
Amount per person
Frying or grilling steak: 6oz (150gm).
Roast meat with bone: 8oz (200gm).
Roast meat without bone: 5–6oz (125–150gm).
Cold meat: 3oz (75gm).
Minced meat: 4oz (100gm).
Cutlets: 2.
Chops: 1.
Stewing meat with bone: 6–8oz (150–200gm).
Stewing meat without bone: 4–5oz (100–125gm).
Liver: 4–6oz (100–150gm).
Roast chicken: 12oz (300gm).
Chicken for made-up dishes: 4–8oz (100–200gm).

The cheaper cuts of meat
Beef
Shin, chuck or shoulder steak. Leg for stewing, braising, pies or puddings. Brisket, topside or top rump (thick flank) for pot roasting. Silverside.

Lamb
Best end of neck for roasts. Middle neck and scrag are cheaper for casseroles and stews. Breast of lamb is a very cheap roast.

Pork
Belly of pork is low priced for roasting and boiling. Hand of pork is a good cheap boiling joint.

Gammon
Slipper, hock and collar are the cheapest gammon joints.

Sausages
Beef sausages are cheaper than pork.

Offal
Ox and pig's liver are cheaper than calf's or lamb's liver and, soaked an hour before use, they are just as good. One ox heart makes enough stew for four people. Kidneys, tripe, pig's or sheep's trotters and oxtail are all good buys.

Poultry
Buy a young bird as this has a pliable breastbone which becomes rigid in older birds.

FISH
Amounts per person
1lb 12oz (700gm) fresh fish equals the same amount in a 13oz (325gm) frozen pack.
Fresh fish with much bone: 6–8oz (150–200gm).
Fresh fish with little bone: 3–4oz (75–100gm).
For made-up dishes: 2–3oz (50–75gm).

Value-for-money varieties of fish
These include herring, mackerel, bass, bream, grey mullet and whiting. Fish roes cost little for breakfast or supper dishes. Smoked fish is economical as it has a stronger taste and therefore a little can be made to go a long way. Coley, often bought for cats, is excellent, and half the price of cod. Fish should be bright in colour and firm fleshed, not dull or limp.

VEGETABLES
Amounts per person
Runner beans: 6oz (150gm).
Brussels sprouts: 6oz (150gm).
Carrots: 4–6oz (100–150gm).
Cabbage: 8oz (200gm).
Onions: 6oz (150gm).
Peas: 8oz (200gm), fresh, 2oz (50gm), dried.
Potatoes: 6–8oz (150–200gm).
Spinach: 8oz (200gm).

MISCELLANEOUS

Fruit
For pies and puddings or stewed: 4–5oz (100–125gm) per person.
Rice
2oz (50gm) per person.
Macaroni
1½oz (37gm) per person.
Spaghetti
2oz (50gm) per person.
Soup
¾ pint (375ml) each serving.
Sauces and gravies
⅛ pint (63ml) per person.
Cheese
At a cheese party 3oz (75gm) per head.
Firm Cheddar types are the most economical. Shops sometimes grate trimmings from pre-packing and sell them cheaply.
Bread
Standard loaves are comparatively cheaper than smaller, fancy-shaped loaves.

DRINKS FOR PARTIES
¼ bottle of wine per person.
One bottle of sherry serves 16 glasses.
One bottle of gin serves 25 glasses (similarly a bottle of fruit juice).
Estimate 5–6 glasses of wine from one bottle.

Meat

Meat is one of the most expensive items on the housewife's shopping list but there are plenty of ways of stretching it, and it pays to know the cheaper cuts.

PEPPERPOT SOUP
Serves 6

A sustaining soup for cold days that is a meal in itself with bread and cheese.

1lb (½ kilo) shin or skirt of beef
4 tablespoons Worcestershire sauce
2 level teaspoons salt
2½ pints (approximately 1¼ litres) water
2 onions, chopped
2 carrots, quartered
3 sticks celery, sliced
bouquet garni
2oz (50gm) tomato purée
2oz (50gm) pasta (spaghetti, noodles or pasta shapes)
1oz (25gm) butter
1oz (25gm) flour

1. Cut beef into 1-inch cubes.
2. Place in a bowl with Worcestershire sauce and marinate for 12 hours in a cool place, turning occasionally.
3. Place meat and sauce in a large saucepan, add salt and water and bring slowly to the boil.
4. Add vegetables, bouquet garni and tomato purée and simmer until meat and vegetables are tender, about 30 minutes.
5. Add pasta and simmer for 30 minutes more.
6. Remove bouquet garni.
7. Work butter and flour to a paste.
8. Remove soup from heat. Divide butter paste into six pieces and stir in each portion separately until dissolved.
9. Return to heat and simmer for 5 minutes.

POTTED BEEF
Serves 4

A pressed meat recipe using a cheap meat cut which can be made in advance for a picnic.

1lb (½ kilo) shin of beef
2 bayleaves
2 cloves
pinch of mace
2 tablespoons water
3oz (75gm) butter
salt and pepper

1. Preheat oven to cool, 300 deg F or gas 2 (150 deg C).
2. Cut meat into small pieces, removing fat and gristle.
3. Place in an ovenproof dish with herbs and water. Cover closely with buttered paper and kitchen foil, all tucked well round the sides and bake in centre of oven for 3–3½ hours till the meat is very tender.
4. Lift out bayleaves and cloves.
5. Put meat twice through the mincer, beat well with the juices and nearly all the butter. Add salt and pepper if required.
6. Press meat in a basin, cover with a layer of melted butter.
7. Store in a cool place.

BROWN ALE BEEF BAKE
Serves 4

1¼lb (500gm) chuck steak
2oz (50gm) beef dripping
8oz (200gm) onions, thinly sliced
4oz (100gm) mushrooms, thickly sliced
1oz (25gm) flour
½ pint (250ml) brown ale
stock or water as required
salt and black pepper
thickly sliced bread
made mustard
3oz (75gm) butter
4oz (100gm) Cheddar cheese, finely grated

1. Preheat oven to very moderate, 325 deg F or gas 3 (170 deg C).
2. Cut the steak into cubes, removing skin and fat. Brown in hot fat in saucepan, then remove from pan.
3. Fry onions and mushrooms.
4. Draw pan from heat, stir in enough flour to absorb fat. Fry over brisk heat, stirring well till browned.
5. Remove from heat, stir in ale slowly. Bring to simmering point and thin as required with stock or water. Season well.
6. Add the meat, then transfer to covered casserole and cook in centre of oven for 1½ hours.
7. For the topping, spread slices of bread lightly with mustard. Cream butter with cheese and a pinch of salt.
8. Spread thickly on one side of bread. Place slices of bread cheese side up on top of stew. Return casserole to oven at moderate to moderately hot, 375 deg F or gas 5 (190 deg C) and bake without lid for a further 15–20 minutes, or till meat is tender and topping crisp and golden.

WINTER BEEF CASSEROLE
(Illustrated on page 17)
Serves 6

2lb (1 kilo) stewing steak, cut in
2-inch pieces
2oz (50gm) flour, seasoned with
salt and pepper
2 tablespoons cooking oil
1lb (½ kilo) leeks, sliced
1 small head of celery, cut in
1-inch pieces
8oz (200gm) carrots, sliced
½ pint (250ml) beer
½ pint (250ml) beef stock
8oz (200gm) self-raising flour
½ level teaspoon salt
1oz (25gm) butter
1½ level teaspoons dried basil
1½oz (37gm) Parmesan cheese,
grated
1½oz (37gm) Cheddar cheese,
grated
¼ pint (125ml) milk

1. Preheat oven to moderate, 350
deg F or gas 4 (180 deg C).
2. Coat steak with seasoned flour.
3. Heat oil in a frying pan, add
meat and fry until brown on all
sides.
4. Add vegetables and cook for a
further 2–3 minutes.
5. Stir in any remaining flour
from the meat. Pour in beer and
stock and bring to the boil.
6. Transfer to a 3-pint
(approximately 1½-litre) casserole,
cover and cook in centre of oven
for about 1½–2 hours until meat is
tender.
7. Meanwhile mix flour and salt
together and rub in butter. Mix in
basil and half the cheese.
8. About 30 minutes before
serving casserole, increase oven
heat to moderate to moderately
hot, 375 deg F or gas 5 (190 deg C).
9. Bind flour and cheese mixture
with milk, then roll out on floured
surface to ½ inch thick. Cut into
triangles.
10. Remove cover from casserole.
Adjust seasoning. Arrange scone
triangles on top. Sprinkle with
remaining cheese. Return to oven
and bake for about 15 minutes,
till golden.
11. Serve at once with green
beans.

BEEF AND APPLE STEW
Serves 4

1oz (25gm) flour
1 teaspoon dry mustard
seasoning
½ teaspoon mixed herbs
1½lb (¾ kilo) chuck steak, cut in
cubes
1oz (25gm) fat
1 onion, sliced
2 carrots, diced
1 tablespoon malt vinegar
1 garlic clove
½ pint (250ml) beef stock
1 cooking apple, chopped

1. Preheat oven to moderate, 350
deg F or gas 4 (180 deg C).
2. Mix flour, mustard and
seasoning together with the herbs.
Coat meat in the flour mixture.
3. Fry meat in hot fat, remove and
fry onion and carrots till golden.
4. Remove vegetables and add
vinegar and garlic. Cook till
vinegar has almost evaporated.
Add stock.
5. Place meat, vegetables and
peeled, chopped apple in a
casserole, pour over the stock and
vinegar liquid.
6. Cover with a close fitting lid
and cook in centre of oven for
about 2 hours till meat is tender.

BOILED BEEF AND CARROTS
Serves 4–6

2–3lb (1–1½ kilo) salted silverside
1½ pints (approximately ¾ litre)
cold water
3 onions
12 peppercorns
1 bayleaf
1 meat stock cube
8oz (200gm) small carrots
4oz (100gm) self-raising flour
¼ teaspoon salt
½ level teaspoon baking powder
2oz (50gm) shredded beef suet
⅛ pint (63ml) cold water to mix

1. Soak meat in cold water for 3
hours or overnight.
2. Put in large saucepan and
cover with fresh cold water.
3. Add onions, peppercorns,
bayleaf and crumbled meat cube.
4. Bring to the boil and simmer
gently for 2–3 hours.
5. Add carrots in the last hour of
cooking.
6. Meanwhile make the
dumplings by sifting flour, salt
and baking powder in a bowl.
7. Add suet and mix lightly. Add
water and mix to a soft paste.
8. Turn out on a floured board.
Knead until smooth and roll out
to ⅛ inch thick.
9. Divide into eight portions,
shape into dumplings and add to
the meat 20 minutes before
serving.

BRAISED BRISKET WITH ONIONS
Serves 6–8

Onion stuffing goes well with economical beef brisket for a weekend family meal.

3 streaky bacon rashers, chopped
4 onion cores, chopped
½oz (12gm) breadcrumbs
salt and pepper
1oz (25gm) butter, melted
4 large onions, cored
3lb (1½ kilo) rolled beef brisket
1oz (25gm) dripping

1. Preheat oven to hot, 450 deg F or gas 8 (230 deg C).
2. Mix together bacon, onion, breadcrumbs, salt, pepper and butter and fill onion centres.
3. Place remaining stuffing in spaces in brisket.
4. Make sure the joint is well tied, then brown all sides in hot dripping in a heavy pan.
5. Remove and wrap in two thicknesses of kitchen foil, sealing edges firmly.
6. Place in dry meat tin in centre of oven for about 2 hours.
7. Add onions for the final 40 minutes placing on a lower shelf.
8. Serve meat with onions and juices from foil.

FRIKADELLER
Serves 4

1lb (½ kilo) potatoes, peeled and grated
1lb (½ kilo) minced beef
1 egg
1 teaspoon Worcestershire sauce
1 medium onion, peeled and grated
salt and pepper
1oz (25gm) dripping
2–3 spring onions, cut into pieces

1. Pour off any excess water from potatoes.
2. Add meat, then mix in egg, Worcestershire sauce, grated onion, salt and pepper.
3. Fry in dripping in the shape of a flat scone until browned underneath. Mark into four sections and turn over halfway during the cooking.
4. Garnish with spring onions and serve.

BUDGET PIE WITH YOGURT TOPPING
Serves 4–5

Yogurt gives minced beef leftovers a dinner-party dress.

1 teaspoon oil
½oz (12gm) butter
1 medium onion, chopped
8oz (200gm) cooked beef, minced
½ teaspoon bouquet garni
2 tablespoons tomato purée
1 teaspoon Worcestershire sauce
1lb (½ kilo) potatoes, cooked
8oz (200gm) tomatoes
8oz (200gm) sweetcorn
salt and pepper
1 egg
1oz (25gm) flour
1 carton (5oz or 125gm) natural yogurt

1. Preheat oven to moderate to moderately hot, 375 deg F or gas 5 (190 deg C).
2. Warm oil and butter in pan. Add onion and cook gently. Add meat, bouquet garni, tomato purée and Worcestershire sauce.
3. Meanwhile cut potatoes into ¼-inch slices. Slice tomatoes.
4. Using a deep, 8-inch (20cm) casserole, put a layer of potato at the bottom, then layers of onion, tomato, meat and sweetcorn, seasoning between the layers. Repeat, finishing with a layer of potato. Cover.
5. Bake in centre of oven for 30 minutes.
6. For the topping, blend together egg and flour. Stir in yogurt and season to taste.
7. Remove pie from oven, pour topping over and bake for a further 30 minutes.

SALISBURY STEAKS
Serves 6

1lb (½ kilo) minced beef
8oz (200gm) sausagemeat
4oz (100gm) boiled long-grain rice (raw weight)
salt and pepper
1 egg, well beaten
1½ pints (approximately ¾ litre) water
1 packet (½ pint or 250ml) onion soup mix
1oz (25gm) flour

1. Preheat oven to hot, 450 deg F or gas 8 (230 deg C).
2. Combine beef, sausagemeat, rice, seasoning and egg. Mix well.
3. Form into 6-inch 'steaks', then place in baking dish or shallow casserole and bake for 20 minutes.
4. Meanwhile heat 1¼ pints (625ml) water. Add onion soup mix and cook in covered pan for 10 minutes.
5. Mix flour with remaining ¼ pint (125ml) water till smooth. Stir into soup gradually.
6. Cook, stirring until thickened.
7. Pour gravy over 'steaks' and bake for a further 20 minutes.

MEATBALLS WITH CREAMED CUCUMBER
Serves 4

1 large cucumber
½ pint (250ml) white sauce, well seasoned (see Basic recipes, page 100)
12oz (300gm) raw minced beef
6oz (150gm) parsley and thyme stuffing mix
1 egg
1½oz (37gm) flour, seasoned with salt and pepper
2oz (50gm) lard

1. Peel and dice the cucumber and cook it in boiling, salted water until tender.
2. Drain and add half a teacupful of the cucumber liquid to the white sauce. Stir in the cucumber.
3. While the cucumber is cooking, mix the beef, stuffing mixture and egg well together and form into small balls.
4. Coat each with seasoned flour and fry gently in lard till brown all over.
5. Serve with the creamed cucumber.

APPLE AND CHEESE BEEFBURGER SUPPER
Serves 4–6

1 small onion, finely chopped
1lb ($\frac{1}{2}$ kilo) minced beef
4 tablespoons tomato pickle
2 egg yolks
salt and pepper
**1 large cauliflower, prepared
and washed**
**$\frac{1}{2}$ pint (250ml) white sauce (see
Basic recipes, page 100)**
**1 can (4$\frac{1}{2}$oz or 112gm) strained
apple**
5oz (125gm) cheese, grated
pinch of cayenne pepper
fat for shallow frying
4 tomatoes, sliced

1. Mix together onion, minced
beef and tomato pickle and bind
with egg yolks. Season with salt
and pepper.
2. Form into 12 beefburgers and
leave in a cool place for 1 hour
before frying.
3. Cook cauliflower in boiling,
salted water for 25–30 minutes.
4. Make white sauce and add
apple and cheese. Season with
salt, pepper and cayenne pepper
and keep warm.
5. Fry beefburgers in fat for 8–10
minutes on each side.
6. Place cauliflower in centre of
serving dish and pour hot sauce
over. Arrange beefburgers around
cauliflower and top each one with
a slice of tomato.

BURGER PIE
Serves 4

**1lb ($\frac{1}{2}$ kilo) potatoes, peeled and
grated**
1lb ($\frac{1}{2}$ kilo) lean minced beef
**1 large onion, peeled and
chopped**
1 can (8oz or 200gm) tomatoes
**1–2 tablespoons chopped
parsley**
salt and pepper

1. Preheat oven to moderate, 350
deg F or gas 4 (180 deg C).
2. Drain off excess moisture from
potatoes.
3. Mix rest of ingredients
together, season well and turn
into a greased shallow pie dish.
4. Bake in centre of oven for 1$\frac{1}{4}$–
1$\frac{1}{2}$ hours.
5. Serve hot or cold with a green
salad.

MINCED BEEF MICHELE
Serves 4

1oz (25gm) dripping
1 onion, minced
1$\frac{1}{2}$lb ($\frac{3}{4}$ kilo) minced beef
$\frac{1}{4}$ pint (125ml) brown ale
$\frac{1}{4}$ pint (125ml) water
1 tablespoon tomato chutney
salt and pepper
1 bayleaf
**8oz (200gm) carrots, cooked
and diced**
2 hard-boiled eggs, diced
1$\frac{1}{2}$oz (37gm) dried breadcrumbs
3oz (75gm) butter, melted

1. Heat dripping in a pan. Cook
onion in it till lightly browned.
2. Add meat, brown ale, water
and tomato chutney mixed
together. Season with salt, pepper
and bayleaf.
3. Simmer for 20 minutes.
4. Remove bayleaf. Turn meat
into a warmed serving dish and
keep hot.
5. Mix carrots and eggs.
6. Fry breadcrumbs in melted
butter and when golden brown,
mix them with the carrot and egg.
7. Top the dish with this mixture
and serve at once.

SALAD LOAF
Serves 4

1lb ($\frac{1}{2}$ kilo) raw potatoes, grated
1lb ($\frac{1}{2}$ kilo) minced beef
1oz (25gm) tomato chutney
1 egg, beaten
salt and pepper
Worcestershire sauce to taste

1. Preheat oven to moderate to
moderately hot, 375 deg F or gas 5
(190 deg C).
2. Well grease a 1-lb ($\frac{1}{2}$-kilo) loaf
tin.
3. Mix potatoes, beef and chutney
together. Bind with egg and add
seasoning and sauce to taste.
4. Turn into the loaf tin and bake
for 1–1$\frac{1}{4}$ hours.
5. Serve hot or cold.

BAKED SAVOURY ROLL
Serves 4

1 large onion
1oz (25gm) fat
12oz (300gm) raw minced beef
1oz (25gm) flour
$\frac{1}{4}$ pint (125ml) beef stock
large pinch of salt
small pinch of pepper
2 tomatoes
**shortcrust pastry made with
8oz (200gm) flour (see Basic
recipes, page 100)**
1 egg, beaten

1. Preheat oven to moderately
hot, 400 deg F or gas 6 (200 deg C).
2. Peel and chop onion and fry
for about 4 minutes in melted fat.
3. Stir in minced beef and fry
until all the particles have
separated.
4. Sprinkle in the flour and cook
for about 3 minutes, then stir in
stock, salt and pepper.
5. Bring to the boil and add
peeled and sliced tomatoes, then
put aside to cool.
6. Make pastry and roll to about
12 inches by 8 inches. Cut off 1
inch from long side and make into
pastry leaves.
7. Brush edges with beaten egg.
8. Spread filling in centre of
pastry and roll up.
9. Carefully transfer to ovenware
dish, brush with egg and decorate
with pastry leaves.
10. Bake in centre of oven for 40
minutes. Reduce heat after 20
minutes' cooking time to
moderate, 350 deg F or gas 4 (180
deg C). Cover with foil and bake
for a further 20 minutes.
11. Serve with a brown gravy,
sprouts, cabbage or leeks.

CORNED BEEF PIE
Serves 6

shortcrust pastry made with
8oz (200gm) flour (see Basic
recipes, page 100)
2 cans (12oz or 300gm each)
corned beef
6oz (150gm) onion, diced
1 tablespoon oil
½ teaspoon salt
freshly ground black pepper
1 teaspoon Tabasco sauce
1 egg
4oz (100gm) carrots, cooked
4oz (100gm) peas

1. Preheat oven to moderately
hot, 400 deg F or gas 6 (200 deg C).
2. Roll out half the pastry and
line a pie dish.
3. Mash up corned beef with a
fork.
4. Fry onion in oil till soft and
transparent.
5. Mix with the corned beef, then
add salt, pepper, Tabasco, egg,
diced carrot and peas.
6. When well mixed, place
mixture in pastry-lined pie dish.
7. Roll out remaining pastry to
make a covering. Damp the pastry
rim and seal to the lid.
8. Cook in centre of oven for
about 30 minutes. Serve hot or
cold.

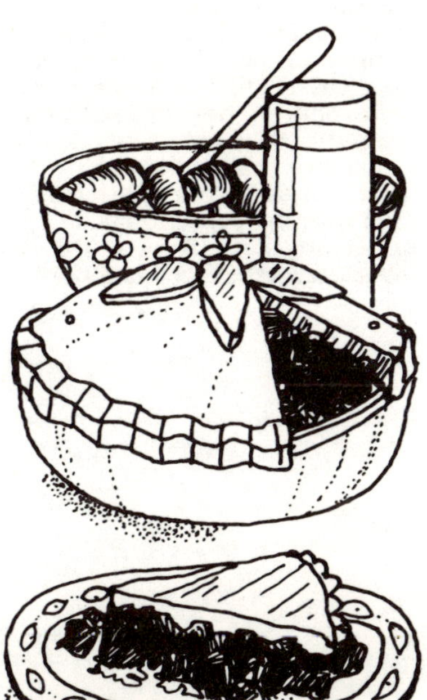

CORNED BEEF AND CHEESE SUPPER
Serves 4

1 large onion, thinly sliced
1 tablespoon oil
1oz (25gm) butter
4oz (100gm) button mushrooms,
sliced
1 can (12oz or 300gm) corned
beef, chilled and cubed
1lb (½ kilo) potatoes, boiled and
diced
1 packet (8oz or 200gm) frozen
green beans, cooked
1 can (5½oz or 137gm)
evaporated milk
1oz (25gm) flour
1 teaspoon dry mustard
1oz (25gm) butter
salt and pepper
4oz (100gm) Cheddar cheese,
grated

1. Fry onion gently in oil and
butter till soft but not brown.
2. Add mushrooms and fry for 2–3
minutes.
3. Stir in the corned beef,
potatoes and green beans. Keep
hot.
4. Make evaporated milk up to ½
pint (250ml) with water and whisk
in flour and mustard.
5. Place in a small saucepan with
the butter and stir over a
moderate heat until the sauce
thickens. Continue to cook,
stirring for a further 2 minutes.
6. Remove from the heat and add
salt, pepper and 3oz (75gm)
cheese.
7. Beat well until cheese melts
and blends.
8. Place corned beef mixture in a
casserole and cover with cheese
sauce. Sprinkle with remaining
cheese and place under grill to
brown.

CORNED BEEF HASH
Serves 4

12oz (300gm) potato, cooked
and diced
2 small onions, chopped
2 cans (12oz or 300gm each)
corned beef, cubed
¼ pint (125ml) beef stock
salt
½ teaspoon Tabasco sauce
1oz (25gm) butter

1. Mix together potato, onions,
corned beef, stock, salt and
Tabasco.
2. Melt butter and spread corned
beef mixture in the pan evenly.
3. Cook slowly until browned on
the bottom.

CORNED BEEF SAVOURY
Serves 4

2 cans (7oz or 175gm) corned
beef
1 large onion
1 tablespoon oil
1 green pepper, sliced and
blanched
8oz (200gm) tomatoes, sliced
salt and pepper
1oz (25gm) butter
1oz (25gm) flour
1 can (3oz or 75gm) evaporated
milk
pinch of mustard powder
4oz (100gm) Cheddar cheese,
grated
8oz (200gm) creamed potatoes

1. Preheat oven to moderately
hot, 400 deg F or gas 6 (200 deg C).
2. Slice the corned beef and onion
and fry onion in oil until soft.
3. Prepare green pepper and
tomatoes and layer with corned
beef and seasoning in a fireproof
dish.
4. Place butter, flour and
evaporated milk made up to ½ pint
(250ml) with water, in a pan.
Heat, stirring well, until
thickened.
5. Add seasoning, mustard and
3oz (75gm) cheese.
6. Pour over the beef and sprinkle
with remaining cheese.
7. Pipe a border of potatoes and
place in centre of oven for 20–25
minutes, or until golden brown.

BREAST OF LAMB WITH APRICOT STUFFING
Serves 4–6

2 breasts of lamb, boned
4oz (100gm) dried apricots
4oz (100gm) seedless raisins
4oz (100gm) white breadcrumbs
1 level teaspoon salt
3oz (75gm) butter, melted

1. Preheat oven to moderate to moderately hot, 375 deg F or gas 5 (190 deg C).
2. Wipe the meat and trim excess fat. Lay skin side down.
3. To make stuffing, snip apricots in small pieces and place with raisins in a saucepan. Cover with cold water, bring to the boil and strain. Add breadcrumbs and salt.
4. Pour melted butter over and blend with a fork.
5. Divide the stuffing between the lamb breasts. Spread evenly to within ½ inch of the edge.
6. Roll up and secure with string.
7. Roast for 1–1½ hours in centre of oven. Remove string and serve.

SWEET AND SOUR LAMB
Serves 4

1 breast of lamb, boned and trimmed
dripping
¼ pint (125ml) vinegar
¼ pint (125ml) stock or pineapple juice
½ teaspoon salt
2oz (50gm) brown sugar
1 medium onion, sliced
1 can (8oz or 200gm) pineapple chunks
2 tablespoons arrowroot

1. Preheat oven to moderate, 350 deg F or gas 4 (180 deg C).
2. Cut the breast of lamb in 1-inch cubes and fry gently for 3–4 minutes.
3. Place in a casserole. Combine the other ingredients, except the arrowroot and pour over the lamb.
4. Bake in centre of oven for 2 hours until tender.
5. When cooked, skim off fat and thicken sauce with arrowroot.

BRISBANE HONEYED ROAST BREAST OF LAMB
Serves 4

4oz (100gm) white breadcrumbs
2 tablespoons onion, finely chopped
1 tablespoon chopped parsley
2oz (50gm) butter
1 egg yolk
1 breast of lamb, boned
3oz (75gm) clear honey
1oz (25gm) flour, seasoned with salt and pepper

1. Preheat oven to hot, 425 deg F or gas 7 (220 deg C).
2. Mix together the breadcrumbs, onion, parsley and butter and bind with egg yolk.
3. Spread breast lightly with some of the honey and the stuffing.
4. Roll and tie securely with string.
5. Roll in seasoned flour and cook in roasting dish in centre of oven for 10 minutes.
6. Remove and spread thickly with remaining honey. Lower oven to cool, 300 deg F or gas 2 (150 deg C).
7. Return to oven and roast for 30 minutes.

LAMB ROLL
Serves 4

1 breast of lamb, boned
4 streaky bacon rashers
1 large cooking apple, peeled and sliced
½oz (12gm) brown sugar
¼ teaspoon thyme
1oz (25gm) breadcrumbs
salt and pepper

1. Preheat oven to moderate, 350 deg F or gas 4 (180 deg C).
2. Place lamb flat on a board, skin side down. Cover with bacon rashers and apple slices.
3. Sprinkle with sugar, thyme and breadcrumbs. Season.
4. Roll meat and tie firmly.
5. Put in a casserole, cover and bake for 1 hour.
6. Remove lid and continue cooking for 30 minutes.

SPRING LAMB ROAST
Serves 4–6

1oz (25gm) margarine
1 medium onion, finely chopped
1 small lemon
3½ tablespoons chopped fresh mint
6oz (150gm) fresh white breadcrumbs
1 egg
salt and pepper
2 breasts of lamb, boned and trimmed
¼ pint (125ml) vinegar
½oz (12gm) caster sugar
1oz (25gm) honey
1 teaspoon soy sauce
1 level teaspoon cornflour
¼ pint (125ml) water

1. Preheat oven to moderately hot, 400 deg F or gas 6 (200 deg C).
2. For the stuffing, melt margarine, add onion and cook gently for 5 minutes.
3. Grate lemon rind, discard pith and cut flesh into ¼-inch cubes. Add to the lemon and onion, 2 tablespoons mint, breadcrumbs, egg and seasoning. Mix well.
4. Divide stuffing between breasts of lamb and spread over meat. Roll up and secure with string. Sprinkle with salt and pepper.
5. Place in roasting dish and cook in centre of oven for 1 hour or until meat is cooked.
6. For the sauce, place vinegar, remaining mint, caster sugar, honey and soy sauce in a pan and bring to the boil. Blend cornflour with water. Stir into sauce, bring to the boil, stirring, and cook for 1 minute.
7. Remove string from lamb before serving. Pour off excess fat from roasting pan. Stir meat juices into sauce. Serve sauce separately with sliced lamb.

GLAZED LAMB'S TONGUES
Serves 4–6

6 lamb's tongues
¾ pint (375ml) beef stock
1 carrot
1 turnip
1 onion
1lb (½ kilo) potatoes
1oz (25gm) butter
1 teaspoon brown sugar
juice of half lemon

1. Soak tongues in cold, salt water for 2 hours. Dry them and put in a stew pan with beef stock and carrot, turnip and onion.
2. Simmer gently for 1½ hours.
3. Cook potatoes then drain and mash with butter.
4. Remove tongues from stock, remove skin and trim the roots. Cut tongues into two lengthways and place on a hot dish.
5. Skim any fat from stock and reduce it to a thick, syrup-like glaze. Add sugar and lemon juice and coat tongues with the glaze.
6. Arrange a border of mashed potato round the tongues and serve at once.

LAMB CUTLETS PORTUGUAISE
(Illustrated on page 17)
Serves 4

8 lamb cutlets
2–3 tablespoons cooking oil
1 medium onion
½oz (12gm) plain flour
½ pint (250ml) stock
2 teaspoons tomato purée
½ teaspoon salt
large pinch of pepper
1 teaspoon sugar
1 can (8oz or 200gm) tomatoes

1. Trim excess fat from cutlets. Fry gently on both sides in 2 tablespoons oil till just brown. Remove from pan.
2. Fry peeled and chopped onion for 3–4 minutes. Add rest of oil and stir in flour. Cook till well browned.
3. Mix stock and purée with salt, pepper and sugar. Add to flour mixture, stirring until it boils and thickens.
4. Cut tomatoes in small pieces. Add to sauce and simmer.
5. Return cutlets to pan. Cover with lid and simmer for 10 minutes till cooked.
6. Serve with creamed potatoes.

TOMATO HOTPOT
Serves 4

1½–2lb (¾–1 kilo) potatoes, peeled
1 onion, peeled and sliced
12oz (300gm) tomatoes, skinned and sliced
salt and pepper
4 middle neck lamb chops
1oz (25gm) flour, seasoned with salt and pepper
pinch of rosemary or mixed herbs
butter or oil
½ pint (250ml) cider

1. Preheat oven to moderate to moderately hot, 375 deg F or gas 5 (190 deg C).
2. Slice half the potatoes; place in a fireproof dish.
3. Add onions and half the tomatoes. Season with salt and pepper.
4. Coat chops with seasoned flour, add to the dish and cover with remaining tomatoes. Add rosemary or mixed herbs.
5. Cut remaining potatoes into thick slices and place on top. Brush with melted butter or oil, season well and pour cider over.
6. Bake in centre of oven without a lid for 2 hours.

NAVARIN OF LAMB
Serves 4

1½lb (¾ kilo) neck, shoulder or breast of lamb
2oz (50gm) butter
2 onions, sliced
2oz (50gm) flour
2 stock cubes
1 pint (approximately ½ litre) hot water
salt and pepper
1 bayleaf
1 garlic clove, chopped
6 new potatoes
6 small carrots
2 small turnips
8oz (200gm) peas

1. Preheat oven to very moderate, 325 deg F or gas 3 (170 deg C).
2. Cut meat into pieces.
3. Melt butter and fry meat and onions till browned.
4. Remove, stir flour into the fat, add stock cubes and water and bring to the boil. Stir till sauce thickens.
5. Replace meat and onions in sauce and season well, adding bayleaf and garlic. Cover and cook in centre of oven for 2 hours.
6. Add potatoes, carrots and turnips and cook for a further 40 minutes.
7. Add peas and continue cooking till meat is tender.

ARIEN LAMB WITH PRUNES
Serves 4–6

Casseroled cutlets spiced with prunes and redcurrant jelly.

**2oz (50gm) butter
1 medium onion, chopped
12 best end neck of lamb cutlets
1½ level tablespoons plain flour
1 level teaspoon ground ginger
½ level teaspoon cinnamon
¾ pint (375ml) beef stock
salt and pepper
2 level tablespoons redcurrant jelly
8oz (200gm) prunes, soaked overnight, halved and stoned
2 tablespoons double cream (optional)**

1. Preheat oven to moderate, 350 deg F or gas 4 (180 deg C).
2. Melt 1½oz (37gm) butter in large frying pan. Add onion and fry for 2–3 minutes.
3. Trim excess fat from cutlets. Coat with flour mixed with ginger and cinnamon and add to pan. Brown on both sides.
4. Transfer cutlets and onion to a casserole. Stir remaining butter, flour and spices into juices in pan and cook for 1 minute.
5. Remove from heat. Stir in stock gradually.
6. Return to heat, bring to the boil, stirring, season and pour over meat in casserole.
7. Cover and cook in centre of oven for about 1 hour.
8. Stir in redcurrant jelly and prunes and cook for a further 15 minutes. If liked, stir in cream just before serving.

LAMB CUTLETS SUZANNE
Serves 6

A cold cheesy cutlet dish for summer meals.

**12 lamb cutlets
2 teaspoons mustard
2 teaspoons soy sauce (optional)
1 small garlic clove, crushed
½ teaspoon ground rosemary
2 teaspoons olive oil
8oz (200gm) cheese, grated
2 eggs
4oz (100gm) breadcrumbs
fat for frying**

1. Trim cutlets.
2. Mix together the mustard, soy sauce, garlic, rosemary, olive oil, half the cheese, and eggs, and coat cutlets with the mixture.
3. Coat with remaining cheese and breadcrumbs mixed, and fry in deep fat for 4–5 minutes, or shallow fat for 7–10 minutes, depending on thickness of meat.
4. Drain on absorbent paper, and serve cold.

LAMBCORN CUTLETS
Serves 4

**8 best end neck of lamb cutlets
flour
1 egg, beaten
2oz (50gm) walnuts or salted peanuts, finely chopped
1oz (25gm) cornflakes, crushed
fat for frying**

1. Trim and flatten cutlets. Clean tops of bones.
2. Dip in flour and then beaten egg.
3. Coat well in mixture of nuts and cornflakes.
4. Fry in shallow fat over high heat for 2–3 minutes, reduce heat and allow a further 5 minutes each side. Alternatively, barbecue the cutlets: grill over glowing charcoal, allowing 10 minutes each side.

GIGOT OF MUTTON
Serves 4

**1lb (½ kilo) potatoes
1 medium onion
salt and pepper
¼ pint (125ml) stock or water
4 loin mutton chops
1 tablespoon oatmeal
dripping**

1. Preheat oven to moderate to moderately hot, 375 deg F or gas 5 (190 deg C).
2. Peel and slice the potatoes and onion finely.
3. Layer potato and onion in an ovenware dish, seasoning well between each layer.
4. Pour stock or water over.
5. Dip chops in oatmeal and brown on both sides in hot dripping. Remove from frying pan and place on top of potato mixture.
6. Bake in centre of oven for 1–1½ hours.

LAMB CURRY
Serves 4

A curry is a sure way of making lamb leftovers into an attractive meal.

**1 large onion, chopped
1 large cooking apple, peeled and chopped
2 tablespoons oil
1 tablespoon curry powder
½ pint (250 ml) stock
1lb (½ kilo) cooked lamb
1 dessertspoon tomato purée
1 level teaspoon cornflour
salt and pepper
8oz (200gm) boiled long-grain rice (raw weight)**

1. Cook onion and apple in oil till soft. Add curry powder and cook for a further 3 minutes.
2. Stir in stock, lamb and tomato purée. Bring to the boil. Cover and simmer for 10 minutes.
3. Blend cornflour with 2 tablespoons water and stir in the curry. Stir till thickened and season to taste. Cook slowly until tender.
4. Serve with rice and curry accompaniments.

BIRYANI
Serves 4–6

1lb (½ kilo) lean lamb, diced
½ carton natural yogurt
1 tablespoon curry powder
1 onion, chopped
oil for frying
1 pint (approximately ½ litre)
stock
2 large potatoes, peeled and
diced
2oz (50gm) long-grain rice
1oz (25gm) sultanas
1oz (25gm) almonds, toasted
and flaked

1. Marinate lamb in yogurt and
curry powder for 2 hours.
2. Preheat oven to moderate, 350
deg F or gas 4 (180 deg C).
3. Fry onion in oil, then place in
a casserole.
4. Fry meat for 3 minutes and add
to casserole.
5. Put stock in frying pan, add
potatoes and bring to boil.
Sprinkle in rice and simmer for 10
minutes.
6. Add sultanas and pour over
lamb in casserole. Cover and cook
in centre of oven for 1 hour.
7. Sprinkle with almonds before
serving.

SUMMER LAMB CASSEROLE
Serves 4

A warm weather way of using up
cooked lamb.

1lb (½ kilo) cooked leg lamb, cut
in 1-inch cubes
1 onion, chopped
1 tablespoon oil
1 small can tomatoes
¼ pint (125ml) chicken stock
1 tablespoon tomato purée
2oz (50gm) carrots
bouquet garni
salt and pepper
2oz (50gm) peas
2oz (50gm) whole green beans
2 pears, peeled, cored and
sliced

1. Trim excess fat off lamb.
2. Fry onion in oil.
3. Add meat, tomatoes, stock,
tomato purée, carrots, bouquet
garni and seasoning. Bring to boil
and simmer for 20 minutes.
4. Add peas, beans and pears.
Simmer for a further 5–10
minutes.
5. Remove bouquet garni before
serving.

MOUSSAKA HOTPOT
Serves 4

A recipe originally from Greece
that can be made with leftover or
fresh minced lamb.

1 large onion, chopped
1 tablespoon oil
1 garlic clove, crushed
1lb (½ kilo) minced lamb
1 can (8oz or 200gm) tomatoes
1 tablespoon tomato purée
salt and black pepper
1 teaspoon mixed herbs
1 tablespoon chopped parsley
1 large aubergine, sliced
1½oz (37gm) butter
1½lb (¾ kilo) potatoes, peeled
and thinly sliced
1oz (25gm) Parmesan cheese

1. Preheat oven to moderate, 350
deg F or gas 4 (180 deg C).
2. Fry onion in oil till tender.
3. Add garlic and meat. Brown
well.
4. Add tomatoes, tomato purée,
seasoning, herbs and parsley.
Bring to boil and simmer for 20–25
minutes.
5. Fry aubergine slices in butter
for 3–4 minutes. Remove and
drain well.
6. Layer meat and aubergine in
casserole alternately. Overlap
potato slices on the top. Sprinkle
with cheese and bake in centre of
oven for 1 hour or till golden.

LAMB COBBLER
Serves 4

12oz (300gm) cooked lamb,
minced
4oz (100gm) mushrooms,
chopped
3 tomatoes, chopped
salt and pepper
4oz (100gm) butter
8oz (200gm) self-raising flour
8oz (200gm) cooked potato,
mashed

1. Preheat oven to hot, 425 deg F
or gas 7 (220 deg C).
2. Mix together meat, mushrooms,
tomatoes, salt and pepper and
place in a pie dish.
3. Rub butter into flour and add
potato.
4. Roll mixture out and cut into
rounds.
5. Place rounds on top of meat in
pie dish and bake in centre of
oven for 25 minutes.

FRIAR TUCK'S SAVOURY PUDDING
Serves 4

1 onion, finely chopped
8oz (200gm) lamb, minced
1 tablespoon oil
1 tablespoon tomato purée
½ teaspoon thyme
salt and pepper
¾ pint (375ml) stock
1 large carrot, grated
suet crust pastry made with
8oz (200gm) flour (see Basic
recipes, page 100)
1oz (25gm) cornflour
gravy browning

1. Fry onion and lamb in oil for 5
minutes, until lamb is brown.
2. Stir in tomato purée, thyme,
salt, pepper and stock. Simmer
for 10 minutes.
3. Drain, reserving the stock. Add
carrot to the lamb mixture.
4. Divide pastry into three
portions. Place one layer in the
bottom of a greased 2-pint
(approximately 1-litre) basin.
5. Place half the lamb mixture on
top and repeat, finishing with a
layer of pastry.
6. Cover with buttered
greaseproof paper or foil and
steam for 2 hours.
7. Mix cornflour to a smooth
paste with 2 tablespoons cold
water and add to the reserved
stock with a few drops of gravy
browning.
8. Bring to the boil, stirring
continuously. Serve gravy with
the pudding.

PORK WITH PRUNES
Serves 6

4lb (2 kilo) belly of pork
1 tablespoon lemon juice
salt and pepper
2oz (50gm) breadcrumbs
grated rind and juice of 1
orange
8oz (200gm) prunes, soaked,
stoned and chopped
salt
1 tablespoon chopped parsley
1 teaspoon cinnamon
8oz (200gm) cooking apples,
peeled, cored and diced
1 egg, well beaten
½ teaspoon Tabasco sauce

1. Preheat oven to moderate to
moderately hot, 375 deg F or gas 5
(190 deg C).
2. Bone the belly of pork and
trim off excess fat. Sprinkle with
lemon juice, salt and pepper.
3. Mix together the breadcrumbs,
orange rind and juice, prunes,
salt, parsley, cinnamon, apples,
egg and sauce. Spread mixture
over the boned side of the meat.
4. Roll up and tie tightly with
string.
4. Rub outside skin with salt and
bake in centre of oven for 40
minutes.
5. Reduce heat to moderate, 350
deg F or gas 4 (180 deg C) for
2–2½ hours.

BOSTON CASSEROLE
Serves 4–6

A traditional dish from America
that adds beans to pork.

6oz (150gm) haricot beans
2lb (1 kilo) belly of pork
2 sticks of celery, sliced
2 large carrots, sliced
1 tablespoon sugar
½ teaspoon dry mustard
seasoning
1 tablespoon syrup
½ pint (250ml) chicken stock

1. Soak beans overnight.
2. Preheat oven to moderate, 350
deg F or gas 4 (180 deg C).
3. Cut pork in fairly large pieces
and place in a casserole,
surround with beans and add
other vegetables.
4. Mix sugar, mustard, seasoning
and syrup with the stock. Pour
into casserole.
5. Cover with lid and bake in
centre of oven for 2½–3 hours.
6. Remove lid to crispen pork 30
minutes before serving.

PORK HOTPOT
Serves 6

2lb (1 kilo) potatoes, sliced
1lb (½ kilo) belly of pork, boned
and sliced
1lb (½ kilo) onions, sliced
salt and pepper
½ pint (250ml) water
¼ packet sage and onion
stuffing
1 egg, beaten
1 large apple, peeled and sliced

1. Preheat oven to moderate to
moderately hot, 375 deg F or gas 5
(190 deg C).
2. Place in a casserole, a layer
each of potatoes, pork and onions.
Season well.
3. Add water, cover with lid and
cook in centre of oven for about
1 hour, until potatoes are soft.
4. Mix stuffing with egg and a
little hot water and spread on top
of hotpot.
5. Arrange slices of apple on top
and brown slowly in oven.

PLUM-STUFFED ROAST
PORK
Serves 4–6

2½lb (1¼ kilo) belly of pork, boned
1 small cooking apple
3–4 damsons
1oz (25gm) breadcrumbs
squeeze lemon juice
salt and pepper
½ teaspoon sugar

1. Preheat oven to moderate, 350
deg F or gas 4 (180 deg C).
2. Flatten meat as much as
possible.
3. Peel, core and chop apple.
4. Stone and chop damsons.
5. Mix with breadcrumbs, lemon
juice, seasoning and sugar.
Spread over the meat.
6. Roll up and secure firmly with
string.
7. Roast in hot dripping for 2
hours.

STUFFED BELLY OF PORK
(Illustrated on page 17)
Serves 4

2lb (1 kilo) belly of pork, boned
2oz (50gm) white breadcrumbs
1oz (25gm) shredded suet
1oz (25gm) sultanas
½ teaspoon mixed herbs
1 small egg, beaten
2oz (50gm) redcurrant jelly
1 can (7½oz or 187gm) apple
purée (or use fresh apples)

1. Preheat oven to moderately
hot, 400 deg F or gas 6 (200 deg C).
2. Trim off excess fat from the
meat. Score the skin.
3. Make stuffing by mixing
breadcrumbs, suet, sultanas, and
herbs together. Bind with egg.
4. Spread stuffing over the meat.
Roll up and secure with string.
5. Wrap pork in foil and place in
a roasting tin in oven for 30
minutes.
6. Lower temperature to
moderate, 350 deg F or gas 5 (190
deg C) and cook a further 1¾
hours.
7. Remove foil. Return to oven
for 15 minutes to brown and crisp
skin.
8. Make sauce by melting
redcurrant jelly and adding apple
purée. Heat through and serve
separately.
9. Garnish with watercress and
serve at once.

Winter beef casserole (see page 8)

Stuffed belly of pork with sauce (see facing page)

Lamb cutlets Portuguaise with boiled rice (see page 13)

Bacon and beef roll (see page 20)

Crunch sausage salad (see page 23)

Creamed kidneys with pasta (see page 27)

Caribbean cocktail (see page 30)

Spiced chicken with rice (see page 33)

PORK CRUMBLE
Serves 4

1½lb (¾ kilo) belly of pork, cut in
cubes
2oz (50gm) flour, seasoned with
salt and pepper
1oz (25gm) lard
12oz (300gm) potatoes, sliced
3 onions, sliced
½ pint (250ml) cider
1 teaspoon marjoram
3oz (75gm) breadcrumbs
3oz (75gm) cheese, grated
cayenne pepper

1. Preheat oven to moderate, 350
deg F or gas 4 (180 deg C).
2. Coat pork in seasoned flour.
3. Heat lard and fry meat till pale
brown.
4. Arrange meat in casserole with
potatoes and onions.
5. Add cider, marjoram and salt
and pepper. Cover with well
fitting lid and bake for 1 hour.
6. Mix together breadcrumbs,
cheese and cayenne pepper in a
bowl.
7. Remove lid from casserole and
sprinkle topping over.
8. Return to oven and cook
without lid for further 30 minutes.

COLD PORK ROLL
Serves 6–8

3lb (1½ kilo) belly of pork,
skinned and boned
6oz (150gm) pork sausagemeat
1 onion, grated
pinch of mixed herbs
salt and pepper
2 hard-boiled eggs
3oz (75gm) browned
breadcrumbs

1. Place meat on board fat side
down.
2. Mix sausagemeat with onion,
herbs and seasoning. Spread over
meat.
3. Cut eggs in half; arrange down
middle of meat.
4. Roll joint up tightly and tie
well with string.
5. Wrap in pudding cloth or foil
and simmer in pan of water for 2
hours.
6. Lift out and leave to cool.
7. When cold, remove cloth or
foil and string and dust with
breadcrumbs.
8. Chill and serve with salad.

PORK AND CIDER CASSEROLE
Serves 4

A casserole dish using hand of
pork.

dripping
1½lb (¾ kilo) hand of pork
1oz (25gm) flour, seasoned with
salt and pepper
2 onions, finely chopped
4 sticks celery, chopped
2 garlic cloves, crushed
(optional)
salt and pepper
¾ pint (375ml) cider
1 carton natural yogurt

1. Melt dripping in a stewpan.
Coat trimmed meat cut in 1-inch
cubes in seasoned flour and fry in
the dripping for a few minutes.
2. Add onions, celery, garlic (if
used) and seasoning. Fry till
lightly browned.
3. Reduce heat and stir in cider.
4. Cover with lid and simmer on
top of the stove for 1½ hours until
the meat is tender.
5. Mix yogurt with a little of the
hot liquid, return to pan and
reheat without boiling.

PORK CUTLET CASSEROLE
Serves 4

1oz (25gm) dripping
4 pork cutlets
1 onion, sliced
8oz (200gm) mushrooms, sliced
4 tomatoes
1 small can mixed vegetable
soup
2 large potatoes

1. Preheat oven to moderate, 350
deg F or gas 4 (180 deg C).
2. Heat dripping and seal cutlets
on both sides. Put cutlets in an
ovenproof dish.
3. Fry onion and mushrooms in
fat and add these to the dish.
4. Skin and slice the tomatoes.
Add to the casserole and pour
soup over.
5. Slice potatoes and cover dish
with these.
6. Bake in centre of oven for
about 1 hour.

BACON SOUP WITH SAUSAGE DUMPLINGS
Serves 8

12oz (300gm) bacon collar or
forehock
2 pints (approximately 1 litre)
water
2 small onions, sliced
1 parsnip, diced
1 bayleaf
½ shredded cabbage heart
2 carrots, diced
salt and pepper
4oz (100gm) pork sausagemeat
4oz (100gm) self-raising flour,
seasoned with salt and pepper

1. Soak the bacon in cold water
for at least 1 hour.
2. Rinse and place in a large pan
with cold water, onions, parsnip
and bayleaf. Simmer for 40
minutes.
3. Remove bacon, cut into strips
and return to pan.
4. Add cabbage, carrots and
seasoning, and bring to boil.
5. To make dumplings divide
sausagemeat into small pieces.
6. Roll into balls and coat in
seasoned flour. Drop into the
liquid.
7. Replace lid and cook for a
further 15 minutes.

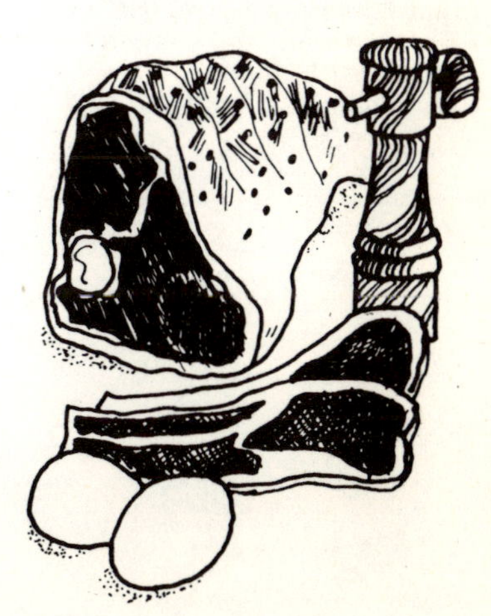

SUMMER BACON SOUP
Serves 6

1 knuckle smoked bacon
1 pig's trotter
1 bouquet garni
10 peppercorns
1 onion stuck with 4 cloves
2 pints (approximately 1 litre)
water
12oz (300gm) mixed summer
vegetables (carrots, peas etc.)
1 glass sherry (optional)

1. Put meats, bouquet garni,
peppercorns and onion in a pan
with the water.
2. Bring to the boil and simmer
for 1¼ hours.
3. Strain and add diced
vegetables.
4. Add sherry, if used, and bacon
cut from the bone.
5. Season again and chill well.

PORKY MEAT LOAF
Serves 4

8oz (200gm) pig's liver
4oz (100gm) lean bacon
8oz (200gm) pork sausagemeat
1oz (25gm) white breadcrumbs
salt and black pepper
4oz (100gm) mushrooms, finely
chopped
¼ teaspoon sage
1 dessertspoon tomato chutney

1. Preheat oven to very moderate,
325 deg F or gas 3 (170 deg C).
2. Remove gristle from liver and
rinds from bacon.
3. Mince liver and bacon and mix
together. Stir in all other
ingredients and mix thoroughly.
4. Press into a 1½-pint
(approximately ¾-litre) basin.
Cover with foil and bake in centre
of oven for 1½ hours.
5. Leave loaf in basin till cold.

BACON AND BEEF ROLL
(Illustrated on page 17)
Serves 4

8oz (200gm) lean raw minced
beef
1 heaped tablespoon finely
chopped parsley
4 firm tomatoes, chopped
2 salad onions, finely chopped
salt and black pepper
8oz (200gm) back bacon,
chopped
1oz (25gm) oatmeal
1 teaspoon made mustard
1 egg

1. Preheat oven to moderately
hot, 400 deg F or gas 6 (200 deg C).
2. Mix all ingredients well
together and shape into a meat
roll.
3. Wrap in foil and bake in centre
of oven for 1½ hours.
4. Serve hot or cold on lettuce,
garnished with cucumber slices
and pineapple pieces.

HIGHLAND BAKE
Serves 4

2 bacon rashers
1 onion, chopped
1oz (25gm) dripping
2 tomatoes, skinned and
chopped
2oz (50gm) fresh breadcrumbs
2oz (50gm) medium oatmeal
salt and pepper
1 egg, beaten
3 tablespoons milk
1lb (½ kilo) beef sausages

1. Preheat oven to moderately
hot, 400 deg F or gas 6 (200 deg C).
2. Remove bacon rinds and cut
rashers into small pieces.
3. Fry bacon and onion in
dripping for 4 minutes, then add
tomatoes and cook for a further
minute.
4. Remove from heat and mix in
crumbs, oatmeal, seasoning, egg
and milk.
5. Place in a shallow, greased tin,
arrange sausages on top and bake
in centre of oven for 30–35
minutes.

CHEF'S SUMMER SALAD
Serves 6

A summery suggestion in which
canned tuna, or cubed firm cheese
can be substituted for meat.

2 large slices white bread ½ inch
thick
2oz (50gm) butter
salt
1 garlic clove
1 large cos lettuce
1 small onion, sliced
1oz (25gm) Parmesan cheese,
grated
2oz (50gm) button mushrooms,
thinly sliced
6oz (150gm) cooked ham, cut in
¼-inch cubes
2oz (50gm) can anchovy fillets,
drained
4 tablespoons olive oil
1 tablespoon lemon juice
2 tablespoons Worcestershire
sauce
1 level teaspoon salt

1. Remove crusts from bread. Cut
bread in ½-inch cubes.
2. Fry in butter till golden brown.
Drain on absorbent paper and
sprinkle with salt.
3. Rub a large salad bowl with
garlic.
4. Tear lettuce into pieces and
place in bowl. Add onion, cheese,
mushrooms, ham and anchovy
fillets and mix carefully together.
5. Blend olive oil, lemon juice,
Worcestershire sauce and salt
well together. Just before serving,
pour dressing over and toss salad.
6. Add bread cubes and mix well.

BACON ROLY POLY
Serves 4

9–10oz (225–250gm) cooked,
leftover bacon joint
1 small onion
$\frac{1}{4}$ level teaspoon mixed herbs
6oz (150gm) self-raising flour
pinch of salt
3oz (75gm) shredded suet
7 tablespoons cold water

1. Mince bacon and onion and
add herbs.
2. Mix flour, salt and suet in a
bowl. Add enough water to make
a soft but not sticky dough.
3. Knead lightly on floured board
till smooth. Roll into an oblong,
12 inches by 8 inches.
4. Spread minced bacon mixture
on dough to about $\frac{1}{2}$ inch of the
edges. Roll up like a Swiss roll.
5. Wrap securely in greased foil
or tie in a pudding cloth.
6. Put in a large saucepan, one
third full of boiling water. Cover
and boil for 1 hour, topping up
water as necessary.

PEASE PUDDING AND
BOILED BACON
Serves 4

8oz (200gm) split peas
salt and pepper
1oz (25gm) butter
1 egg, beaten
pinch of sugar
3lb (1$\frac{1}{2}$ kilo) bacon forehock or
collar

1. Wash peas and soak overnight
in cold water.
2. Tie loosely in a cloth and place
in saucepan with salt. Cover with
boiling water.
3. Boil for 2$\frac{1}{2}$–3 hours till soft.
Sieve peas or liquidize in a
blender. Add butter, egg, salt,
pepper and sugar.
4. Beat together lightly, then tie
up tightly in floured cloth and
boil for a further 30 minutes.
5. Boil bacon joint for 25 minutes
per pound ($\frac{1}{2}$ kilo) plus an extra 25
minutes with bayleaves, cloves
and sliced onion added to the
cooking water.
6. Serve bacon joint hot with
pease pudding.

HEARTY BEAN BAKE
Serves 4

1 onion, chopped
1 tablespoon oil
$\frac{1}{2}$oz (12gm) flour
1 medium can tomatoes
1 medium can baked beans
salt and pepper
Worcestershire sauce to taste
1 tablespoon chopped parsley
1 teaspoon mixed herbs
1lb ($\frac{1}{2}$ kilo) cooked ham, cut
into cubes
1 large cooking apple, peeled,
cored and sliced

1. Fry onion in oil till tender. Add
flour and stir in tomatoes and
baked beans.
2. Season and add Worcestershire
sauce, parsley and herbs.
3. Bring to the boil and stir in
ham and apple.
4. Simmer for 20 minutes,
stirring occasionally.

LEEK AND BACON HOTPOT
Serves 4

8 leeks
1oz (25gm) butter
8oz (200gm) mushrooms
$\frac{1}{2}$ teaspoon thyme
8oz (200gm) streaky bacon
rashers
1lb ($\frac{1}{2}$ kilo) potatoes, peeled
$\frac{1}{3}$ pint (170ml) dry cider

1. Preheat oven to moderately
hot, 400 deg F or gas 6 (200 deg C).
2. Clean leeks thoroughly and
slice thinly.
3. Heat butter in a fireproof dish
or pan. Fry leeks for about 3
minutes.
4. Quarter mushrooms and add to
dish. Sprinkle with thyme and
cover with bacon rashers. Top
with sliced potatoes which may be
parboiled first. Then pour on
cider.
5. Bake in centre of oven for
about 45 minutes.

SPICED BANANA AND HAM
ROLLS
Serves 4

8 slices canned chopped ham
4 tablespoons sweet chutney
4 large bananas
1 can mulligatawny soup
6oz (150gm) long-grain rice
$\frac{1}{2}$ teaspoon powdered ginger
yellow colouring (optional)
1$\frac{1}{2}$oz (37gm) raisins

1. Preheat oven to moderate to
moderately hot, 375 deg F or gas 5
(190 deg C).
2. Spread each ham slice with
chutney.
3. Cut bananas in halves,
lengthways, and wrap each half
in a slice of ham.
4. Place in a shallow ovenproof
dish and pour mulligatawny soup
over.
5. Place in centre of oven and
cook for 20 minutes.
6. Meanwhile, cook the rice,
flavoured with ginger, in boiling,
salted water, adding a little
yellow colouring, if wished. Drain
and add raisins.
7. Spoon rice on to a serving dish
and top with the ham rolls.

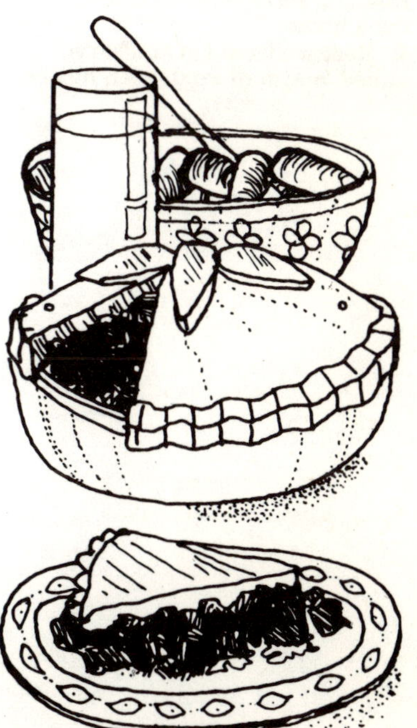

WILTSHIRE TEABREAD
Serves 4–6

The first of two recipes using
bacon in savoury breads for tea
or breakfast.

**4oz (100gm) streaky bacon, rind
removed and finely chopped
4 sticks celery, finely chopped
1 small onion, grated
1lb (½ kilo) self-raising flour
¼ level teaspoon salt
pepper
2oz (50gm) dripping
2 level tablespoons chopped
parsley
½ pint (250ml) milk, less 2
tablespoons
1 egg, beaten**

1. Preheat oven to moderate to
moderately hot, 375 deg F or gas 5
(190 deg C).
2. Place bacon in a pan and fry
gently for 2 minutes.
3. Add celery and onion. Fry
gently for 5 minutes. Leave to
cool.
4. Sift together flour, salt and
pepper and rub in dripping until
mixture resembles fine
breadcrumbs.
5. Stir bacon mixture into flour
with parsley. Beat together milk
and egg and stir into flour.
6. Knead very lightly on floured
surface. Shape into a rectangle
and place in a greased 2-lb (1-kilo)
loaf tin. Bake in centre of oven
for 1 hour.
7. Remove from tin and serve
sliced, warm or cold, with butter.

BUFFINS
Makes 8

**8oz (200gm) streaky bacon
rashers, de-rinded
8oz (200gm) self-raising flour
2oz (50gm) butter
1oz (25gm) cheese, grated
pinch of cayenne pepper
little milk
1 egg yolk**

1. Preheat oven to hot, 425 deg F
or gas 7 (220 deg C).
2. Grill bacon rashers until crisp,
then chop finely.
3. Sift flour into a basin and rub
in butter.
4. Add bacon, cheese, cayenne
pepper and mix to a dry dough
with a little milk.
5. Roll out on a floured board to a
square, ½ inch thick.
6. Cut into four squares, then
eight triangles. Place on a
greased baking tray.
7. Brush with egg yolk and bake
12–15 minutes in centre of oven.
8. Serve hot, split and buttered.

HAM AND PORK RISSOLES
Serves 6

**1 can (7oz or 175gm) chopped
ham with pork
1lb (½ kilo) potatoes, boiled and
mashed
1 egg, separated
milk
salt and pepper
flour
dried breadcrumbs
2oz (50gm) butter
1 tablespoon oil
parsley sprigs
tomato wedges
cucumber twists**

1. Break up chopped ham with
pork with a fork. Mix with
mashed potatoes.
2. Add egg yolk and sufficient
milk to make a firm mixture. Bind
together and season with salt and
pepper.
3. Shape, with floured hands, into
6 rounds, ¾ inch thick and coat
with lightly whisked egg white
and breadcrumbs.
4. Fry in butter and oil for about
4 minutes, on each side, until
golden brown. Drain.
5. Garnish with parsley sprigs,
tomato wedges and cucumber
twists and serve with creamed
spinach and carrots.

HAM AND PORK CASSEROLE
Serves 4

**1 can (12oz or 300gm) chopped
ham with pork
1 level teaspoon dried onion
1 can (14oz or 350gm) peeled
tomatoes
1 can (13oz or 325gm) celery
hearts, drained**

1. Preheat oven to moderate, 350
deg F or gas 4 (180 deg C).
2. Cut chopped ham with pork
into small cubes and put into an
ovenproof 3–4-pint (approximately
1½–2-litre) casserole.
3. Add dried onion, roughly
chopped tomatoes with the juice,
and roughly chopped celery
hearts.
4. Cover with lid or foil and bake
in centre of oven for 1¼ hours.

COUNTRY VEGETABLE BAKE
Serves 4

**1oz (25gm) butter or margarine
1lb (½ kilo) potatoes
2 parsnips or 1 small swede,
peeled and cut in 1-inch dice
1lb (½ kilo) beef sausages
½ pint (250ml) chicken stock
salt and pepper**

1. Preheat oven to moderately
hot, 400 deg F or gas 6 (200 deg C).
2. Melt butter or margarine in
medium-sized saucepan. Add
vegetables and cover pan.
3. Fry for 10 minutes, then turn
into greased casserole.
4. Lay sausages – do not prick
them – across the top. Pour stock
and seasoning over.
5. Cover with foil or casserole lid
and bake in centre of oven for 45
minutes.
6. Remove lid and bake for a
further 15 minutes.

BEEF SAUSAGE PLATTER
Serves 4

**1lb (½ kilo) large beef
sausages**
1½lb (¾ kilo) cabbage, shredded
½ pint (250ml) chicken stock
salt
1 teaspoon minced onion
2 tablespoons soured cream
**1 tablespoon grated
horseradish**

1. Grill the sausages.
2. Cook cabbage in the stock.
Season with salt. When tender,
drain well, reserving the stock.
3. Put ¼ pint (125ml) stock in a
pan, add onion and boil rapidly
for 1 minute. Stir in the cream
and horseradish till well mixed.
4. Turn cabbage on to a hot dish.
Arrange sausages on it and pour
the sauce over.

SAUSAGE AND BACON
RISOTTO
Serves 4

2oz (50gm) butter
1 large onion, chopped
**6oz (150gm) streaky bacon, rind
removed and chopped**
2 sticks celery
6oz (150gm) long-grain rice
1¼ pints (625ml) beef stock
**4oz (100gm) button mushrooms,
cut in quarters**
**2 tomatoes, skinned and
quartered**
2 tablespoons spicy sauce
salt and pepper
8 sausages

1. Melt butter and fry onion and
bacon gently for 5 minutes. Chop
celery and cook in boiling water
for 1 minute, then drain.
2. Add rice to onion and bacon
and cook, stirring for 2 minutes.
3. Add stock, bring to the boil,
stirring. Simmer gently for 15
minutes. Stir in celery and
mushrooms. Simmer a further 5–8
minutes until all stock is
absorbed.
4. Stir in tomatoes and sauce and
adjust seasoning.
5. Meanwhile fry or grill
sausages.
6. Serve sausages on top of rice.

COUNTRY PORK AND
BACON LOAF
Serves 4–6

This and the following recipe are
ideal pennywise picnic fare. This
one can be served hot too.

1oz (25gm) lard or bacon fat
2 onions, chopped
4 sticks celery, chopped
1½lb (¾ kilo) pork sausagemeat
4oz (100gm) white breadcrumbs
**2 level tablespoons chopped
parsley**
salt and pepper
2 egg yolks
¼ pint (125ml) milk
**3oz (75gm) streaky bacon
rashers, rind removed**
**1oz (25gm) butter or
margarine**
**4oz (100gm) flat mushrooms,
peeled and chopped**
½oz (12gm) flour
½ pint (250ml) beef stock
1 teaspoon soy sauce

1. Preheat oven to moderate, 350
deg F or gas 4 (180 deg C).
2. Melt fat and fry half the onion
and the celery gently for 5
minutes.
3. Mix together with
sausagemeat, breadcrumbs,
parsley and seasoning.
4. Blend together egg yolks, milk
and mix into sausagemeat
mixture.
5. Stretch bacon with back of
a knife and arrange rashers along
base of a greased 2-lb (1-kilo) loaf
tin.
6. Turn sausagemeat mixture into
tin, pressing down well.
7. Cover tin with foil and place in
baking tin half filled with hot
water. Bake in centre of oven for
1¼ hours.
8. For the sauce melt butter or
margarine in pan and fry
remaining onion gently for 5
minutes. Add mushrooms and fry
a further 3 minutes.
9. Stir in flour, remove pan from
heat and blend in beef stock.
Bring to the boil, stirring, and
simmer gently for 1 minute.
Season well and add soy sauce.
10. Turn out loaf on to warmed
plate and serve hot with sauce or
cold with salad.

SAUSAGE PLAIT
Serves 4

**shortcrust pastry made with
8oz (200gm) flour (see Basic
recipes, page 100)**
6oz (150gm) sausagemeat
1 onion, finely chopped
**4oz (100gm) mushrooms, finely
chopped**
2 tablespoons chopped parsley
dash of Worcestershire sauce
salt and pepper

1. Preheat oven to moderately
hot, 400 deg F or gas 6 (200 deg C).
2. Roll out pastry into a
rectangle, about 10 inches wide by
9 inches long. Mark into three
lengthways.
3. Mix remaining ingredients
together and place down the
centre section.
4. Cut ½-inch diagonal strips each
side of the filling, moisten with
water and plait over the sausage
mixture.
5. Glaze with a little milk and
bake on a baking tray in centre of
oven for 40–45 minutes.
6. Serve hot or cold.

CRUNCH SAUSAGE SALAD
(Illustrated on page 18)
Serves 4

1lb (½ kilo) pork sausages
1oz (25gm) lard
4 slices white bread, diced
**4oz (100gm) mushrooms,
chopped**
1 garlic clove, crushed
2 tablespoons vinegar
3 tablespoons single cream
salt and pepper
1 lettuce
½ cucumber

1. Fry sausages gently in the
lard, then drain and leave to cool.
Slice into thick rings.
2. Fry bread, mushrooms and
garlic. Drain and leave to cool.
3. Make dressing with vinegar,
cream, salt and pepper.
4. Stir in the sausage rings,
bread, mushrooms and garlic.
5. Chill and serve heaped in
lettuce leaves, with thinly sliced
cucumber.

SAUSAGE KIEV
Serves 6

2oz (50gm) margarine
¼ teaspoon tomato purée
¼ teaspoon mixed herbs
1lb (½ kilo) sausagemeat or
sausages
1 egg, beaten
breadcrumbs to coat
oil for deep frying

1. Mix together margarine,
tomato purée and herbs and chill.
2. Divide sausagemeat into six
flattened circles. Place a little of
the chilled margarine mixture in
the centre of each.
3. Roll up into balls. Brush with
beaten egg and coat in
breadcrumbs.
4. Fry in hot oil for 10 minutes.
Drain and serve with rice.

SAUSAGE BEAN SCRAMBLE
Serves 4–6

1 can (16oz or 400gm) pineapple
slices
1lb (½ kilo) pork chipolata
sausages
1oz (25gm) fat
1 large onion, peeled and
chopped
1 green pepper, deseeded and
chopped
1 can (16oz or 400gm) baked
beans
1 level tablespoon mild
continental mustard
salt and pepper

1. Drain pineapple slices and
reserve syrup.
2. Gently fry sausages in fat until
brown on all sides. Remove from
pan and keep warm.
3. In the same pan fry onion and
pepper until soft and the onion is
golden.
4. Stir in the baked beans and
heat through. Place in a fireproof
serving dish.
5. Arrange sausages and
pineapple slices on top, each slice
with a cooked sausage threaded
through it.
6. Heat together 4 tablespoons
reserved syrup, mustard, salt and
pepper to taste and pour over
pineapple.
7. Put under a hot grill for a few
minutes to brown.

PORKY PUDDING
Serves 4

½ packet sage and onion
stuffing
¼ pint (125ml) boiling water
8oz (200gm) sausagemeat
2oz (50gm) lean bacon, chopped
1 egg, beaten
½ level teaspoon dry mustard
salt and pepper

1. Prepare stuffing as directed on
packet, using the boiling water,
and leave to stand for about 10
minutes.
2. Add all the other ingredients
and mix well.
3. Turn into a greased 1-pint
(approximately ½-litre) basin and
cover with greased greaseproof
paper or foil.
4. Steam until cooked. Serve hot
or cold.

SAUSAGE AND BACON
KEBABS WITH CRANBERRY
SAUCE
Serves 4

1lb (½ kilo) pork sausages
8 streaky bacon rashers
4 button onions
4 button mushrooms
1 small green pepper
8 bayleaves
oil
1 jar or can (8oz or 200gm)
cranberry sauce
2 tablespoons stock
1 teaspoon chopped parsley

1. Twist each sausage in half and
cut at the join.
2. Trim rind off bacon and wrap
each rasher round a sausage.
3. Skin and parboil onions for 5
minutes.
4. Trim mushrooms and cut green
pepper into chunks.
5. Thread all these ingredients on
to four skewers alternately with
bayleaves.
6. Brush kebabs with oil and grill
for 10–15 minutes, turning
occasionally and brushing with
more oil.
7. Heat cranberry sauce with
stock and hand separately.
8. Sprinkle kebabs with parsley
and serve with jacket potatoes.

SAUSAGE BURGERS
Serves 4

1 medium onion, chopped
½oz (12gm) butter
8oz (200gm) sausagemeat
2 heaped tablespoons fresh,
white breadcrumbs
1 cooking apple, peeled and
grated or chopped
½ level teaspoon salt
pepper
¼ level teaspoon dried sage
1 egg
½oz (12gm) lard
4 hamburger buns
butter
prepared mustard

1. Fry onion in butter till tender.
2. Mix sausagemeat,
breadcrumbs, apple, cooked
onion, salt, pepper, and dried
sage. Bind together with beaten
egg.
3. Shape into four rounds on a
floured board.
4. Melt lard and fry burgers for
about 7 minutes each side. Serve
in warmed, buttered buns with
mustard.

SAUSAGE SIZZLE
Serves 4

1lb ($\frac{1}{2}$ kilo) chipolata sausages
5 streaky bacon rashers
4oz (100gm) button mushrooms
5 tablespoons white vinegar
2 tablespoons redcurrant jelly
1 level tablespoon made
mustard
2 level tablespoons demerara
sugar
1 teaspoon Worcestershire
sauce

1. Twist chipolata sausages in
half and cut at the join. Wrap in
small pieces of bacon.
2. Grill these and remaining
sausages and the mushrooms
under a medium heat for about
10–15 minutes, turning frequently.
3. Meanwhile, prepare a sauce by
heating together vinegar,
redcurrant jelly, mustard, sugar
and Worcestershire sauce.
4. Simmer together, stirring
occasionally, until sauce is of a
coating consistency.
5. Place cooked sausages and
mushrooms on cocktail sticks and
serve sauce separately as a dip.

**SAUSAGE AND MINCE
LOAF**
Serves 4

2oz (50gm) margarine
4oz (100gm) mushrooms,
chopped
1 small onion, chopped
3oz (75gm) breadcrumbs
2 tablespoons tomato purée
6oz (150gm) sausagemeat
6oz (150gm) minced beef
$\frac{1}{2}$ teaspoon mixed herbs
1 egg, beaten
salt and pepper
2 hard-boiled eggs, sliced

1. Preheat oven to moderate to
moderately hot, 375 deg F or gas 5
(190 deg C).
2. Melt margarine in a pan and
add mushrooms and onion. Fry
for a few minutes then drain.
3. Mix in all remaining
ingredients except hard-boiled
eggs.
4. Line a 1-lb ($\frac{1}{2}$-kilo) loaf tin with
foil. Place slices of egg at bottom.
5. Fill with the mixture and bake
in centre of oven for $\frac{3}{4}$–1 hour.

SAUSAGES WITH BEER
Serves 4

2 streaky bacon rashers, cut
into strips
1 onion, chopped
1 carrot, thinly sliced
1 stick celery, sliced
1 large tomato, skinned and
chopped
1 medium cooking apple,
peeled, cored and diced
$\frac{1}{4}$ pint (125ml) stock
1oz (25gm) mushrooms, peeled
and sliced
1lb ($\frac{1}{2}$ kilo) sausages
salt and pepper
$\frac{1}{4}$ pint (125ml) stout

1. Preheat oven to moderate, 350
deg F or gas 4 (180 deg C).
2. Fry bacon lightly, then
transfer to a casserole and keep
warm.
3. Add onion, carrot and celery to
bacon fat and fry until golden
brown, then add tomato, apple,
stock and mushrooms. Cook for a
further 2–3 minutes.
4. Turn this mixture into the
casserole, place sausages on top,
season well and pour stout over.
5. Cover and cook in centre of
oven for 45 minutes. Remove lid
and continue cooking for a
further 15 minutes to brown
sausages.

SAUSAGE CASSEROLE
Serves 4

1oz (25gm) dripping
1lb ($\frac{1}{2}$ kilo) sausages
1 onion, finely chopped
1 small white cabbage, coarsely
shredded
1 large cooking apple, peeled,
cored and sliced
$\frac{1}{4}$ pint (125ml) stock or water
salt and pepper
3 tomatoes, skinned and
quartered

1. Melt fat in a large saucepan.
Add sausages and onions and fry
quickly for about 5 minutes, or
until golden brown.
2. Add cabbage, apple, stock or
water and seasoning, cover and
simmer for 15 minutes.
3. Stir in the tomatoes, cover and
simmer for a further 5 minutes.
4. Arrange in a warm dish and
serve piping hot.

CURRIED FRUIT SAUSAGES
Serves 4

1oz (25gm) dripping
1lb ($\frac{1}{2}$ kilo) pork sausages
1 level teaspoon curry powder
4 bananas, sliced
2oz (50gm) raisins

1. Melt dripping in a frying pan
and fry sausages gently, without
pricking, for about 20 minutes
until brown. Remove from the pan
and keep hot.
2. Add curry powder to remaining
fat and mix well.
3. Add bananas and raisins and
fry, turning frequently in the fat,
until bananas are tender.
4. Serve arranged around the
sausages on a warm dish.

SAUSAGE AND EGG PIE
Serves 6

1lb (½ kilo) chipolata sausages
2oz (50gm) fat or dripping
shortcrust pastry made with
12oz (300gm) flour (see Basic
recipes, page 100)
3 streaky bacon rashers
1 small onion
4 eggs
1 tablespoon finely chopped
parsley
salt and pepper
a little extra beaten egg to
glaze

1. Preheat oven to hot, 425 deg F
or gas 7 (220 deg C).
2. Gently fry sausages in fat for
about 8 minutes until an even
brown all over. Drain on
absorbent paper and leave to get
cold.
3. Roll out just over half the
pastry and use it to line an 8-inch
(20-cm) pie plate or flan dish.
4. Cut sausages in half and
arrange in the bottom of the pie
case.
5. Remove rind from bacon and
chop roughly.
6. Chop onions and fry with the
bacon in the fat left from
sausages. Drain.
7. Hard boil one of the eggs and
leave to cool. Shell and chop it
roughly. Mix with bacon and
onion and place on top of
sausages in pie dish.
8. Beat remaining eggs together
with parsley, salt and pepper.
Pour into pie dish.
9. Roll remainder of the pastry to
fit top of pie. Place the lid in
position and glaze with a little
beaten egg. Add pastry leaves
made from any leftover pastry and
glaze with egg. Make a small hole
in the top.
10. Bake in centre of oven for 10
minutes, then reduce oven
temperature to moderate to
moderately hot, 375 deg F or gas 5
(190 deg C) and cook for a further
20 minutes, or until pastry is
golden.
11. Serve hot or cold.

BRAISED SAUSAGES
Serves 4–6

½oz (12gm) fat or dripping
1lb (½ kilo) beef or pork
sausages
2 medium onions, sliced
12oz (300gm) carrots, sliced
1 pint (approximately ½ litre)
boiling water
3 tablespoons cider
salt and pepper
1lb (½ kilo) cabbage, shredded
2–3 tomatoes, peeled and
quartered

1. Melt fat or dripping in a
saucepan and quickly fry
sausages until brown, turning
frequently, for about 5 minutes.
Remove sausages and keep warm.
2. Drain off surplus fat and add
onions, carrots, water, cider and
seasoning. Simmer for 15 minutes.
3. Add cabbage and tomatoes and
lay sausages on top. Cover and
cook for a further 15 minutes.
4. Adjust seasoning, turn
sausages and vegetables into a
warm casserole and serve at once.

STUFFED SAUSAGE BREAKFAST
Serves 4

1lb (½ kilo) pork sausages
chutney
8 streaky bacon rashers
3 large tomatoes
4oz (100gm) small mushrooms
sprigs of parsley to garnish

1. Preheat oven to moderately
hot, 400 deg F or gas 6 (200 deg C).
2. Slit sausages lengthways with
a sharp knife without cutting
right through. Put a small
amount of chutney into centre of
each.
3. Wrap a bacon rasher round
each sausage.
4. Cut tomatoes in half and place
on a baking tray with the
prepared sausages.
5. Add mushrooms brushed with
oil and bake in centre of oven for
20–30 minutes until sausages are
brown and bacon is cooked.
6. Serve on a hot dish garnished
with sprigs of parsley.

SAUSAGE WHEEL
Serves 4

1lb (½ kilo) beef sausages
1 onion, sliced
½oz (12gm) dripping
1 can (8oz or 200gm) tomatoes
1 small cooking apple, peeled
and cut into cubes
1 bayleaf
salt and pepper
1½lb (¾ kilo) creamed potato

1. Fry sausages and onion slowly
in melted dripping for about 20–30
minutes, turning frequently.
2. Put tomatoes, apple, bayleaf
and seasoning in a pan, cover and
simmer for 12–15 minutes until
apple is soft. Remove bayleaf.
3. Pile creamed potato on to a
serving plate and make a deep
hollow in the centre.
4. Top with onions, then
sausages arranged in a wheel
pattern.
5. Pour sauce into the hollow and
serve at once.

SAVELOYS AND SAUERKRAUT GARNI
Serves 4

1 can sauerkraut
3 teaspoons made mustard
1 tablespoon creamed
horseradish
1 carton natural yogurt
1 tablespoon lemon juice
1 tablespoon caraway seeds
2 dessert apples, cored and
sliced
4 saveloys

1. Preheat oven to moderate to
moderately hot, 375 deg F or gas 5
(190 deg C).
2. Combine sauerkraut, mustard,
horseradish, yogurt, lemon juice
and caraway seeds.
3. Transfer to a casserole and
arrange in layers with apple and
saveloys.
4. Place in centre of oven and
cook for about 25 minutes.

CREAMED KIDNEYS WITH PASTA
(Illustrated on page 18)
Serves 4

A low cost dinner party dish.

8oz (200gm) pasta shapes
2½oz (72gm) butter
1 onion, finely chopped
8 lamb's kidneys
½oz (12gm) flour
4oz (100gm) mushrooms, sliced
3 tablespoons sharp sauce
¼ beef stock cube dissolved in
¾ pint (375ml) water
salt and pepper
2 tablespoons single or double
cream

1. Cook pasta in plenty of boiling,
salted water for 10–15 minutes.
2. Melt 1½oz (37gm) butter in a
pan. Fry onion gently until soft.
3. Meanwhile skin, core and slice
kidneys.
4. Toss in flour and add to onions
with mushrooms.
5. Fry, turning frequently for 3
minutes. Add sauce, stock, salt
and pepper. Bring to boil,
stirring.
6. Cook for 2 minutes, then stir in
almost all the cream.
7. Toss drained pasta in
remaining butter.
8. Pile pasta around kidney
mixture. Pour remaining cream
over the top and serve at once.

KIDNEY AND MUSHROOM BAKE
Serves 4

4 lamb's kidneys
1lb (½ kilo) tomatoes
1 tablespoon oil
salt and pepper
12oz (300gm) mushrooms
¼ pint (125ml) meat stock
4oz (100gm) butter
1 garlic clove
4oz (100gm) breadcrumbs

1. Preheat oven to moderate, 350
deg F or gas 4 (180 deg C).
2. Skin and core kidneys and cut
into ½-inch strips.
3. Skin and slice tomatoes.
4. Put tomatoes and kidneys into
an ovenproof dish, pour oil over
and sprinkle with salt and pepper.
5. Cover with sliced mushrooms,
and pour stock over.
6. Heat butter in a pan and add
finely crushed garlic and
breadcrumbs. Stir over a medium
heat for a moment, then cover the
mushrooms with this mixture.
7. Bake in centre of oven for 35
minutes.

BAKED LAMB'S HEARTS
Serves 4

4 lamb's hearts
1 teaspoon horseradish sauce
4 salad onions, minced
1oz (25gm) lean bacon, minced
1oz (25gm) porridge oats
1 teaspoon dried sage
salt and pepper
1 egg
6oz (150gm) fatty bacon

1. Preheat oven to moderate, 350
deg F or gas 4 (180 deg C).
2. Soak hearts in cold water for
about 30 minutes. Remove tubes
and dry.
3. Mix horseradish sauce with
onion, bacon, oats, sage and
seasoning. Bind with egg.
4. Stuff mixture into heart
cavities. Wrap bacon round each,
securing with cotton or fine
string.
5. Put hearts in fireproof dish,
cover and bake in centre of oven
for 1½–2 hours till hearts are
cooked.

LIVER AND BACON ROLL
Serves 4

suet crust pastry made with
8oz (200gm) flour (see Basic
recipes, page 100)
4oz (100gm) bacon rashers
8oz (200gm) calf's liver
1 onion, chopped
pinch mixed herbs
salt and pepper

1. Roll out pastry on floured
surface to about 12 inches by 8
inches.
2. Arrange rashers on dough.
3. Chop liver, mix with onion,
herbs and seasoning and spread
over rashers 1 inch from edge.
4. Moisten edges of dough, roll up
(from longer side) and pinch ends
to seal.
5. Wrap in double thickness,
greased greaseproof paper, folding
in a large pleat for expansion.
6. Wrap loosely in kitchen foil
and steam for 2 hours.

MOCK GOOSE
Serves 4–6

2lb (1 kilo) potatoes
1lb (½ kilo) liver or pig's fry
½oz (12gm) flour, seasoned with
salt and pepper
2 onions, chopped
1 apple, peeled and chopped
1 teaspoon powdered sage
¾ pint (375ml) boiling stock or
water

1. Preheat oven to moderate, 350
deg F or gas 4 (180 deg C).
2. Wash and peel potatoes, then
cut into slices. Wipe liver or pig's
fry and cut in ½-inch thick slices.
3. Coat liver in seasoned flour.
4. Mix together onion, apple and
sage. Grease a casserole, put in
layers of potato, liver and onion
mixture, seasoning between each
layer; top with potato.
5. Pour stock or water over and
cover with greased paper and lid.
Bake in centre of oven for 1 hour.
6. Remove lid and bake for a
further 20 minutes to brown
potatoes.

KIDNEY AND LIVER PUDDING
Serves 4–6

8oz (200gm) kidneys
8oz (200gm) sheep's liver
4oz (100gm) bacon
½oz (12gm) flour, seasoned with
salt, pepper, nutmeg and mace
suet crust pastry made with
8oz (200gm) flour (see Basic
recipes, page 100)
½ pint (250ml) beef stock or
gravy

1. Wash kidneys and liver. Dry
and cut into small pieces. Remove
rind from bacon and cut in small
pieces.
2. Cook bacon for a few minutes.
Remove from pan and drain.
3. Coat liver and kidney pieces
with seasoned flour. Fry in bacon
fat, adding dripping if necessary.
4. When brown, place on plate
with bacon.
5. Cut one third suet pastry for
top, then roll out rest into circle
to line a greased 1½-pint
(approximately ¾-litre pudding
basin. Fill with meat. Add ¼ pint
(125ml) stock or gravy.
6. Add pastry top and seal. Cover
with greased paper and steam for
2½–3 hours.
7. Serve with remaining gravy.

SWEET AND SOUR LIVER
Serves 4

1oz (25gm) margarine
4 streaky bacon rashers,
chopped
1 small onion, chopped
1lb (½ kilo) liver, sliced and
tossed in flour
½oz (12gm) plain flour
½ pint (250ml) cider
¼ pint (125ml) stock
1 small green pepper, sliced
1 dessertspoon tomato purée
salt and pepper
chopped parsley to garnish

1. Melt margarine in a pan and
fry bacon, onion and liver for 4–5
minutes.
2. Stir in flour, cider and stock
and bring to the boil.
3. Add pepper and purée and
simmer for 20 minutes.
4. Season to taste and sprinkle
with parsley.

LIVER AND BACON – STUFFED MARROW RINGS
Serves 4

1 large marrow, peeled
6 large slices white bread,
crusts removed, and broken in
pieces
¼ pint (125ml) milk
2oz (50gm) oil
2 onions, chopped
8oz (200gm) pig's liver, chopped
5oz (125gm) streaky bacon,
rind removed and chopped
½ level teaspoon dried mixed
herbs
salt and pepper
2 celery sticks, finely chopped
1 can (14oz or 350gm) peeled
tomatoes
¼ level teaspoon sugar

1. Preheat oven to moderate to
moderately hot, 375 deg F or gas 5
(190 deg C).
2. Cut marrow into 4 slices, each
at least 3 inches thick and remove
seeds and pith.
3. Place in large pan of boiling,
salted water. Cover and simmer
for 10 minutes.
4. Drain well, then place slices in
greased, ovenproof dish.
5. For the stuffing, soak bread in
milk and leave to stand for 30
minutes.
6. Beat well with a fork.
7. Heat 1oz (25gm) oil in a pan
and fry half the onion gently for
5 minutes.
8. Add liver, 4oz (100gm) bacon
and ¼ teaspoon mixed herbs. Fry
for a further 5 minutes.
9. Add to soaked bread and mix
well. Season and spoon mixture
into marrow slices. Bake in centre
of oven for 25–30 minutes.
10. For the sauce, heat remaining
oil in a pan and fry rest of onion,
the celery, and rest of bacon
gently for 5 minutes.
11. Stir in tomatoes and rest of
herbs. Bring to the boil, cover and
simmer for 10 minutes. Reduce to
a purée.
12. Add sugar, season well and
reheat. Serve sauce separately.

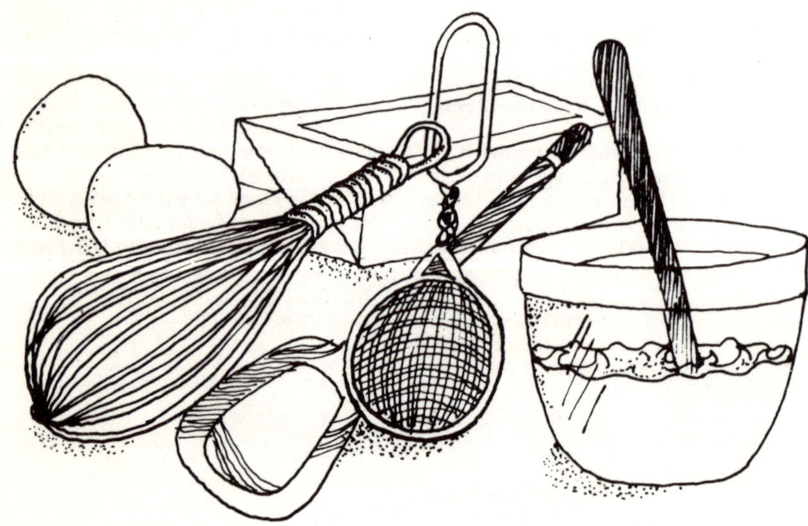

LIVER AND BACON PATE
Serves 4–6

6 streaky bacon rashers
8oz (200gm) pig's liver
8oz (200gm) fat bacon
1 garlic clove
1 large onion
3oz (75gm) butter
½ pint (250ml) milk
2 blades mace
4 bayleaves
2–3 peppercorns
1oz (25gm) flour
salt and pepper

1. Preheat oven to moderate, 350 deg F or gas 4 (180 deg C).
2. Remove rinds from streaky bacon and stretch on a board with the back of a knife.
3. Lay rashers at the bottom and round the sides of a greased terrine or straight-sided dish.
4. Fry liver, de-rinded fat bacon, garlic and roughly chopped onion in 2oz (50gm) butter for 10 minutes. Mince or put into a blender.
5. Put milk into a pan with mace, 1 bayleaf and peppercorns. Bring to the boil very slowly, leave to stand for 10 minutes, then strain.
6. Melt remaining butter in a pan, add flour and cook for 1 minute. Remove from heat and gradually stir in milk.
7. Return to heat and bring to the boil, stirring all the time until sauce bubbles and thickens. Add to liver mixture and blend well. Season to taste.
8. Turn into prepared dish and top with rest of bayleaves. Cover with foil and lid, stand dish in a roasting tin of hot water and bake for 1 hour.
9. Leave to become quite cold then serve with toast.

BRAISED OXTAIL
Serves 3–4

1 oxtail
2oz (50gm) flour
2oz (50gm) dripping or bacon fat
1 carrot
1 onion
1 stick celery
bunch of herbs
1½ pints (approximately 1¼ litres) stock or water
1 tablespoon sherry or lemon juice

1. Trim any superfluous fat from oxtail, put pieces of meat into a saucepan with cold water and bring to the boil.
2. Cook for 15 minutes, then rinse and dry well.
3. Coat pieces of oxtail with flour and fry in dripping or bacon fat until brown on all sides.
4. Add sliced vegetables and herbs and stock or water to cover and cook very gently for at least 3 hours. When the tail is tender lift on to a hot serving dish.
5. Reduce sauce by rapid boiling and add sherry or lemon juice. Pour over oxtail and serve.

MOCK CASSOULET
Serves 4

12oz (300gm) black pudding
6 streaky bacon rashers
1 can broad beans
1 medium can baked beans
2 tablespoons chopped parsley
1 tablespoon tomato purée
8 slices French bread
butter
grated Parmesan cheese

1. Preheat oven to moderate to moderately hot, 375 deg F or gas 5 (190 deg C).
2. Cut black pudding into slices, ¾ inch thick.
3. Form bacon rashers into rolls and grill lightly for 2–3 minutes, to remove excess fat.
4. Combine broad beans, baked beans, parsley and tomato purée. Add black pudding and bacon rolls and transfer to a casserole.
5. Butter the slices of bread and sprinkle with grated Parmesan cheese. Arrange on top of casserole.
6. Place in centre of oven and cook for 25 minutes.

Poultry

Poultry is very much a cost-conscious food, for every bit of it can be used right down to the carcass and giblets.

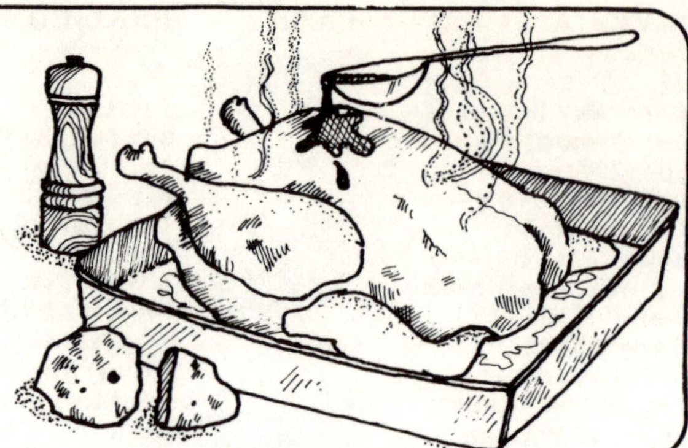

TAUNTON CHICKEN SOUP
Serves 6

A substantial soup that makes good use of leftover chicken.

**1 large carrot, grated
1 medium onion, finely chopped
2 sticks celery, chopped
1oz (25gm) butter
2¼ pints (1⅛ litres chicken stock
¾ pint (375ml) dry cider
4oz (100gm) cooked chicken, finely diced
1½oz (37gm) small soup pasta (stars, alphabets, rings)
salt and pepper**

1. Gently fry carrot, onion and celery in butter for 4–5 minutes.
2. Add chicken stock and cider, and bring to the boil. Cover and simmer gently for 15–20 minutes.
3. Add chicken, pasta and seasoning. Continue to simmer for 6–10 minutes or until pasta is cooked.

CHICKEN CHOWDER
Serves 4

**1 pint (½ litre) chicken stock
¼ pint (125ml) milk
8oz (200gm) potatoes, peeled and diced
1 large carrot, diced
1 celery stick, chopped
salt and pepper
1 can (7oz or 175gm) sweetcorn
6oz (150gm) cooked chicken, diced**

1. Mix stock and milk together and bring to boil in a pan.
2. Add potatoes, carrot, celery, salt and pepper. Cook for 15 minutes.
3. Drain can of sweetcorn and add with chicken meat. Heat through for 5 minutes.

CARIBBEAN COCKTAIL
(Illustrated on page 18)
Serves 4

A cooked chicken and grapefruit mixture to get a dinner party going.

**2 grapefruit
4oz (100gm) cooked chicken, diced
3 sticks celery, finely chopped
1 small can pineapple pieces
3 tablespoons mayonnaise
salt and pepper
5 tablespoons mango chutney
4 glacé cherries**

1. Halve grapefruit. Remove pulp and discard pith and pips.
2. Cut flesh into segments and combine with rest of ingredients.
3. Fill grapefruit shells, decorate each with a cherry and serve chilled.

ORIENTAL CHICKEN BROTH
Serves 4

A Chinese-style soup that makes use of the goodness in chicken bones.

**1 chicken carcass
1½ pints (approximately ¾ litre) water
½ onion, peeled
1 carrot, diced
1 bayleaf
pinch of garlic salt
pinch of celery salt
pepper
2 teaspoons lemon juice
2 teaspoons soy sauce
8 salad onions, trimmed**

1. Simmer chicken carcass with water, onion, carrot, bayleaf, salts and pepper for 1 hour.
2. Strain the broth and add lemon juice and soy sauce. Taste and add more seasoning if necessary. Add salad onions.
3. Simmer a further 15 minutes.

CURRIED CHICKEN AND APPLE PANCAKES
Serves 4–6

½ pint (250ml) pancake batter
(see Basic recipes, page 100)
1oz (25gm) butter
1oz (25gm) flour
1 tablespoon curry powder
½ pint (250ml) milk
salt and pepper
8oz (200gm) cooked chicken,
chopped
2 medium cooking apples,
peeled, cored and chopped

1. Make pancakes as usual in a
well-greased frying pan, stacking
them in a clean teatowel and
keeping hot.
2. Place butter, flour, curry
powder, milk and seasoning in a
pan.
3. Bring to the boil, stirring all
the time, until thick and smooth.
Cook for 1–2 minutes.
4. Add chicken and apple and
cook for a further 4–5 minutes.
Adjust seasoning.
5. Spread mixture over each
pancake and fold in half and half
again to form a fan shape.

POULET ROTI
Serves 4–6

1 roasting chicken (4lb or 2
kilo)
3oz (75gm) lard
1 onion, sliced
1 carrot, sliced
1 stick celery, sliced
1 can (15½oz or 387gm) cream of
chicken soup

1. Preheat oven to moderately
hot, 400 deg F or gas 6 (200 deg C).
Place chicken and lard in roasting
tin and roast for 1 hour 40
minutes, basting occasionally.
2. After 40 minutes add
vegetables.
3. Transfer cooked chicken to
serving dish and keep warm.
4. Add vegetables to chicken
soup and heat thoroughly. Sieve
or put in the blender to make
purée. Reheat if necessary.
5. Serve sauce separately, with
the chicken.

ROAST CHICKEN WITH CIDER
Serves 4–6

1 roasting chicken (3lb or 1½
kilo)
salt and pepper
1 garlic clove, crushed
(optional)
1oz (25gm) margarine
8oz (200gm) tomatoes, skinned
and sliced
2 medium onions, sliced
1oz (25gm) black olives, stoned
½ pint (250ml) cider
½oz (12gm) flour
2 tablespoons tomato purée

1. Preheat oven to moderate to
moderately hot, 375 deg F or gas 5
(190 deg C).
2. Wipe chicken, sprinkle inside
with salt and pepper and rub
outside with garlic, if used.
3. Fry chicken on all sides in
margarine till golden. Place in
casserole with tomatoes, onions
and olives.
4. Add salt and pepper and cider
and bake in centre of oven for 1½
hours till tender.
5. Strain liquid into saucepan.
Blend flour with a little water and
stir into pan. Add tomato purée.
6. Bring to boil, simmer for 1
minute stirring. Pour sauce over
chicken.

ROAST CHICKEN TARRAGON
Serves 4

1 roasting chicken (3lb or
1½ kilo)
6oz (150gm) butter
4oz (100gm) fresh breadcrumbs
grated rind of 1 lemon
4 level teaspoons tarragon
salt and pepper
1 level teaspoon chopped
parsley
1 teaspoon lemon juice

1. Preheat oven to moderately
hot, 400 deg F or gas 6 (200 deg C).
2. Prepare chicken. Put 4oz
(100gm) butter, breadcrumbs,
lemon rind, 3 teaspoons tarragon,
and seasoning in a basin and mix
together well. Stuff chicken with
this mixture.
3. Place chicken in a large piece
of foil. Make herb butter by
creaming together remaining
butter and tarragon, parsley and
lemon juice.
4. Spread butter over the chicken.
Wrap loosely in foil and cook in
centre of oven for about 1½ hours.
For last 30 minutes open foil to
allow chicken to brown. Serve
with rice.

CHICKEN FRICASSEE
Serves 4–6

1 small boiling fowl (about 2½lb
or 1¼ kilo)
2 egg yolks
3 tablespoons double cream,
fresh or canned
salt and pepper
pinch of cayenne pepper
1 pint (approximately ½ litre)
white sauce (see Basic recipes,
page 100)
1 teaspoon lemon juice
triangles of fried bread
parsley
slices of lemon

1. Simmer chicken in lightly
salted water until tender. Cut
into small joints and slices and
keep hot.
2. Mix egg yolks, cream,
seasoning and cayenne pepper
together in a basin.
3. Add to white sauce, reheat very
slowly and add lemon juice.
4. Pour sauce over chicken,
garnish with fried bread, parsley
and lemon slices. Serve with
boiled rice.

CHICKEN IN HONEY LEMON SAUCE
Serves 4

1 medium onion
4oz (100gm) butter
6oz (150gm) long-grain rice
1 pint ($\frac{1}{2}$ litre) stock
1 teaspoon mixed herbs
salt and pepper
fresh rosemary
4 chicken joints or 2 small
chickens, halved
4oz (100gm) clear honey
juice of 1 lemon

1. Preheat oven to moderately
hot, 400 deg F or gas 6 (200 deg C).
2. Chop and fry onion in 2oz
(50gm) butter until soft.
3. Stir in rice and add stock,
herbs and seasoning.
4. Transfer to casserole, add a
little rosemary, cover and bake in
centre of oven for 20 minutes.
5. Melt rest of butter in large
frying pan. Gently brown chicken
all over, then cover and cook on
low heat for about 20 minutes or
till tender. Remove and keep hot.
6. Heat honey, lemon juice and
4 small sprigs of rosemary with
juices in pan. Boil gently until
syrupy.
7. Pour sauce over chicken.
Serve with the herb rice.

ROAST CHICKEN WITH APRICOT STUFFING
Serves 6–8

3 tablespoons apricot chutney
4oz (100gm) fresh breadcrumbs
$\frac{1}{4}$ level teaspoon mixed spice
1 tablespoon lemon juice
3oz (75gm) butter
1 egg
1 large roasting chicken (6lb or
3 kilo)
$\frac{1}{4}$ lemon
salt and pepper
3 streaky bacon rashers

1. Preheat oven to moderate to
moderately hot, 375 deg F or gas 5
(190 deg C).
2. Mix chutney with breadcrumbs,
mixed spice and lemon juice. Melt
1oz (25gm) butter and pour over
mixture. Bind with egg.
3. Press stuffing into neck cavity
of chicken securing with a skewer.
Place lemon in body cavity.
4. Rub rest of butter over chicken
and sprinkle with salt and pepper.
5. Place chicken in roasting tin
and cover with bacon.
6. Cook in centre of oven for
about 2 hours basting frequently.
7. Remove bacon 15 minutes.
before serving to allow breast
meat to brown.

PINEAPPLE WALNUT – STUFFED ROAST CHICKEN
Serves 6–8

1 roasting chicken (4lb or 2
kilo)
$2\frac{1}{2}$oz (62gm) butter
2oz (50gm) stale white
breadcrumbs
4oz (100gm) pineapple, drained
and chopped
2oz (50gm) walnuts, chopped
1 level teaspoon salt
finely grated rind of $\frac{1}{2}$ lemon
a little pineapple juice

1. Preheat oven to moderate to
moderately hot, 375 deg F or gas 5
(190 deg C). Prepare chicken.
2. Make stuffing by melting $1\frac{1}{2}$oz
(37gm) butter in a pan, add
breadcrumbs and stir. Cook for a
minute or two.
3. Stir in pineapple, walnuts, salt
and lemon rind, adding pineapple
juice if required to give a moist
consistency.
4. Pack stuffing loosely in neck or
body cavity. Secure neck flap with
skewer. Put giblets (except liver)
in tin round chicken.
5. Spread remaining butter all
over chicken, then cover with
buttered paper. Cook chicken,
allowing 20 minutes per pound
($\frac{1}{2}$ kilo) plus 20 minutes extra.
6. Remove paper 20 minutes
before end of cooking time, baste
thoroughly and put liver in
roasting tin.
7. When cooked, put chicken on
warmed serving dish. Make gravy
from $\frac{1}{2}$ pint (250ml) water added
to roasting tin and giblets. Boil
for 5 minutes. Season and strain.

CHICKEN IN CIDER
Serves 4

2oz (50gm) butter
4 chicken portions
4 onions
8oz (200gm) mushrooms
salt and pepper
8oz (200gm) carrots
bouquet garni
1 level tablespoon flour
$\frac{1}{4}$ pint (125ml) chicken stock
$\frac{1}{2}$ pint (250ml) dry cider

1. Preheat oven to moderate to
moderately hot, 375 deg F or gas 5
(190 deg C).
2. Heat butter in large pan. Turn
chicken in butter till golden
brown.
3. Add quartered onions and
whole mushrooms. Season well.
4. Place in casserole with
quartered carrots, and bouquet
garni.
5. Stir flour in remaining fat in
pan, add stock, cider and season.
Bring to the boil.
6. Pour into the casserole, cover
and cook in centre of oven for
about 1$\frac{1}{4}$ hours until meat is
tender. Remove bouquet garni
before serving.

ORANGE CHICKEN
Serves 4

4 chicken joints
2oz (50gm) flour, seasoned with
salt and pepper
2oz (50gm) fat
$\frac{3}{4}$ pint (375ml) chicken stock
1 small can orange juice

1. Preheat oven to moderate, 350
deg F or gas 4 (180 deg C).
2. Coat chicken pieces with
seasoned flour and fry in fat till
brown. Put in ovenproof dish.
3. Stir remaining flour into fat in
pan, add stock and orange juice.
Bring to the boil, stirring until it
thickens. Pour over the chicken.
4. Cook in centre of oven for 50
minutes.

CHICKEN MARYLAND
Serves 4

4 chicken joints
2 eggs, beaten
4oz (100gm) fresh, white
breadcrumbs
2 small bananas
cooking fat for deep frying
3oz (75gm) self-raising flour
small pinch salt
1 egg
1 tablespoon cooking oil
1 can (8oz or 200gm) sweetcorn

1. Remove chicken skin. Brush
with egg and coat in crumbs. Pat
crumbs well in and keep chicken
on one side in frying basket.
2. Cut bananas in eight pieces,
dip in egg and crumbs. Heat fat.
3. Meanwhile mix flour, salt, egg
and oil in a bowl. Stir in
sweetcorn. (Mixture should be of
a stiff batter consistency.)
4. Fry chicken in hot deep fat for
8–10 minutes till brown and
tender. Drain and keep hot.
5. Fry bananas for about 1$\frac{1}{2}$
minutes till golden brown. Drain
well.
6. Heat fat to 375 deg F (190 deg
C) and drop spoonfuls of fritter
batter into it. Allow to puff up
and brown for about 3 minutes.
Drain well.
7. Serve chicken surrounded with
fried bananas and sweetcorn
fritters.

SPICED CHICKEN
(Illustrated on page 18)
Serves 4

4 chicken breasts
1oz (25gm) butter
1 tablespoon cooking oil
1 small onion, chopped
$\frac{1}{2}$oz (12gm) flour
salt and pepper
$\frac{1}{2}$ level teaspoon ground ginger
1 level teaspoon paprika
$\frac{3}{4}$ pint (375ml) cider
1 tablespoon tomato purée
$\frac{1}{4}$ teaspoon sugar
1 tablespoon chopped parsley

1. Preheat oven to very moderate,
325 deg F or gas 3 (170 deg C).
2. Fry chicken in butter and oil
till browned.
3. Remove and fry onion till soft.
4. Work in flour, seasonings,
ginger and paprika.
5. Add cider and stir in tomato
purée, sugar and parsley.
6. Return chicken to the pan,
baste well, cover and simmer for
20 minutes or cook in the oven for
30 minutes.
7. Remove chicken from pan and
place with rice on a serving
dish. Stir sauce well then pour
into a sauceboat.
8. Serve chicken with the sauce.

CHICKEN AND SWEETCORN
Serves 4

4 chicken joints
2oz (50gm) flour, seasoned with
salt and pepper
2oz (50gm) margarine
2 streaky bacon rashers
$\frac{3}{4}$ pint (375ml) chicken stock
1 packet or can sweetcorn
1 teaspoon cornflour

1. Coat chicken with seasoned
flour.
2. Melt margarine and fry
chicken on both sides to brown.
3. Remove rind and chop bacon,
add to the pan and cook for a few
minutes.
4. Pour stock over chicken. Cover
and simmer gently for 25 minutes.
5. Add sweetcorn for the last 10
minutes. Remove chicken and
keep it warm.
6. Blend cornflour with a little
cold water and stir into the stock.
Bring to the boil and pour over
the chicken.

CHICKEN WITH LEMON CIDER RICE
Serves 4

4 chicken joints
1 garlic clove, crushed
1½oz (37gm) Parmesan cheese, grated
1 teaspoon salt
1 teaspoon black pepper
3oz (75gm) butter
2oz (50gm) cooking oil
1 stick celery, chopped
1 large onion, chopped
½ pint (250ml) cider
⅛ pint (63ml) lemon juice
1 tablespoon grated lemon peel
1¼ teaspoons salt
pinch of chervil
4oz (100gm) long-grain rice

1. Rub chicken lightly with garlic.
2. Mix cheese with salt and black pepper in a shallow dish. Roll chicken in this, then fry gently for about 30 minutes in 2oz (50gm) butter and oil.
3. Meanwhile make lemon cider rice by frying celery and onion in remaining butter over low heat in covered pan, taking care not to brown.
4. Add liquids, grated peel, salt and chervil. Bring to the boil and add rice.
5. Reduce heat and simmer for 25 minutes till liquid is absorbed and rice is tender. Stir occasionally to prevent rice sticking. Serve with chicken.

CHINESE PINEAPPLE CHICKEN
Serves 4

1 can (12oz or 300gm) pineapple cubes
4 chicken joints
4 tablespoons corn oil
1 dessertspoon soy sauce
1 dessertspoon Worcestershire sauce
8oz (200gm) flat ribbon noodles
1 small packet frozen peas
1 dessertspoon gravy powder

1. Preheat oven to moderately hot 400 deg F or gas 6 (200 deg C).
2. Drain and reserve syrup from pineapple cubes.
3. Brush chicken pieces with oil and place in a roasting tin.
4. Sprinkle with soy and Worcestershire sauce and bake in centre of oven for about 25 minutes.
5. Turn chicken pieces, baste with a little pineapple syrup and bake for a further 20 minutes.
6. Meanwhile cook noodles in plenty of boiling, salted water for about 10 minutes until just tender. Drain and place on a hot serving dish.
7. Cook peas.
8. Arrange chicken on the serving dish surrounded with a border of noodles.
9. Mix gravy powder with a little pineapple syrup, stir into juices in pan and add sufficient syrup to make a thick sauce.
10. Bring sauce to the boil and stir in the pineapple cubes and cooked peas.
11. Heat through and spoon over the chicken. Serve any leftover sauce separately.

BANANA CHICKEN
Serves 6–8

2 small spring chickens
1 pint (approximately ½ litre) milk
1 small onion, stuck with 2 cloves
1 level dessertspoon flour
1 egg, beaten
salt and pepper
2 hard-boiled eggs, sliced
2 small, under-ripe bananas
cooked peas

1. Cover chickens with warm water in a saucepan, season with salt and bring to the boil. Remove any scum, replace lid and cook gently for 35 minutes.
2. Drain off liquid and pour in milk. Add onion and simmer gently for 30 minutes. Remove chickens and keep hot.
3. Thicken the milk with flour then stir in beaten egg. Cook and stir over gentle heat until smooth and creamy. (Do not allow it to boil.) Season to taste with salt and pepper.
4. Pour a little sauce over chickens, garnish with slices of egg and thinly sliced banana rings.
5. Arrange peas around chickens and serve rest of sauce separately.

CREAMY CHICKEN PAPRIKA
Serves 4

4 chicken joints
2oz (50gm) flour, seasoned with salt and pepper
4 tablespoons oil
2 onions, sliced
1 can (10½oz or 262gm) condensed tomato soup
4oz (100gm) mushrooms, sliced
3 teaspoons paprika
1 bayleaf
salt and pepper
1 carton soured cream

1. Skin chicken, coat in seasoned flour and fry in oil till golden.
2. Remove from pan and fry onions till golden.
3. Add soup and half can water. Stir in mushrooms, paprika, bayleaf and seasoning.
4. Return chicken to pan, cover and simmer for 30–40 minutes, stirring occasionally.
5. Remove bayleaf. Stir in soured cream and reheat but do not allow to boil.

Chicken luan served with chutney (see page 39)

Curried chicken salad with assorted salads (see page 40)

Turkey tetrazzini (see page 41)

Turkey salad (see page 42)

Herrings with red cabbage (see page 55)

Creamy kipper scallops (see page 56)

Crunchy cod casserole (see page 47)

Grilled halibut with spiced sauce (see page 59)

PIQUANT TOMATO CHICKEN
Serves 4

2 tablespoons olive oil
4 chicken joints
1 head of celery
8oz (200gm) bacon, cut in 2-inch
slices
12 silverskin onions
1 can (15½oz or 387gm) cream of
tomato soup
salt and pepper

1. Preheat oven to very moderate,
325 deg F or gas 3 (170 deg C).
2. Heat oil, fry chicken till golden
brown and drain.
3. Chop celery and blanch in
boiling water.
4. Fry bacon till brown.
5. Place chicken, celery, bacon
and onions in casserole. Cover
with the tomato soup and season.
6. Bake in centre of oven for
about 1 hour.

MUMBLES PIE
Serves 4

2 chicken legs
6oz (150gm) bacon flank,
chopped
½ pint (250ml) white sauce (see
Basic recipes, page 100)
2 leeks
salt and pepper
shortcrust pastry made with
10oz (250gm) flour (see Basic
recipes, page 100)

1. Simmer chicken and bacon for
1 hour. Leave to cool, then chop
meat.
2. Preheat oven to moderately
hot, 400 deg F or gas 6 (200 deg C).
3. Make white sauce using
chicken liquor.
4. Simmer the sliced leeks in
sauce for 10 minutes. Check
seasoning.
5. Line a deep tart plate with half
the pastry, fill with chicken,
bacon and cooled sauce.
6. Cover with remaining pastry
and bake in centre of oven for 35
minutes. Serve hot or cold.

CHICKEN MORNAY
Serves 4

4 chicken joints
1oz (25gm) flour, seasoned with
salt and pepper
2½oz (62gm) butter
½ pint (250ml) milk
½oz (12gm) flour
4oz (100gm) cheese, crumbled
½ teaspoon made mustard
2oz (50gm) fresh white
breadcrumbs

1. Preheat oven to moderately
hot, 400 deg F or gas 6 (200 deg C).
2. Coat chicken in seasoned flour
and put in ovenproof dish. Dot
with 2oz (50gm) butter and bake
in centre of oven for 20 minutes.
3. Heat milk, remaining butter
and flour together, stirring till
sauce thickens.
4. Stir in cheese and season to
taste with salt, pepper and
mustard. Simmer gently for 2–3
minutes.
5. Drain liquid from cooked
chicken into sauce, stir well and
pour sauce over chicken.
6. Sprinkle breadcrumbs over
top, brown under grill and serve.

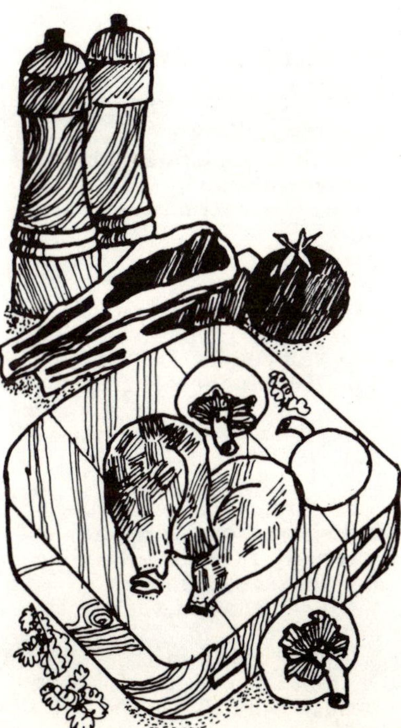

CHICKEN AND MARROW CASSEROLE
Serves 4

4 chicken joints
2 tablespoons cooking oil
1 medium marrow, peeled,
deseeded and diced
1 large onion, peeled and sliced
large pinch of dried herbs
1 can (15oz or 375gm)
mushroom soup
salt and pepper

1. Preheat oven to moderate, 350
deg F or gas 4 (180 deg C).
2. Fry chicken in oil till golden.
3. Put in casserole with marrow
and onion. Sprinkle with herbs.
4. Pour soup over the meat.
5. Bake in centre of oven for 1
hour or till tender. Add seasoning
to taste.

CHICKEN GOULASH
Serves 4

4 chicken joints
salt and pepper
2 tablespoons cooking oil
1 medium onion, finely chopped
1 teaspoon paprika
2 teaspoons tomato purée
1 can (8oz or 200gm) tomatoes
chicken stock
½oz (12gm) flour
¼ pint (125ml) natural yogurt

1. Season chicken. Fry in oil till
golden brown, then remove from
pan.
2. Fry onion till tender. Add
paprika and tomato purée.
3. Strain tomatoes and make
juice up to ½ pint (250ml) with
stock.
4. Stir into saucepan with
tomatoes. Bring to the boil and
replace chicken. Cover and cook
for 40–45 minutes until tender.
5. Blend flour with a little water
and stir into saucepan. Bring to
boil and cook for 1 minute stirring
all the time.
6. Stir in yogurt and pour sauce
over chicken.

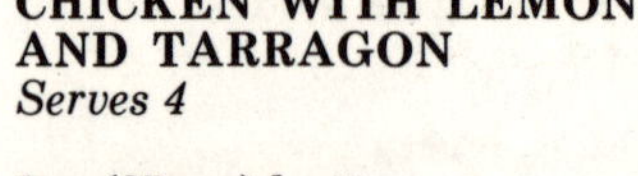

CHICKEN AND BACON CASSEROLE
Serves 4

1 chicken stock cube
1 bayleaf
12oz (300gm) smoked streaky
bacon
1 onion
2oz (50gm) butter
4 chicken joints
1oz (25gm) flour, seasoned with
salt and pepper
2oz (50gm) peas

1. Preheat oven to moderate, 350
deg F or gas 4 (180 deg C).
2. Make a stock from chicken
cube, bayleaf and ¼ pint (125ml)
water.
3. De-rind bacon and cut into
1½-inch cubes.
4. Peel and slice onion.
5. Fry bacon and onion in butter
till well browned. Drain and
place in casserole.
6. Dip chicken in seasoned flour.
Fry in butter for 5–6 minutes till
brown. Place in casserole with
chicken stock.
7. Cover and cook in centre of
oven for 45 minutes.
8. Add the peas 5 minutes before
end of cooking time.

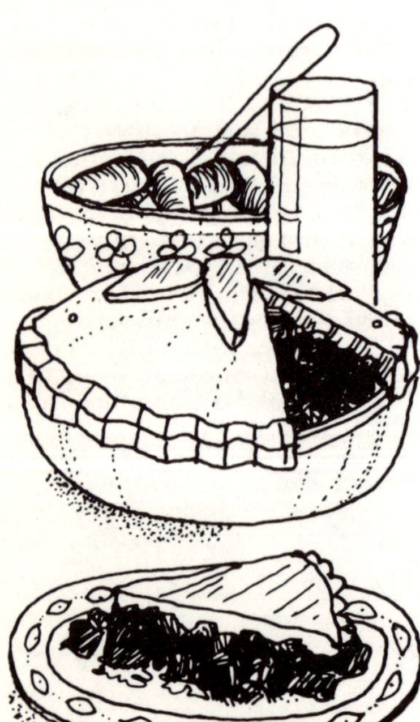

CHICKEN WITH LEMON AND TARRAGON
Serves 4

1oz (25gm) butter
4 chicken joints
1 onion, chopped
1oz (25gm) flour
¾ pint (375ml) chicken stock
1 level teaspoon dried tarragon
juice of 1 lemon
1 can (8oz or 200gm) butter
beans, drained
2 tablespoons cream, fresh or
canned
salt and pepper

1. Preheat oven to moderate to
moderately hot, 375 deg F or gas 5
(190 deg C).
2. Melt butter in a pan and fry
chicken joints gently for 10
minutes, turning once. Remove
from pan and place in a casserole.
3. Add onion to pan and fry
gently for 5 minutes. Remove pan
from heat, stir in flour and blend
in stock.
4. Add tarragon and lemon juice
and return pan to heat. Bring to
the boil, stirring.
5. Pour over the chicken, cover
and cook in centre of oven for 30
minutes.
6. Stir in butter beans, cream and
seasoning and return to oven for
5 minutes to reheat.

CHICKEN AU GRATIN
Serves 4

2oz (50gm) butter
2 small onions, finely chopped
2oz (50gm) flour
1 pint (approximately ½ litre)
milk
8oz (200gm) cooked chicken,
diced
2 hard-boiled eggs, sliced
12oz (300gm) long-grain rice
salt and pepper
4oz (100gm) cheese, grated

1. Melt butter and fry onions till
soft.
2. Stir in flour and cook slowly
for 2 minutes without colouring.
3. Remove from heat, stir in milk
gradually, then stir till boiling.
Boil for several minutes.
4. Fold in chicken, egg and rice.
Season well.
5. Either mix in cheese and serve
or transfer to shallow casserole,
sprinkle with cheese and grill till
golden.

CHICKEN BAKE
Serves 4–6

8oz (200gm) cooked chicken,
diced
4oz (100gm) cooked rice (raw
weight)
½ pint (250ml) chicken stock
2oz (50gm) margarine
4oz (100gm) flour
2 teaspoons baking powder
1 teaspoon salt
1oz (25gm) sugar
¼ pint (125ml) milk

1. Preheat oven to moderate, 350
deg F or gas 4 (180 deg C).
2. Mix first three ingredients
together. Melt margarine in
casserole.
3. Meanwhile mix rest of
ingredients together.
4. Pour into casserole.
5. Spoon chicken mixture in
centre.
6. Bake in centre of oven for 50
minutes.

CHICKEN PILAU
Serves 4

2oz (50gm) butter
1 medium onion, sliced
1 garlic clove, crushed
2 streaky bacon rashers, cut in
strips
2 large tomatoes, skinned and
chopped
2 level tablespoons currants
8oz (200gm) cooked chicken
1 level teaspoon salt
1 tablespoon chopped parsley
8oz (200gm) rice

1. Melt butter, and add onion and
garlic. Cook till soft without
browning.
2. Add bacon and cook for 2
minutes until lightly brown.
3. Add tomatoes, currants,
chicken, salt and parsley and heat
through for about 10 minutes.
4. Meanwhile cook rice in boiling,
salted water; drain and add to
chicken mixture and heat
through.

CURRY SUPREME
Serves 4

4 teaspoons curry powder
2 teaspoons chilli powder
2 teaspoons mixed spice
pinch of ginger and garlic
(optional)
2 small cans tomato purée
1 cup vinegar
4 tablespoons cooking oil
1 large onion, sliced
salt
2lb (1 kilo) cooked chicken
8oz (200gm) boiled rice (raw
weight)

1. Put curry powder, chilli
powder, mixed spice, ginger and
garlic (if used) into a bowl. Mix
with a little water and put on one
side.
2. Empty purée into cup and mix
with vinegar. Put on one side.
3. Heat cooking oil, add onion
and fry till golden.
4. Add spices, tomato purée and
salt. Stir over low heat till all oil
appears on the surface.
5. Add cubed chicken. Simmer
gently for 10 minutes, then add ½
pint (250ml) water.
6. Simmer till meat is tender, then
serve with rice.

CHICKEN LUAN
(Illustrated on page 35)
Serves 4

4oz (100gm) butter or
margarine
1 large stick celery, chopped
4 level teaspoons curry powder
1oz (25gm) flour
2 cans (10oz or 250gm) cream of
chicken soup
salt and pepper
12oz (300gm) cooked chicken,
diced
2 cans (8oz or 200gm each)
pineapple pieces, drained
8oz (200gm) rice
watercress to garnish

1. Melt butter or margarine in a
pan. Add celery and curry powder
and fry for 3–4 minutes.
2. Add flour and cook for 1
minute.
3. Stir in chicken soup, seasoning,
chicken and pineapple and heat
gently.
4. Meanwhile, cook rice in
boiling, salted water till tender,
drain and serve the chicken on it.
Garnish with watercress.

MACARONI CHICKEN
Serves 4

6oz (150gm) macaroni
3 streaky bacon rashers,
de-rinded and chopped
4oz (100gm) mushrooms, sliced
8oz (200gm) cooked chicken,
diced
3 tomatoes, skinned and sliced
½ pint (250ml) white sauce (see
Basic recipes, page 100)
4oz (100gm) cheese, grated

1. Preheat oven to moderate, 350
deg F or gas 4 (180 deg C).
2. Cook macaroni in boiling,
salted water until tender. Drain
and place in casserole.
3. Fry bacon and mushrooms till
tender. Add to macaroni.
4. Place chicken on bacon and
mushrooms. Arrange tomatoes on
top and pour white sauce over.
5. Sprinkle with cheese and heat
through for 15 minutes in centre
of oven.

CRISP CHICKEN BALLS
Serves 4

2oz (50gm) streaky bacon,
de-rinded
1 small onion, finely chopped
2oz (50gm) mushrooms, diced
8oz (200gm) cooked chicken
2oz (50gm) butter
2oz (50gm) flour
¼ pint (125ml) chicken stock
¼ pint (125ml) milk
½ teaspoon prepared mustard
salt and pepper
1 teaspoon chopped parsley
1oz (25gm) flour
1 egg, beaten
browned breadcrumbs
fat for deep frying

1. Fry bacon, then remove from
pan.
2. Fry onion and mushrooms till
tender. Mince bacon with chicken.
3. Melt butter and stir in flour.
Add stock and milk gradually.
Bring to the boil, stirring all the
time and simmer for 2 minutes.
4. Add mustard, salt, pepper,
parsley, bacon, chicken, onion and
mushrooms.
5. Spread mixture on plate and
leave to cool.
6. Form mixture into eight balls
and roll in flour.
7. Dip in egg and coat with
breadcrumbs.
8. Fry in deep fat until golden
brown. Drain on kitchen paper.

PARSLEY AND THYME
FLAN
Serves 4–6

1 packet parsley and thyme
stuffing
1 small egg, beaten
1oz (25gm) butter, melted
½ pint (250ml) white sauce (see
Basic recipes, page 100)
8oz (200gm) cooked chicken,
diced
1 can (7½oz or 187gm) button
mushrooms, drained

1. Preheat oven to moderately
hot, 400 deg F or gas 6 (200 deg C).
2. Make up stuffing using ⅓ pint
(170ml) water. Add egg and press
into well greased 8-inch (20-cm)
flan ring. Leave to stand for 10
minutes.
3. Brush with melted butter. Line
with foil and beans and bake
blind in centre of oven for 25
minutes.
4. Remove foil and beans and
bake for a further 10 minutes.
5. Make up white sauce, then add
chicken and mushrooms.
6. Ease flan from ring. Pour filling
into ring and serve hot.

SWEET AND SOUR
CASSEROLE
Serves 4

1 chicken (1½lb or ¾ kilo)
1oz (25gm) dripping
4 tablespoons tomato ketchup
½oz (12gm) flour
juice of ½ lemon
2 level teaspoons sugar
¼ level teaspoon black pepper
12 pickled onions
4oz (100gm) mushrooms, halved
¾ pint (375ml) stock or water

1. Preheat oven to moderate, 350
deg F or gas 4 (180 deg C).
2. Cut chicken into pieces. Fry
in hot dripping in heavy casserole
until lightly browned.
3. Add tomato ketchup and cook
for a further 5 minutes over gentle
heat.
4. Stir in flour, lemon juice, sugar,
black pepper, pickled onions and
mushrooms.
5. Add stock or water, cover and
continue to cook in centre of oven
until meat is tender.

CHICKEN AND EGG PIE
Serves 6–8

A deep pie for picnic or buffet.

1oz (25gm) butter
1 onion, finely chopped
6oz (150gm) button mushrooms,
chopped
3lb (1½ kilo) cooked chicken
meat
1 level teaspoon mixed dried
herbs
salt and pepper
shortcrust pastry made with
10oz (250gm) flour (see Basic
recipes, page 100)
4 hard-boiled eggs, sliced
½ pint (250ml) chicken stock
1 egg, beaten

1. Preheat oven to moderately
hot, 400 deg F or gas 6 (200 deg C).
2. Melt butter or margarine in
pan and gently fry onion for 5
minutes.
3. Add mushrooms and cook for a
further 2 minutes.
4. Add chicken meat, herbs and
seasoning to taste. Leave to cool.
5. Turn pastry on to a floured
board and knead lightly until
smooth. Roll out a circle about 13
inches in diameter then cut out a
quarter section. Line a round
cake tin 7 inches (18cm) in
diameter and 3 inches (7·5cm)
deep, joining cut edges.
6. Spoon half chicken mixture
into this and press down. Arrange
hard-boiled eggs on top and top
with rest of chicken.
7. Spoon 4 tablespoons chicken
stock over. Roll out pastry for lid
and cover pie. Press dampened
edges together. Brush with beaten
egg and make hole in centre of
pie.
8. Bake in centre of oven for 30
minutes. Reduce heat to moderate,
350 deg F or gas 4 (180 deg C) for a
further 30 minutes.
9. Leave to cool in tin, then
remove from tin. Pour stock
through hole till full, then leave
to set.

TOMATO CHICKEN CASSEROLE
Serves 4–6

1 boiling fowl (about 3lb or 1½
kilo)
1 can (14oz or 350gm) tomato
juice
¾ pint (375ml) chicken stock
1 bayleaf
2 medium onions, sliced
2–3 peppercorns
salt and pepper
1 garlic clove, crushed
2 tablespoons tomato purée
3 tablespoons white wine

1. Wash and wipe fowl and place
in the bottom of a large pan.
2. Pour on tomato juice, stock
and add bayleaf, onion,
peppercorns, seasoning and garlic.
3. Cover closely and simmer
gently until fowl is tender.
4. Remove fowl from juice. Joint
as required. Place portions in
oven to keep hot.
5. Strain juice into clean pan, stir
in tomato purée, simmer gently
for 5 minutes, then add wine.
6. Pour sauce over chicken and
serve.

HOT BAKED CHICKEN SALAD
Serves 4

8oz (100gm) cooked chicken,
chopped
4oz (100gm) celery, diced
2oz (50gm) almonds or pecans,
chopped
2 teaspoons chopped onion
1 teaspoon grated lemon rind
1 tablespoon lemon juice
pepper
mayonnaise to taste (about 4oz
or 100gm)
2½oz (62gm) Cheddar cheese,
grated
3oz (75gm) potato crisps or
cornflakes, crushed

1. Preheat oven to moderate to
moderately hot, 375 deg F or gas 5
(190 deg C).
2. Place chicken, celery, nuts,
onion, lemon rind, lemon juice
and pepper in a mixing bowl.
3. Add mayonnaise and toss
mixture with two forks.
4. Divide between four individual
casseroles or put in one large one.
5. Sprinkle cheese on top and
arrange crushed crisps or
cornflakes round rim or over the
cheese.
6. Bake in centre of oven for 25
minutes.

CURRIED CHICKEN SALAD
(Illustrated on page 35)
Serves 4

1lb (½ kilo) cooked chicken
2oz (50gm) salted nuts
2oz (50gm) sultanas
1 teaspoon curry powder
½ pint (250ml) natural yogurt
1 teaspoon chopped chives
salt

1. Cut chicken roughly. Lightly
chop nuts. Mix together and add
sultanas.
2. Mix curry powder, yogurt and
chives together, and season with
a little salt. Add this to chicken
mixture.
3. Serve chicken with a lettuce
and watercress salad and an egg
and tomato salad.

SPRING CHICKEN SALAD
Serves 4

6oz (150gm) long-grain rice
1 small packet frozen peas or
mixed vegetables
2oz (50gm) sultanas
1 large chicken joint, cooked
6 tablespoons salad cream
4 tablespoons top of milk
¼ teaspoon curry powder
½ teaspoon salt

1. Cook rice in boiling, salted
water for 5 minutes.
2. Add vegetables and sultanas
and cook for a further 5 minutes
until tender.
3. Drain rice mixture when
cooked and allow to cool.
4. Cube chicken and add to rice.
5. Mix salad cream, milk, curry
powder and salt and pour over
rice mixture. Combine well
together.
6. Pile into salad bowl and serve.

SALAD TOSS
Serves 4

1 medium potato, cooked
1 apple
juice of 1 lemon
4oz (100gm) cooked chicken,
diced
4oz (100gm) cheese, diced
¼ small cabbage, shredded
1 tablespoon mixed pickles
1 carton (5oz or 125gm) soured
cream or natural yogurt

1. Dice potato. Peel and dice
apple. Dip in lemon juice and mix
with chicken.
2. Add cheese and cabbage.
3. Stir in mixed, chopped pickles.
Chill.
4. Top with spoons of soured
cream or yogurt.

HUNGARIAN SPICED TURKEY
Serves 4

Some ideas for using up Christmas
or leftover turkey.

4oz (100gm) butter
2 medium onions, chopped
1lb (½ kilo) cooked turkey,
minced
4oz (100gm) fresh white
breadcrumbs
salt and pepper
1 egg, beaten
2 tablespoons oil
1½ level tablespoons paprika
⅛ teaspoon cayenne pepper
1oz (25gm) flour
½ pint (250ml) chicken stock
12oz (300gm) tomatoes, roughly
chopped
1 level teaspoon sugar
salt
2 cartons (5oz or 125gm each)
natural yogurt

1. Melt 1oz (25gm) butter in
saucepan and cook half the onion
for 3 minutes.
2. Combine turkey, breadcrumbs
and onion. Season well and bind
with egg.
3. Turn mixture on to floured
surface and shape into 16
even-sized balls.
4. Heat oil and 2oz (50gm) butter
in pan and fry meat mixture for
10–15 minutes, turning, to brown
evenly.
5. Remove and keep hot.
6. For sauce, melt remaining
butter and cook rest of onion for 3
minutes. Add spices and cook for
a further minute.
7. Stir in flour, remove from heat
and blend in stock.
8. Return to heat, stir till sauce
thickens and add tomatoes.
9. Bring to boil, add sugar and
salt to taste. Simmer for 5–10
minutes.
10. Pass through sieve into clean
saucepan. Stir in yogurt. Warm
through and pour over turkey
balls.

TURKEY TETRAZZINI
(Illustrated on page 35)
Serves 4–6

8oz (200gm) spaghetti
1 celery stick, chopped
1 small onion, chopped
1 can mushrooms, thinly sliced
3oz (75gm) butter
1 can (10oz or 250gm) cream of
chicken soup
¼ pint (125ml) milk
2oz (50gm) sharp Cheddar
cheese, grated
2 tablespoons sherry (optional)
salt and pepper
8oz (200gm) turkey, cooked
and diced
grated Parmesan cheese

1. Preheat oven to moderate, 350
deg F or gas 4 (180 deg C).
2. Cook spaghetti in boiling,
salted water till tender. Drain
and keep hot.
3. Cook celery, onion, and
mushrooms in butter till tender.
4. Add soup, milk, cheese and
sherry if used. Season well.
5. Cook over low heat till cheese
has melted. Add turkey and pour
over spaghetti.
6. Stir and place in casserole.
Sprinkle with Parmesan and bake
in centre of oven for 20–25
minutes.

TURKEY FRIED RICE
Serves 4–6

3 tablespoons cooking oil
1 garlic clove, crushed
1 medium onion
3oz (75gm) celery, chopped
4oz (100gm) mushrooms
8oz (200gm) turkey, cooked
4oz (100gm) cooked rice (raw
weight)
4–5 tablespoons soy sauce
salt and pepper
2 eggs

1. Heat oil in large pan and add
garlic, onion, celery and
mushrooms. Fry gently for
2 minutes.
2. Add turkey and brown slightly.
3. Add rice, soy sauce, salt and
pepper and heat through.
4. Quickly add eggs, one at a
time, and mix in thoroughly.
Serve at once, piping hot.

RAINBOW RISOTTO
Serves 4–6

2oz (50gm) butter
1 medium onion, chopped
8oz (200gm) long-grain rice
1 pint (approximately ½ litre)
chicken stock
4½oz (112gm) peas
12oz (300gm) cooked turkey
1 can (1lb or ½ kilo) sliced
peaches, drained and cut in
½-inch pieces
salt and pepper

1. Melt butter in large pan, add
onion and fry until tender but not
browned. Stir in rice.
2. Add stock, bring to boil, cover
and simmer for 15 minutes.
3. Add peas, cover and simmer for
a further 5 minutes.
4. Add turkey, peaches and
seasoning. Cover and cook a
further 5 minutes.

TURKEY SCRAMBLE
Serves 4

12oz (300gm) mushrooms
1oz (25gm) butter
1 teaspoon chopped gherkins
½ teaspoon sage
½ teaspoon garlic salt
salt and pepper
8 large thin turkey slices
¼ pint (125ml) turkey stock
6 eggs
4 tablespoons cream

1. Preheat oven to very moderate,
325 deg F or gas 3 (170 deg C).
2. Chop mushrooms and cook in
half the butter with gherkins,
sage and garlic salt until liquid
has nearly evaporated. Add salt
and pepper.
3. Sandwich turkey slices
together with mushroom mixture.
4. Place in ovenproof dish and
add stock. Cover and bake in
centre of oven for 20 minutes.
5. A few minutes before turkey is
ready, scramble eggs in remaining
butter and add cream. Cover
turkey with eggs.

TURKEY MUSHROOM PIE
Serves 4–6

1 packet (13oz or 325gm) frozen
puff pastry (or see Basic
recipes, page 100)
½ pint (250ml) white sauce (see
Basic recipes, page 100)
6oz (150gm) cooked turkey,
diced
4oz (100gm) mushrooms,
quartered
salt and pepper
1 egg, beaten

1. Preheat oven to hot, 425 deg F
or gas 7 (220 deg C).
2. Roll out half pastry and line
pie dish. Roll out rest for lid and
put on one side.
3. Prepare white sauce and add
turkey, mushrooms, salt and
pepper. Heat gently for 2–3
minutes.
4. Pour into pastry-lined dish.
Cool. Cover with pastry lid and
dampen to seal. Trim edges and
flute them.
5. Brush top of pie with egg and
bake in centre of oven for 15
minutes. Reduce heat to moderate
to moderately hot, 375 deg F or
gas 5 (190 deg C) for a further
10 minutes.

TURKEY SALAD
(Illustrated on page 35)
Serves 4

4 tablespoons oil
1 teaspoon curry powder
salt and pepper
1 lemon
1 tablespoon chopped parsley
8oz (200gm) cooked turkey,
diced
1 can (10oz or 250gm) potatoes,
drained and sliced

1. Place oil, curry powder, salt,
pepper, grated rind of half lemon
and juice from whole lemon and
parsley in a screw-topped jar.
Shake well till ingredients are
blended.
2. Mix together turkey and
potatoes.
3. Pour dressing over turkey
mixture. Toss well and leave,
covered, for 1 hour. Serve on
lettuce, garnish with tomato
slices and watercress.

TURKEY LOAF
Serves 6

2oz (50gm) long-grain rice
8oz (200gm) cooked turkey,
minced
4 streaky bacon rashers,
de-rinded and minced
salt and pepper
1 egg
½ packet parsley and thyme
stuffing
grated rind of ½ lemon
1 teaspoon paprika

1. Preheat oven to moderate to
moderately hot, 375 deg F or gas 5
(190 deg C).
2. Cook rice in boiling, salted
water for 10 minutes.
3. Mix turkey and bacon with
salt, pepper and egg.
4. Drain rice, add to turkey
mixture and beat well until
blended.
5. Prepare stuffing, add lemon
rind and paprika and mix well.
6. Place half turkey mixture in
greased loaf tin. Spread with
stuffing, then cover with
remaining turkey mixture. Cover
with greased foil and bake in
centre of oven for 35 minutes.
7. Serve hot or cold.

Fish

Like meat, fish can be made to go further with the addition of rice, pasta and vegetables, and even the traditional cobbler scone topping can go on a quick fish pie.

FISH SOUP
Serves 4–6

1 cod or hake's head
2oz (50gm) butter
1 large onion
3 sticks celery
2 pints (approximately 1 litre) fish stock (see method)
pinch of saffron
salt and pepper
¼ pint (125ml) milk
1 heaped tablespoon chopped parsley
12oz (300gm) cod or coley

1. Cover fish head with water and simmer for 25 minutes. Drain and reserve stock.
2. Melt butter and fry chopped onion and celery quickly until transparent but not brown. Add fish stock, saffron and seasoning.
3. Simmer for 10 minutes.
4. Stir in milk and parsley.
5. Skin fish and cut into small pieces.
6. Add to soup and simmer for 5 minutes. Season and serve.

SOVEREIGN FISH PUDDING
Serves 4

1 large and 1 small packet cod fillets
2oz (50gm) margarine
2 eggs
1 onion, grated
salt and pepper
1oz (25gm) flour
3 tablespoons milk

1. Skin the cod, remove bones and put uncooked fish twice through a mincer, so it is fine and smooth.
2. Melt margarine and stir into the fish with all remaining ingredients.
3. Put mixture into 1½-pint (approximately ¾-litre) pudding basin. Cover with greaseproof paper or foil.
4. Steam for 1 hour and serve hot or cold.

FISH AND CELERY PANCAKES
Serves 4

½ pint (250ml) pancake batter (see Basic recipes, page 100)
2 sticks celery, chopped
1oz (25gm) butter
8oz (200gm) cod, cooked and flaked
salt and pepper
½ pint (250ml) white sauce (see Basic recipes, page 100)

1. Cook pancakes and keep warm.
2. Cook celery in the butter till tender. Add cod and seasoning.
3. Fill pancakes with this mixture and roll them up. Place on a serving dish.
4. Pour white sauce over pancakes.

POTATO FISH SOUFFLE
Serves 4

12oz (300gm) potatoes
1oz (25gm) butter
8oz (200gm) white fish, cooked and flaked
1oz (25gm) cheese, grated
1 teaspoon chopped parsley
2 egg yolks
3 egg whites
salt and pepper

1. Preheat oven to moderate to moderately hot, 375 deg F or gas 5 (190 deg C).
2. Peel and boil potatoes until tender, then drain and sieve them.
3. While hot stir in the butter, fish, cheese, parsley, egg yolks, stiffly beaten egg whites, salt and pepper.
4. Pour mixture into lightly greased soufflé dish and bake in centre of oven for 30 minutes.

KEDGEREE
Serves 4

4 hard-boiled eggs
4oz (100gm) butter or
margarine
4oz (100gm) cod or haddock,
cooked and flaked
8oz (200gm) boiled rice (raw
weight)
lemon juice

1. Shell and chop eggs finely.
2. Heat butter or margarine in
pan. Add fish, rice, lemon juice
and egg.
3. Heat through for a few
minutes before serving.

BREAKFAST SAVOURY
Serves 4

8oz (200gm) smoked cod fillet
a little milk
$\frac{1}{4}$oz (6gm) butter
1 can (15$\frac{1}{4}$oz or 381gm)
macaroni in cheese sauce
1 hard-boiled egg (optional)

1. Poach fish in milk and butter
in a pan. Remove any skin and
bones.
2. Add macaroni, then cover and
heat thoroughly.
3. Place in serving dish and
garnish with egg, if used.

FISH CAKES
Serves 4

1lb ($\frac{1}{2}$ kilo) cod or other white
fish, cooked and flaked
1lb ($\frac{1}{2}$ kilo) potato, mashed
1oz (25gm) butter, melted
1 egg yolk
salt and pepper
lemon juice
flour
fat for shallow frying

1. Mix fish, potato, butter and egg
yolk together. Season and add a
squeeze of lemon juice.
2. Shape when cool into flat
round cakes, roll in flour and fry
till golden brown on both sides.
3. Drain on absorbent paper.

BAKED COD AND BACON
Serves 4

4 cod steaks or fillets
pepper
prepared mustard
8 streaky bacon rashers

1. Preheat oven to moderate, 350
deg F or gas 4 (180 deg C).
2. Place two cod steaks or fillets
in buttered ovenproof dish.
Season with pepper and a smear
of mustard.
3. Lay over them 4 bacon rashers.
Place other two fish steaks on top
then remainder of bacon.
4. Cover and bake in centre of
oven for 30 minutes.
5. Remove lid and let top bacon
layer brown.

SCALLOPED FISH CHEESE
Serves 4

1lb ($\frac{1}{2}$ kilo) cod or white fish,
cooked
1 pint (approximately $\frac{1}{2}$ litre)
white sauce (see Basic recipes,
page 100)
2$\frac{1}{2}$oz (62gm) Cheddar cheese,
grated
1 hard-boiled egg
2 tablespoons chopped parsley

1. Preheat oven to hot, 425 deg F
or gas 7 (220 deg C).
2. Mix flaked fish with white
sauce and add 1oz (25gm) cheese.
3. Spoon into scallop shells or
individual ovenproof dishes.
4. Make stripes on fish with rest
of cheese.
5. Bake in centre of oven for
15–20 minutes till heated
through. Before serving, sprinkle
with chopped hard-boiled white of
egg mixed with parsley arranged
in stripes.
6. Arrange slices of egg yolk on
the dishes.

POTATO FISH NIÇOISE
Serves 4

1lb ($\frac{1}{2}$ kilo) cod or white fish,
cooked
$\frac{1}{2}$ pint (250ml) white sauce (see
Basic recipes, page 100)
squeeze lemon juice
salt and pepper
1lb ($\frac{1}{2}$ kilo) boiled potatoes
$\frac{1}{2}$ can anchovy fillets
2oz (50gm) cheese, grated

1. Heat fish in the sauce.
2. Add lemon juice to taste.
3. Season, then stir in potatoes
and heat carefully to keep whole.
4. Place mixture in ovenproof
dish, cover with anchovy fillets
in a lattice pattern.
5. Sprinkle the cheese over the
top, then grill till cheese melts.

SPAGHETTI FISH RING
Serves 4

8oz (200gm) spaghetti
12oz (300gm) cooked white fish
¼ pint (125ml) white sauce (see
Basic recipes, page 100)
¼ pint (125ml) cream, fresh or
canned
seasoning
2oz (50gm) butter
1 teaspoon chopped parsley
paprika

1. Cook spaghetti in boiling,
salted water for 10–15 minutes
until tender. Drain well.
2. Add flaked fish to white sauce
and beat well. Add cream and
seasoning.
3. Melt butter in a saucepan and
toss spaghetti in it. Heat through.
4. Heat fish mixture gently and
pile in the centre of a serving
dish. Surround with spaghetti.
5. Sprinkle with parsley and
paprika and serve immediately.

SUPPER FISH BAKE
Serves 4

1 large packet frozen cod
fillets
4 large potatoes, thinly sliced
2 large onions, thinly sliced
salt and pepper
¼ pint (125ml) single cream

1. Preheat oven to moderate to
moderately hot, 375 deg F or gas 5
(190 deg C).
2. Skin cod. Remove any bones
and cut into strips.
3. Arrange layers of fish, potato
and onion in an ovenproof dish.
Season well and finish with a
layer of potato.
4. Pour cream over fish mixture
and bake in centre of oven for 45
minutes until top is golden.
Serve with buttered carrots.

FISH MOULD
Serves 4

1lb (½ kilo) white fish, cooked
and flaked
8oz (200gm) potato, cooked and
sieved
2oz (50gm) shredded suet
2 eggs, beaten
¼ pint (125ml) milk
squeeze lemon juice
salt and pepper

1. Mix all ingredients together to
a soft consistency.
2. Pile into buttered basin, cover,
and steam for 1–1¼ hours.

FISH LOAF
Serves 4

1 large packet frozen cod
fillets
2oz (50gm) white breadcrumbs
1 egg, beaten
1 onion, chopped
1 small can condensed
mushroom soup
salt and pepper
1oz (25gm) margarine
1oz (25gm) flour
1 small can tomatoes

1. Preheat oven to moderate to
moderately hot, 375 deg F or gas 5
(190 deg C).
2. Skin cod, remove any bones
and mince finely. Mix with
breadcrumbs, egg, onion, soup
and seasoning.
3. Put mixture into greased 1-lb
(½-kilo) loaf tin.
4. Cover and bake in centre of
oven for 45 minutes until top is
firm to the touch.
5. Meanwhile, melt margarine in
a pan. Add flour and cook gently
for 1 minute. Remove from heat
and stir in tomatoes.
6. Heat again, stirring, till thick.
7. Serve fish loaf with tomato
sauce.

BOTANY BAY FISH BAKE
Serves 4–6

2oz (50gm) butter
1½lb (¾ kilo) filleted white fish,
such as cod or haddock
1lb (½ kilo) tomatoes, skinned
and sliced
2 tablespoons lemon juice
salt and pepper
grated nutmeg
pinch of thyme
3 level tablespoons browned
crumbs
2 eggs

1. Preheat oven to moderate to
moderately hot, 375 deg F or gas 5
(190 deg C).
2. Use ½oz (12gm) butter to grease
a 2-pint (approximately 1-litre)
casserole dish.
3. Skin fish and cut into pieces.
Place half fish on base of dish and
put half the tomatoes on top.
4. Sprinkle with 1 tablespoon
lemon juice, seasonings and a
good pinch each of nutmeg and
thyme.
5. Top with remaining fish,
tomatoes, lemon juice, seasoning,
nutmeg and thyme as before.
6. Sprinkle crumbs on top and dot
with remaining butter. Cover and
bake in centre of oven for about
30 minutes or till fish is cooked.
7. Remove cover. Beat eggs and
pour over mixture in casserole.
8. Return to oven for a further
10–15 minutes, until egg is set.

COD CELESTE
Serves 4

2lb (1 kilo) tail end of cod
1 level dessertspoon prepared
mustard
½oz (12gm) plain flour
3oz (75gm) butter, melted
salt and pepper
4 tablespoons dry white wine
chopped parsley

1. Preheat oven to moderate to
moderately hot, 375 deg F or gas 5
(190 deg C).
2. Clean cod and remove bones
and fins.
3. Spread inside and out with
mustard, then place in ovenproof
casserole.
4. Sprinkle with flour, pour
melted butter over fish and
season. Cover and bake in centre
of oven for about 35 minutes.
5. Transfer fish to serving dish
and keep warm.
6. Add wine and parsley to butter
and fish juices. Heat in a small
pan until boiling.
7. Pour sauce over fish or serve
separately.

MAHARANEE PIE
Serves 4

1lb (½ kilo) cod fillet
1oz (25gm) butter
1 medium onion, chopped
1oz (25gm) flour
2 level teaspoons curry powder
4 tablespoons milk
1 medium cooking apple,
peeled, cored and cut in ½-inch
cubes
4oz (100gm) frozen peas
1½oz (37gm) raisins
salt and pepper
1 tablespoon lemon juice
2 hard-boiled eggs, chopped
13oz (325gm) frozen puff pastry
(or see Basic recipes, page 100)
1 egg, beaten

1. Preheat oven to hot, 425 deg F
or gas 7 (220 deg C).
2. Place cod in shallow pan and
cover with water. Poach gently
for 8–10 minutes.
3. Drain and flake cod, keeping ½
pint (250ml) liquor for sauce.
4. Melt butter in pan, add onion
and cook gently for 3 minutes.
5. Stir in flour and curry powder
and cook for 1 minute.
6. Remove from heat. Blend in
fish liquor and milk and bring to
the boil, stirring. Add apple, peas
and raisins.
7. Simmer for 3 minutes, then
season. Add lemon juice, flaked
fish and egg.
8. Spoon into a 1½-pint
(approximately ¾-litre) pie dish
and leave to cool.
9. Roll out pastry and cover pie.
Glaze with beaten egg.
10. Bake in centre of oven for
20–25 minutes until the pastry is
well risen and golden.

SAVOURY FISH PIE
Serves 4–6

1lb (½ kilo) white fish, cooked
½ pint (250ml) cheese sauce (see
Basic recipes, page 100)
2oz (50gm) butter
salt and pepper
pinch of grated nutmeg
a little milk
1½lb (¾ kilo) potato, cooked and
sieved

1. Preheat oven to hot, 425 deg F
or gas 7 (220 deg C).
2. Mix together fish and cheese
sauce. Pour into lightly greased
pie dish.
3. Beat butter, seasoning and
milk into hot potato.
4. Pile potato on top of fish and
fork up roughly.
5. Bake in centre of oven for 15
minutes.

COUNTRY FISH GRILL
Serves 4

2lb (1 kilo) potatoes
1lb (½ kilo) cod
¾ pint (375ml) water
1 packet thick vegetable soup
mix
1–2 tablespoons milk
½oz (12gm) margarine
salt and pepper
2oz (50gm) cheese, grated

1. Boil potatoes for 20 minutes
until cooked. Drain.
2. Poach fish in water for 10–15
minutes until flakes fall apart
easily.
3. Drain off liquor and make up
to ¾ pint (375ml) with water. Mix
in the soup and bring to boil.
Cover and simmer for 20 minutes.
4. Cream potatoes with milk,
margarine and seasoning. Fork
round edges of a 1½–2-pint
(approximately ¾–1-litre)
ovenproof dish.
5. Stir fish into cooked soup and
pour in dish. Sprinkle with grated
cheese and grill till golden.

SPAGHETTI WITH FISH AND APPLE BALLS
Serves 4

12oz (300gm) cod, cooked and
flaked
2 apples, finely chopped
1 packet white sauce mix
2oz (50gm) flour, seasoned with
salt and pepper
1 egg
½ pint (250ml) milk
4oz (100gm) plain flour
fat for deep frying
8oz (200gm) spaghetti
2½oz (62gm) butter
1 small onion, chopped
1 small apple, grated
1 tube or can tomato purée
2 teaspoons cornflour
½ pint (250ml) water
salt and pepper
1 can tomatoes, roughly
chopped
pinch of sugar

1. Add fish and apple to sauce
mix. To make up sauce, use half
the stated amount of liquid to
give a thick, binding sauce.
2. Divide mixture into equal
portions. Roll into balls using
seasoned flour to prevent sticking.
3. Beat egg and milk into flour to
make batter and coat fish balls.
4. Fry these in deep fat till
golden. Drain on absorbent paper.
5. Meanwhile cook spaghetti in
boiling, salted water till just
tender.
6. Drain, return to pan and toss
in 1½oz (37gm) melted butter.
7. While spaghetti is cooking,
make the sauce. Heat remaining
butter, fry onion and add apple.
Then add the tomato purée,
cornflour blended with water and
seasoning.
8. Bring to boil and stir till
smooth. Simmer for 5 minutes
then add tomatoes. Cook for a
further 5 minutes.
9. Re-adjust seasoning and add
sugar. Serve fish balls on
spaghetti topped with sauce.

COD CREOLE
Serves 4

1oz (25gm) butter
1 onion, finely chopped
2 sticks celery, chopped
½oz (12gm) flour
1 can (12oz or 300gm) tomatoes
4 tablespoons tomato purée
¼ pint (125ml) chicken stock
Tabasco sauce
pinch of sugar
pinch of salt
bouquet garni
1lb (½ kilo) cod, cut in wedges

1. Melt butter and fry onion and
celery till soft.
2. Stir in flour and add tomatoes,
tomato purée, stock, Tabasco,
sugar, salt and bouquet garni.
3. Add the cod, bring to the boil
and simmer for 15 minutes.
4. Adjust seasonings, and serve.

COD CASSEROLE
Serves 4

1½lb (¾ kilo) cod fillet
4oz (100gm) bacon
4oz (100gm) mushrooms
1 small bottle cider
2oz (50gm) butter
salt and pepper

1. Preheat oven to moderate to
moderately hot, 375 deg F or gas 5
(190 deg C).
2. Wipe fish and cut into 1½-inch
cubes.
3. Dice bacon and cut mushrooms
into quarters.
4. Put into a casserole. Add the
cider, butter and seasonings.
5. Cover and bake in centre of
oven for 45–50 minutes.

CRUNCHY COD CASSEROLE
(Illustrated on page 36)
Serves 4

1lb (½ kilo) fillet of cod, or 1
packet (13oz or 325gm) frozen
cod fillets
1 large onion, chopped
1oz (25gm) butter
2oz (50gm) button mushrooms,
sliced
1 can (14oz or 350gm) tomatoes
or 8oz (200gm) fresh tomatoes,
skinned and sliced
1 tablespoon chopped parsley
salt and pepper
4 slices bread, crusts removed
and well buttered
1oz (25gm) Cheddar cheese,
grated

1. Preheat oven to moderate, 350
deg F or gas 4 (180 deg C).
2. Arrange cod in buttered,
shallow, ovenproof dish.
3. Fry onion in butter till soft.
Add mushrooms and fry another
minute.
4. Stir in tomatoes (drain juice
from canned tomatoes), parsley
and seasoning.
5. Pour over fish and bake,
covered in centre of oven for
about 40 minutes.
6. Cut slices of bread into
triangles and arrange on a
baking sheet close together.
7. Sprinkle with grated cheese
and bake in oven on shelf below
fish.
8. Arrange bread round the
outside of fish before serving.

COLEY CASSEROLE
Serves 4

1lb ($\frac{1}{2}$ kilo) potatoes
1$\frac{1}{2}$lb ($\frac{3}{4}$ kilo) coley
salt and pepper
4oz (100gm) butter
8oz (200gm) onions
8oz (200gm) carrots
12oz (300gm) mushrooms
2 tablespoons chopped parsley
1 pint (approximately $\frac{1}{2}$ litre)
fish stock

1. Preheat oven to moderate to
moderately hot, 375 deg F or gas 5
(190 deg C).
2. Peel potatoes, drop into
boiling, salted water for 3
minutes, then drain.
3. Cut fish into four portions and
season well.
4. Heat butter in a pan and cook
the fish for about 30 seconds each
side. Put aside and keep warm.
5. Slice onions and carrots, put
into butter, turn for a few minutes
over heat, then remove from pan.
6. Toss sliced mushrooms and
parsley in remaining fat for 1
minute.
7. Put potatoes into the bottom of
a buttered, ovenproof dish, cover
with onion and carrot and place
fish on top. Scatter mushrooms
and parsley on top.
8. Pour fish stock over, cover the
dish and cook in centre of oven
for about 45 minutes.

SEAFOOD SCALLOPS
Serves 6

8oz (200gm) cod or haddock
1 can (8oz or 200gm) tomatoes
2oz (50gm) butter
1 medium onion, chopped
4oz (100gm) mushrooms, sliced
4oz (100gm) prawns or
shrimps, peeled
2 teaspoons cornflour
2 tablespoons Worcestershire
sauce
salt and pepper
1 packet (3oz or 75gm) instant
potato

1. Preheat oven to moderate to
moderately hot, 375 deg F or gas 5
(190 deg C).
2. Poach fish in juice drained
from tomatoes.
3. Melt butter in a pan, add
onion and cook gently until
transparent. Add mushrooms and
prawns or shrimps and cook for 2
minutes.
4. Stir in tomatoes, flaked fish
with the liquor, and cornflour
blended with Worcestershire
sauce. Bring to the boil, stirring
gently, to thicken. Season to
taste.
5. Spoon mixture into six scallop
shells or individual dishes.
Prepare instant potato following
directions on the packet. Pipe
potato round edge of shells.
6. Bake in centre of oven for 15
minutes until potato is brown on
top and filling is hot.

HADDOCK AND RICE
SALAD
Serves 4

12oz (300gm) haddock fillets,
cooked and flaked
4oz (100gm) mushrooms,
blanched
2 tomatoes, chopped
4oz (100gm) boiled long-grain
rice (raw weight)
4 tablespoons natural yogurt
4 tablespoons salad cream
1 teaspoon salt
$\frac{1}{4}$ teaspoon pepper
2 tablespoons capers

1. Combine fish, mushrooms,
tomatoes and rice.
2. Make a sauce by mixing the
remaining ingredients. Stir into
the rice mixture and serve chilled.

SMOKED CURRY SALAD
Serves 4

1 packet frozen smoked
haddock, cooked
3 tablespoons salad cream
1 teaspoon curry powder
1oz (25gm) cooked rice (raw
weight)
2 tomatoes, chopped
1 stick celery, sliced
1 hard-boiled egg and
watercress to garnish

1. Skin and flake fish and mix
with salad cream and curry
powder.
2. Stir in rice, tomatoes and
celery and pile in a serving dish.
3. Garnish with egg slices and
watercress.

HADDOCK CHOWDER
Serves 4

½oz (12gm) margarine
1 onion, chopped
2 carrots, sliced
2oz (50gm) mushrooms, sliced
1 small can tomatoes
¾ pint (375ml) water
1 large packet frozen haddock
fillets
2 large potatoes, diced
salt and pepper
1 tablespoon chopped parsley

1. Melt margarine and fry onion,
carrot and mushrooms till soft but
not brown.
2. Add tomatoes and water. Stir
well.
3. Skin haddock, remove any
bones and cut into large chunks.
4. Gently stir fish and potatoes
into the soup. Cover and simmer
for 7–10 minutes without stirring.
5. Season and top with parsley.

SMOKED HADDOCK
SOUFFLE
Serves 4

6oz (150gm) smoked haddock
½ pint (250ml) milk
½oz (12gm) flour
½oz (12gm) butter
4 eggs
salt and pepper
½ teaspoon prepared mustard

1. Preheat oven to moderately
hot, 400 deg F or gas 6 (200 deg C).
2. Poach haddock in milk till it
flakes easily. Remove skin and
bones.
3. Put fish, milk, flour and butter
in a large pan. Heat, stirring
continuously, till sauce thickens.
4. Separate yolks from egg whites
and stir yolks into sauce.
5. Season with salt, pepper and
mustard.
6. Whisk egg whites till very
stiff. Fold into sauce. Pour
mixture into buttered 2-pint
(approximately 1-litre) soufflé
dish.
7. Bake in centre of oven for
20–25 minutes.

SMOKED HADDOCK PATE
Serves 6

A delicious party starter dish.

12oz (300gm) smoked haddock
2oz (50gm) butter, melted
7½oz (187gm) double cream
2 teaspoons lemon juice
1 teaspoon Worcestershire
sauce
pepper and cayenne pepper
2 tablespoons butter, melted

1. Wipe fish, then poach it in
boiling water for 10 minutes.
Drain, skin and flake fish.
2. Mash fish with 2oz (50gm)
butter and pass through a sieve
or purée in a liquidizer.
3. Whip cream till almost thick.
4. Fold in fish and season with
lemon juice, Worcestershire
sauce and peppers.
5. Pour into dish and allow to set.
Cover top with melted butter and
leave to set.

SMOKED HADDOCK
CRUNCH
Serves 4

1lb (½ kilo) smoked haddock
2½oz (62gm) butter
¼ teaspoon pepper
¼ pint (125ml) evaporated milk
2oz (50gm) flour
1 can (7oz or 175gm) sweetcorn
1oz (25gm) Cheddar cheese,
grated
1 small packet plain crisps,
roughly crushed

1. Preheat oven to moderately
hot, 400 deg F or gas 6 (200 deg C).
2. Place smoked haddock in a pan
with ¾ pint (375ml) water, ½oz
(12gm) butter and pepper. Bring
to the boil and poach for 10–15
minutes until tender.
3. Drain fish, retaining the stock.
Remove skin and bones and flake
the haddock with a fork.
4. Make evaporated milk up to 1
pint (approximately ½ litre) with
the fish stock and whisk in flour.
5. Place in a saucepan with
remaining butter and stir over
moderate heat until sauce boils
and thickens.
6. Carefully stir in the haddock
and sweetcorn and check
seasoning.
7. Place in a 2-pint
(approximately 1-litre) pie dish,
sprinkle with cheese and top
with crisps.
8. Bake in centre of oven for 15
minutes.
9. Serve with baked potatoes.

POTATO KEDGEREE
Serves 4

2lb (1 kilo) smoked haddock
½ pint (250ml) milk
3oz (75gm) butter
1lb (½ kilo) potatoes, boiled
and sliced
3 tomatoes, skinned and sliced
2 tablespoons chopped parsley
1½oz (75gm) blanched almonds
2 eggs, beaten
salt and pepper
1 hard-boiled egg to garnish

1. Poach haddock in milk and
butter. Leave to cool, then flake
fish.
2. Put all ingredients (including
milk and butter) into a large pan.
3. Heat through, stirring gently.
Cook for about 5 minutes.
4. Serve garnished with sliced
egg.

FILLETS WITH EGG AND DILL SAUCE
Serves 4

1½lb (¾ kilo) haddock or
whiting fillets
½ pint (250ml) milk
1 teaspoon dill
salt and pepper
1oz (25gm) butter
1oz (25gm) flour
1 hard-boiled egg

1. Divide fish into four portions.
2. Place in a saucepan and cover
with milk. Add dill and seasoning.
Simmer gently for 8–10 minutes.
3. Drain, reserving liquid. Keep
fish hot.
4. Melt butter, stir in flour and
cook for 2 minutes. Remove pan
from heat and add reserved
liquid. Stir well. Return pan to
heat, stir till sauce thickens and
season well.
5. Chop the egg and stir into the
sauce.
6. Pour sauce over fish and serve.

HADDOCK COBBLER
Serves 4–6

1lb (½ kilo) smoked haddock,
poached
¾ pint (375ml) cheese sauce (see
Basic recipes, page 100)
2oz (50gm) margarine
8oz (200gm) self-raising flour
1 level teaspoon baking powder
pinch of chopped chives
¼ teaspoon mustard
7 tablespoons milk
milk to glaze

1. Preheat oven to moderately
hot, 400 deg F or gas 6 (200 deg C).
2. Place haddock in ovenproof
dish and pour cheese sauce over.
3. To make scone topping place
rest of ingredients in mixing bowl.
Mix to form a scone dough.
4. Turn out on floured board and
knead lightly.
5. Roll out to ½ inch thickness
and cut in 2-inch rounds.
6. Place round edge of dish.
Glaze with milk and bake in
centre of oven for 15–20 minutes.

LATTICE FISH PIE
Serves 4–6

1¼lb (600gm) haddock fillets
1oz (25gm) margarine
1½oz (37gm) flour
½ pint (250ml) milk
salt and pepper
1 small packet instant mashed
potato
1 hard-boiled egg

1. Poach the fish. Drain, reserving
the liquid, then skin and flake fish
coarsely.
2. Melt margarine in pan, stir
in flour, then gradually blend in
milk and ¼–½ pint (125–250ml) fish
liquor, stirring all the time.
3. Bring to boil. Simmer gently
for 2 minutes. Season and add
fish. Heat through gently.
4. Make up mashed potato (or
use equivalent in fresh).
5. Turn fish into a shallow,
ovenproof dish. Pipe potato to
form lattice pattern on top and
place a thick slice of egg in
alternate squares.

SMOKED HADDOCK PIE
Serves 4–6

2oz (50gm) margarine
2oz (50gm) flour
¾ pint (375ml) milk made up to
1 pint (approximately ½ litre)
with water
14oz (350gm) smoked haddock
½ teaspoon onion salt
salt and pepper
3 tomatoes, skinned and
chopped
2 hard-boiled eggs, chopped
1 packet (4 portions) instant
potato

1. Preheat oven to moderate to
moderately hot, 375 deg F or gas 5
(190 deg C).
2. Melt margarine over low heat.
Blend in flour and stir in milk and
water. Bring to boil and simmer
for 1 minute.
3. Cut fish into cubes and stir into
the sauce with seasonings,
tomatoes and eggs.
4. Pour into a 2½-pint
(approximately 1¼-litre) pie dish.
5. Make up potato and pipe round
edge of dish. Bake in centre of
oven for about 30 minutes.

RUSSIAN FISH PIE
Serves 4

8oz (200gm) smoked haddock
5 tablespoons milk
½oz (12gm) margarine
1 tablespoon plain flour
1 hard-boiled egg
2 teaspoons chopped parsley
salt and pepper
1 packet (7½oz or 187gm)
frozen puff pastry, thawed (or
see Basic recipes, page 100)
milk to glaze

1. Preheat oven to hot, 425 deg F
or gas 7 (220 deg C).
2. Poach haddock in milk for 10
minutes. Drain, then make up
liquid to ¼ pint (125ml) with milk
or water.
3. Melt margarine in a saucepan.
Add flour, cook for 1 minute then
remove from heat. Add fish
liquor, beating well. Return to
heat and stir till sauce thickens.
4. Flake fish and chop egg. Add to
the sauce with parsley and
seasoning. Allow to cool.
5. Roll pastry out to a 10-inch
square. Spread fish filling
diagonally across centre of pastry.
Damp edges of pastry all round,
then fold corners to centre and
seal.
6. Brush the top with milk and
bake for 45 minutes till golden
and crisp.
7. Serve hot or cold.

CREAMY FISH PIE
Serves 4

1lb (½ kilo) haddock fillets
salt and pepper
¼ pint (125ml) plus 2
tablespoons evaporated milk
1oz (25gm) flour
1oz (25gm) butter
6oz (150gm) Cheddar cheese,
grated
1lb (½ kilo) potatoes, boiled and
mashed

1. Place haddock in a wide,
shallow pan. Just cover with
water and add salt and pepper.
2. Poach gently for about 15
minutes until haddock is tender.
3. Make ¼ pint (125ml) evaporated
milk up to ½ pint (250ml) with
strained fish stock and whisk in
the flour.
4. Place in a saucepan with
butter and stir over a moderate
heat until sauce boils and
thickens.
5. Remove from heat and add 4oz
(100gm) cheese. Beat well until
cheese melts. Check seasoning.
6. Drain and flake the fish and
add to the sauce. Place in a 2-pint
(approximately 1-litre) dish and
keep hot.
7. Cream potatoes with remaining
evaporated milk and season to
taste with salt and pepper.
8. Pile or pipe on to fish mixture
and top with remaining cheese.
9. Place under a hot grill to
brown and serve at once.

FISH AND BACON PIE
Serves 4

12oz (300gm) cod or haddock,
skinned and filleted
a little milk
4oz (100gm) butter
1½lb (¾ kilo) potatoes
4oz (100gm) streaky bacon,
chopped
1½oz (37gm) plain flour
¾ pint (375ml) milk, made up
from the milk that the fish is
cooked in
1 teaspoon lemon juice
1 hard-boiled egg, chopped

1. Preheat oven to moderate, 350
deg F or gas 4 (180 deg C).
2. Place fish in ovenproof dish
with a little milk. Dot with 1oz
(25gm) butter and bake in centre
of oven for 20–30 minutes.
Increase oven setting to
moderately hot, 400 deg F or gas 6
(200 deg C).
3. Drain and flake fish. Keep milk
for sauce. Boil potatoes in salted
water.
4. Fry bacon lightly.
5. Melt 2oz (50gm) butter in a
pan. Add flour and cook for 1
minute. Remove from heat and
stir in milk and lemon juice
gradually. Return to heat and
bring to boil, stirring.
6. Cook for 1 minute then stir in
fish, bacon and egg.
7. Drain potatoes and mash with
2 tablespoons milk and remaining
butter.
8. Turn fish into a 1½-pint
(approximately ¾-litre) pie dish.
Top with mashed potato and bake
in centre of oven for about 30
minutes until top is browned.

FINNAN RICE
Serves 4

1 packet frozen smoked
haddock
3 hard-boiled eggs, chopped
1 onion, chopped
1 tablespoon chopped parsley
3oz (75gm) cooked long-grain
rice (raw weight)
1 teaspoon chopped capers
2 gherkins, chopped
2 tablespoons salad cream
4 tomatoes, cut in wedges

1. Cook haddock as directed on
packet. Remove bones and flake.
Leave to cool.
2. Mix together fish, eggs, onion,
parsley, rice, capers, gherkins and
salad cream.
3. Arrange in dish with tomato
wedges as a border.

HADDOCK PROVENCALE
Serves 4

½oz (12gm) margarine
1 onion, chopped
2 sticks celery, chopped
2oz (50gm) mushrooms, sliced
1 small can tomatoes
1 large packet haddock fillets
salt and pepper
8oz (200gm) shell pasta or
spaghetti

1. Melt margarine and fry the
onion, celery and mushrooms till
soft.
2. Add tomatoes and stir well.
3. Skin haddock then add whole
fillets to the sauce mixture.
4. Cook gently for 10–15 minutes
without stirring. Season.
5. Meanwhile, cook the pasta in
boiling, salted water for about
10–15 minutes until tender.
Drain and arrange on a serving
dish with the fish mixture in the
centre.

CREAMY HADDOCK AND
MUSHROOM SUPPER
Serves 4

1lb (½ kilo) fresh haddock
1 onion, sliced
4 peppercorns
1 small blade of mace
½ teaspoon salt
4oz (100gm) button
mushrooms, sliced
1½oz (37gm) butter
½ pint (250ml) evaporated milk
1½oz (37gm) flour
lemon slices and parsley to
garnish

1. Place fish, onion, peppercorns,
mace and salt in a saucepan with
just enough water to cover.
2. Poach gently for 10–15 minutes
until haddock is just cooked.
3. Drain fish, reserving stock.
Remove any skin or bones from
fish and place in a serving dish.
Keep hot.
4. Fry mushrooms gently in
butter for 3–4 minutes.
5. Make evaporated milk up to 1
pint (approximately ½ litre) with
the reserved fish stock and whisk
in the flour.
6. Add to the mushrooms and stir
constantly over a moderate heat
until sauce thickens. Continue to
cook, stirring over a low heat for
a further 2 minutes.
7. Check seasoning and pour
sauce over the haddock.
8. Garnish with lemon slices and
parsley.

ENGLISH HERRINGS
Serves 4

4 herrings, split and boned
3oz (75gm) butter
1 teaspoon dry mustard
salt and pepper
4 tomatoes, halved and topped
with a piece of butter

1. Preheat oven to moderate to
moderately hot, 375 deg F or gas 5
(190 deg C).
2. Wipe herrings and open out
flat.
3. Cream butter, mustard and
seasoning together. Spread on
each fish. Fold the fish in half and
wrap in foil.
4. Place on baking sheet with the
tomatoes and bake in centre of
oven for 25–30 minutes.
5. Remove foil and serve.

HONEYED HERRING
KEBABS
Serves 4

4 whole herrings, boned
8 button mushrooms
4 tomatoes
1 eating apple
2oz (50gm) clear honey
1 teaspoon mixed herbs

1. Cut herrings down back into
two fillets. Cut each in half again
crossways.
2. Wash mushrooms and remove
stalks. Cut tomatoes in half.
Core and cut apple into quarters.
3. Thread folded herring pieces,
mushroom, tomato and apple on
four skewers. Make sure
ingredients are tightly pressed
together.
4. Make glaze by mixing honey
with herbs. Brush kebabs with
this. Grill under medium heat for
25 minutes turning frequently and
reglazing half way through.

Breakfast pancakes (see page 61)

Edam and apple cocktail (see page 65)

Bean soufflette (see page 62)

Cheese and cider fondue (see page 68)

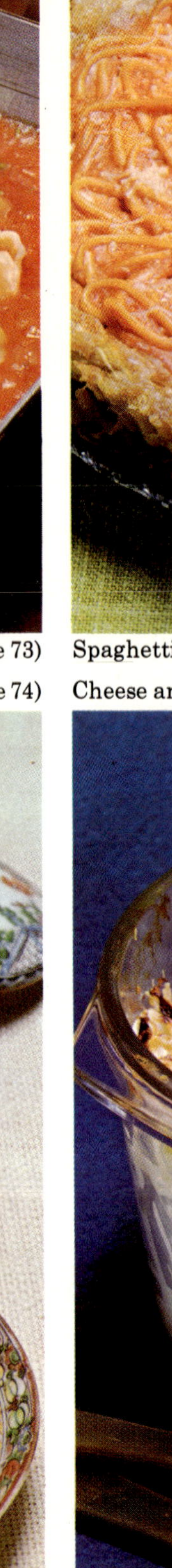

Frypan casserole (see page 73)   Spaghetti supper dish (see page 69)

Cream of corn soup (see page 74)   Cheese and cabbage casserole (see page 77)

CROFTER CASSEROLE
Serves 4

A layered fish, onion and potato pie.

**4 large herrings
salt and pepper
2 large onions
4 medium potatoes, thinly
sliced
2oz (50gm) butter**

1. Preheat oven to hot, 425 deg F or gas 7 (220 deg C).
2. Scale, clean and bone fish. Season well.
3. Put herrings in greased ovenproof dish. Cover with a layer of sliced onions, then add a layer of potato slices. Season and dot with butter. Repeat onion and potato layers. Season and butter again.
4. Cover dish and bake in centre of oven for 50 minutes.
5. Remove cover and bake for a further 10 minutes to brown potato top.

SCANDINAVIAN HERRINGS
Serves 4

Herrings, served whole, in a thick sauce.

**4 large herrings
1 tablespoon prepared mustard
1 tablespoon tomato purée
½ teaspoon sugar
2 tablespoons single cream
pinch of mixed herbs
salt and pepper
melted butter
lemon to garnish**

1. Preheat oven to moderate, 350 deg F or gas 4 (180 deg C).
2. Scale, clean and bone fish, leaving tails on. Open out each fish flat.
3. Blend mustard, tomato purée, sugar, cream and herbs. Season and spread over inside of each fish.
4. Make a small cut at place of last fin on back of fish. Roll tail up and push through the slit, tucking flap underneath, so that fish remains in rolled-up shape. Alternatively, roll fish up and secure with a cocktail stick.
5. Arrange in greased ovenproof dish. Brush with melted butter and bake in centre of oven for 20–30 minutes.

**BAKED HERRINGS
PROVENÇALE**
Serves 4

**4 herrings
salt and pepper
2 small onions
1oz (25gm) butter, melted
1lb (½ kilo) tomatoes
2 tablespoons vinegar
black pepper
1 teaspoon sugar
1 teaspoon chopped parsley**

1. Preheat oven to moderate to moderately hot, 375 deg F or gas 5 (190 deg C).
2. Clean herrings, take off heads, trim fins and tails. Make light slashes in each side. Season well.
3. Skin onions and slice in thin wedges. Fry in half the butter for 5 minutes.
4. Plunge tomatoes in boiling water. Remove skins and cut in wedges.
5. Make a layer of tomato and onion at bottom of greased, ovenproof dish.
6. Sprinkle with vinegar, salt, black pepper and sugar.
7. Arrange fish on top and brush with rest of melted butter. Cover and bake in centre of oven for 45 minutes.
8. Sprinkle with parsley and serve.

CIDER-BAKED HERRINGS
Serves 6

A first course or high-tea dish.

**6 herrings
salt and pepper
½ pint (250ml) cider
1 tablespoon mixed pickling
spice
4 bayleaves
2 small onions, cut in rings**

1. Preheat oven to cool, 275 deg F or gas 1 (140 deg C).
2. Clean, split and fillet herrings. Season well. Roll up, skin inwards, beginning at the tail.
3. Place close together in ovenproof dish.
4. Cover with cider, sprinkle with pickling spice, and add bayleaves and onion rings.
5. Cover and bake in centre of oven for about 1½ hours.
(By substituting malt vinegar for cider, this makes a good Soused Herring recipe.)

HERRINGS WITH RED CABBAGE
(Illustrated on page 36)
Serves 4

**1oz (25gm) butter
2 medium onions, chopped
1½lb (¾ kilo) red cabbage, finely
shredded
3oz (75gm) soft brown sugar
4 tablespoons wine vinegar
salt and pepper
4 herrings**

1. Preheat oven to moderate, 350 deg F or gas 4 (180 deg C).
2. Melt butter, add onion and fry for about 5 minutes without browning.
3. Add red cabbage and cook a further 5 minutes.
4. Stir in sugar, vinegar, salt and pepper. Transfer to casserole, cover and bake in oven for 2 hours or till tender.
5. Clean herrings and place on top of red cabbage for last 20 minutes of cooking time.

TOMATO HERRING CASSEROLE
Serves 4

4 medium herrings, filleted
1 tablespoon tomato ketchup
1 small onion, chopped
1oz (25gm) cooking fat
1 can (8oz or 200gm) tomatoes
2 level teaspoons cornflour
juice of ½ lemon
¼ pint (125ml) water
2 bayleaves (optional)
salt and pepper

1. Preheat oven to moderate, 350 deg F or gas 4 (180 deg C).
2. Spread herrings with ketchup, roll up and place in ovenproof dish.
3. Fry onion in fat till tender. Add tomatoes.
4. Blend cornflour with lemon juice. Add water and bring to boil, stirring continuously.
5. Add bayleaves if used and season. Pour over herrings.
6. Cover and bake in centre of oven for 30 minutes.

KIPPER PATE
Serves 4

A tasty and tempting dinner party meal opener.

4oz (100gm) raw kipper fillets, skinned
2 tablespoons dry white wine
freshly milled black pepper
4oz (100gm) softened butter

1. Marinate kipper in white wine for 12–24 hours in a cool place.
2. Mash with a fork well.
3. Add pepper and blend with the butter.

CREAMY KIPPER SCALLOPS
(Illustrated on page 36)
Serves 4

Another way of dressing up kippers for dinner parties.

1lb (½ kilo) kipper fillets
2¼oz (56gm) butter
1½oz (37gm) flour
¾ pint (375ml) milk
finely grated rind of 1 lemon
12oz (300gm) potatoes
2 tablespoons milk

1. Cut kipper fillets into ½-inch cubes and divide equally between four large scallop shells.
2. Melt 1½oz (37gm) butter in a pan. Stir in flour and cook for 2–3 minutes without browning.
3. Remove from heat and gradually stir in milk. Bring to boil and cook for 3–4 minutes.
4. Stir in lemon rind. Divide sauce equally over kipper pieces.
5. Mash potatoes with remaining butter and the milk and pipe it round edge of shells.
6. Put under a hot grill just before serving.

KIPPER SOUFFLE
Serves 4

2 packets of kipper fillets
2oz (50gm) margarine
2oz (50gm) flour
½ pint (250ml) milk
4 eggs, separated
salt and pepper

1. Preheat oven to moderate to moderately hot, 375 deg F or gas 5 (190 deg C).
2. Mince kippers finely.
3. Melt margarine, add flour and cook gently for 1 minute. Gradually add milk stirring all the time and bring to the boil until it thickens.
4. Stir in fish and egg yolks. Season well.
5. Whisk egg whites till stiff. Fold them into kipper mixture. Pour into greased 7-inch (18-cm) soufflé dish and bake for 40 minutes in centre of oven until risen and golden.

KIPPER PIZZA
Serves 4–6

8oz (200gm) self-raising flour
½ teaspoon salt
1½oz (37gm) butter
¼ pint (125ml) milk
4oz (100gm) cheese, grated
1 teaspoon powdered mustard
½ teaspoon dried oregano
½ teaspoon dried basil
8oz (200gm) tomatoes, sliced
salt and pepper
8 kipper fillets
6 black olives (optional)
little oil

1. Preheat oven to moderately hot, 400 deg F or gas 6 (200 deg C).
2. Sift flour and salt together. Rub in butter till mixture resembles breadcrumbs.
3. Bind together with milk to make a soft dough. Roll out to a 12-inch circle and place on greased baking sheet.
4. Mix together cheese, mustard and herbs and sprinkle over dough. Arrange tomatoes on top, and season.
5. Arrange kipper fillets radially on the tomatoes. Stud top with olives, if used.
6. Brush kipper fillets with oil, then bake in centre of oven for about 30 minutes till pastry is cooked and the cheese is bubbling and golden.

KIPPER TRICORN
Serves 4

1 small packet (3oz or 75gm)
instant potato
1 packet (7oz or 175gm) kipper
fillets
black pepper
1 packet (13oz or 325gm) puff
pastry (or see Basic recipes,
page 100)
1 egg, beaten

1. Preheat oven to hot, 450 deg F
or gas 8 (230 deg C).
2. Make up potato according to
packet directions.
3. Flake kipper fillets and add to
potato. Season.
4. Roll out pastry to size of large
dinner plate. Pile kipper and
potato mixture in centre.
5. Wet edges of pastry and join
together to form a triangular
shape.
6. Brush with beaten egg and
bake in centre of oven for about
30 minutes, till puffed and
golden.

KIPPER RAMEKINS
Serves 4–6

Kippers in cheese soufflé sauce
makes an unusual hors d'oeuvre.

8oz (200gm) kippers, boned
1oz (25gm) butter
½oz (12gm) flour
¼ pint (125ml) milk
salt, pepper and mustard
2 eggs, separated
1oz (25gm) cheese, grated

1. Preheat oven to hot, 425 deg F
or gas 7 (220 deg C).
2. Cook kippers. Skin fillets and
mash with juices.
3. Melt butter in a pan. Add flour
and cook for 1 minute.
4. Remove from heat and
gradually add milk, stirring well.
Return to heat, stir and bring to
boil. Allow to thicken, then
season well.
5. Remove from heat. Add egg
yolks, cheese and kipper.
6. Fold in stiffly whisked egg
whites, place in small ovenproof
dishes (about ¼ pint or 125ml
each) and bake in centre of oven
for 15 minutes till brown and well
risen.

KIPPER CURRY SALAD
Serves 4–6

8oz (200gm) kipper fillets
4 tablespoons mayonnaise or
salad cream
1 teaspoon curry powder
1 teaspoon vinegar
2oz (50gm) boiled rice (raw
weight)
8oz (200gm) tomatoes, skinned
and diced
4 sticks celery, diced
salt and pepper
2 hard-boiled eggs

1. Skin kippers and cut into
2-inch strips.
2. Mix mayonnaise or salad
cream with curry powder and
vinegar.
3. Stir in kipper, rice, tomatoes
and celery. Season, and blend
well.
4. Pile into a serving dish and
garnish with slices of egg.

KIPPER TOMATO BAKE
Serves 4–6

4oz (100gm) macaroni
1 onion, finely chopped
1oz (25gm) butter
1oz (25gm) flour
¼ pint (125ml) chicken stock
1 can (8oz or 200gm) tomatoes
1 tablespoon prepared mustard
10oz (250gm) kipper fillets
2oz (50gm) cheese, grated

1. Preheat oven to moderate to
moderately hot, 375 deg F or gas 5
(190 deg C).
2. Partly cook macaroni in
boiling, salted water for 5
minutes, then drain.
3. Cook onion in butter for 2–3
minutes. Stir in flour and cook
gently for 2 minutes. Gradually
add stock, tomatoes and mustard.
4. Bring to boil and simmer for 5
minutes.
5. Cut kipper fillets into 1-inch
pieces.
6. Layer macaroni, kipper and
sauce alternately in a 2-pint
(approximately 1-litre) casserole.
Finish with a layer of kippers,
topped with tomato sauce.
7. Sprinkle with cheese and bake
in centre of oven for 40 minutes.

KIPPER CHEESE PUDDING
Serves 4

1 medium onion
1oz (25gm) butter
3 eggs, separated
1 teaspoon prepared mustard
pepper
⅓ pint (170ml) milk
2oz (50gm) cheese, grated
4oz (100gm) white breadcrumbs
8oz (200gm) kipper fillets

1. Preheat oven to moderate, 350
deg F or gas 4 (180 deg C).
2. Chop onion finely and fry in
butter for 2–3 minutes till soft.
3. Leave to cool slightly, then add
egg yolks, mustard, pepper, milk,
cheese and breadcrumbs.
4. Remove skins from kippers and
cut in ½-inch pieces. Add to
mixture.
5. Whisk egg whites till just stiff.
Fold carefully into kipper
mixture, then pour into well
greased 2-pint (approximately
1-litre) soufflé dish.
6. Bake in centre of oven for 45
minutes till just golden brown
and set.

TUNA MOUSSE
Serves 8

1 can (7oz or 175gm) tuna
1oz (25gm) butter
1oz (25gm) flour
¾ pint (375ml) milk
3 level teaspoons powdered
gelatine in 2 tablespoons water
2 tablespoons Worcestershire
sauce
2 tablespoons lemon juice
salt and pepper
2 egg whites

1. Mash tuna finely with fork.
2. Melt butter in pan and stir in
flour. Add milk gradually,
stirring, to make a smooth sauce.
3. Bring to boil, stirring. Cook
for 2 minutes. Leave to cool
covered with foil.
4. Heat gelatine and water gently
in a pan till gelatine dissolves.
5. Add tuna to sauce, then stir in
Worcestershire sauce, lemon
juice, seasoning and gelatine.
6. Beat egg whites till just firm.
Fold into tuna mixture when just
on point of setting. Turn into
2-pint (approximately 1-litre) dish
and leave to set.

TUNA RICE RING
Serves 4

1oz (25gm) butter
6oz (150gm) long grain rice
1 can (7oz or 175gm) tuna,
drained
2 tablespoons mayonnaise
1 can (5oz or 125gm) garden
peas
salt and pepper
lemon and cucumber slices to
garnish

1. Well grease a ring mould with
butter.
2. Boil and drain rice, allow to
cool and mix with three-quarters
of the tuna.
3. Press into the mould and leave
in a cool place overnight.
4. Next day, turn out and fill
centre of ring mould with
remainder of tuna mixed with
mayonnaise and drained peas.
Season to taste.
5. Garnish with lemon and
cucumber slices.

BAKED TUNA SALAD
Serves 6

1 can (7oz or 175gm) tuna,
drained and flaked
1 small green pepper, chopped
(optional)
4oz (100gm) shelled prawns
4 sticks celery, chopped
1 small onion, chopped finely
7oz (175gm) mayonnaise
¼ level teaspoon salt
1 teaspoon Worcestershire
sauce
1½oz (37gm) cornflakes
1oz (25gm) butter, melted
paprika

1. Preheat oven to moderate, 350
deg F or gas 4 (180 deg C).
2. Put tuna, pepper, if used,
prawns, celery, onion,
mayonnaise, salt and
Worcestershire sauce in a basin.
Mix well together.
3. Spread mixture in six scallop
shells or ovenproof dishes.
4. Lightly crush cornflakes and
combine with melted butter.
Spoon a little over each shell and
sprinkle with paprika.
5. Bake in centre of oven for
about 30 minutes.

TUNA POTATO CASSEROLE
Serves 4–6

1 can (7oz or 175gm) tuna
3 medium potatoes
1 medium onion, sliced
1 can (10oz or 250gm) cream of
mushroom soup
¼ pint (125ml) milk
pepper
1oz (25gm) butter

1. Preheat oven to moderate to
moderately hot, 375 deg F or gas 5
(190 deg C).
2. Drain and flake tuna.
3. Slice potatoes thinly.
4. Arrange tuna, potatoes and
onion in alternate layers in a
large, greased casserole,
beginning and ending with a
potato layer.
5. Blend soup, milk and pepper
and pour into casserole.
6. Dot with butter and bake in
centre of oven for 1 hour until
potatoes are tender.

TUNA FISH PILAFF
Serves 4

2¾oz (86gm) butter
1 large onion, finely sliced
8oz (200gm) long-grain rice
salt and pepper
1¼ pints (625ml) chicken stock
1 can (7oz or 175gm)
mushrooms
squeeze of lemon juice
1 can tuna, flaked

1. Heat 2oz (50gm) butter in a pan
and fry onion until soft.
2. Add rice and fry till it looks
transparent. Season.
3. Add stock, bring to boil, cover
tightly and simmer for 20
minutes.
4. Melt the remaining butter in a
pan. Add mushrooms and lemon
juice.
5. Toss over a brisk heat for 2
minutes, then add tuna.
6. Season and cook a further 2
minutes.
7. When ready to serve, put rice
mixture into a ring mould and
press lightly with a plate to make
rice cling together. Turn it out
and fill centre with tuna.

TUNA MACARONI
Serves 4

1 medium onion, chopped
2 bacon rashers, chopped
½oz (12gm) margarine
1 can (8oz or 200gm) tomatoes
salt and pepper
¼ pint (125ml) stock
1 can (7oz or 175gm) tuna
1 small packet frozen peas
4oz (100gm) freshly boiled
macaroni

1. Fry onion and bacon in the
margarine.
2. Add tomatoes, seasoning and
stock. Simmer for 10 minutes.
3. Add tuna and peas and cook
for a further 5 minutes. Take care
not to break the fish.
4. Serve fish mixture in centre of
hot macaroni.

TUNA CRUNCH
Serves 4

A simple-to-make dish using
potato crisps as a pie topping.

1oz (25gm) margarine
1oz (25gm) plain flour
½ pint (250ml) milk
1 level teaspoon curry powder
1 can (8oz or 200gm) tuna
4oz (100gm) cooked peas
2 hard-boiled eggs, sliced
1 small packet potato crisps

1. Preheat oven to moderate, 350
deg F or gas 4 (180 deg C).
2. Place margarine, flour, milk
and curry powder in a pan and
bring to the boil, whisking all the
time.
3. Add drained tuna, peas and
eggs and place in ovenproof dish.
4. Top with potato crisps and
bake in middle of oven for 25
minutes.

SARDINE SAUCERS
Serves 4

2 cans sardines
2 tablespoons oil
1 onion, chopped
1 garlic clove
½ pint (250ml) tomato pulp
6oz (150gm) mushroom, sliced
1½oz (37gm) butter
breadcrumbs

1. Preheat oven to moderately hot, 400 deg F or gas 6 (200 deg C).
2. Arrange sardines in four scallop shells or individual ovenproof dishes.
3. Heat oil in a pan, add onion, crushed garlic and tomato pulp and simmer gently until onion is just tender.
4. Fry mushrooms in butter in another pan and add to tomato mixture.
5. Pour over the sardines, then top with breadcrumbs.
6. Bake in centre of oven until crumbs are crisp and golden.

FLOWERED MACKEREL
Serves 4

Rich mackerel gets a sharp fruit sauce.

4 mackerel, split and boned
3oz (75gm) butter
2oz (50gm) fresh breadcrumbs
3 level tablespoons chopped watercress
salt and pepper
1 can (15½oz or 387gm) gooseberries
small piece of butter
2oz (50gm) sugar

1. Preheat oven to moderate to moderately hot, 375 deg F or gas 5 (190 deg C).
2. Wipe mackerel and open.
3. Cream butter and add breadcrumbs, watercress and seasoning.
4. Spread inside of fish with this mixture. Fold in half and place in shallow, ovenproof dish. Cover and bake in centre of oven for 30–35 minutes until tender.
5. Pulp gooseberries in their syrup. Heat through with the butter and sugar. Pour over the fish and serve.

GRILLED HALIBUT WITH SPICED SAUCE
(Illustrated on page 36)
Serves 4

4 halibut or cod steaks, about 6oz (150gm) each
1oz (25gm) plain flour, seasoned with salt and pepper
3oz (75gm) butter
½ level teaspoon powdered basil
½ level teaspoon marjoram
pinch of mixed spice
¼ level teaspoon powdered mustard
1 level teaspoon tomato purée
2 tablespoons lemon juice
lemon slices to garnish

1. Wash and dry fish. Coat with seasoned flour.
2. Melt 1oz (25gm) butter in grill pan or shallow ovenware dish and lay fish in it.
3. Spoon a little butter over fish and grill them under medium heat. Add another 1oz (25gm) butter and increase heat a little. Grill till golden on both sides.
4. Meanwhile, melt remaining butter in pan and blend in herbs, spice and mustard. Add tomato purée, lemon juice and salt and pepper to taste.
5. Spoon sauce over fish. Lower grill heat and cook for 5 minutes.
6. Garnish with lemon slices and serve.

PARTY RICE
Serves 12

A way of making a few expensive prawns go a long way at a party.

10oz (250gm) long-grain rice
6oz (150gm) butter
pinch of garlic salt
pinch of mixed herbs
2 sticks celery, diced
1 packet (8oz or 200gm) frozen peas and carrots, cooked
2oz (50gm) peeled prawns

1. Cook rice in boiling, salted water for 10–15 minutes, until tender. Drain.
2. Melt butter in a large pan. Add rice, garlic salt and mixed herbs. Fry for about 4 minutes.
3. Add remaining ingredients and cook for a few minutes to heat through.

WHITING WITH MUSTARD SAUCE
Serves 4

4 whiting
salt and pepper
2 small shallots
1 level tablespoon French mustard
4 tablespoons dry white wine
juice of ½ lemon
1oz (25gm) butter
1 tablespoon chopped parsley

1. Preheat oven to moderate, 350 deg F or gas 4 (180 deg C).
2. Place fish in greased, ovenproof dish. Season well.
3. Peel shallots, chop finely and scatter over fish.
4. Blend together mustard and wine and pour over fish. Cover and bake in centre of oven for 20–30 minutes, till fish is cooked.
5. Drain cooking liquor into a pan. Stir in lemon juice and heat for 2–3 minutes stirring well to reduce liquid. Stir in butter and parsley and pour over fish.

SARDINE AND TOMATO PIZZA
Serves 4

8oz (200gm) self-raising flour
½ level teaspoon salt
2oz (50gm) butter
½ pint (250ml) milk
2 jars sardine and tomato spread
1 small can sardines in tomato sauce
2 tomatoes, sliced
black olives

1. Preheat oven to hot, 450 deg F or gas 8 (230 deg C).
2. Sift flour and salt into a bowl. Rub in butter until mixture resembles fine breadcrumbs.
3. Add milk and mix to a soft dough with a knife. Knead lightly on a floured board until smooth.
4. Shape into a circle about ½ inch thick and place on a greased baking sheet.
5. Spread evenly with sardine and tomato spread and arrange sardines with tails to centre.
6. Add tomatoes and black olives and bake near top of oven for about 10 minutes until well risen and golden brown.

Eggs, cheese and pasta

These economical products are essential standbys from which a meal can always be made in a hurry, and the products used to enhance and stretch higher-priced foods.

POTATO AND HAM OMELETTE
Serves 4–6

3oz (75gm) butter
8oz (200gm) potatoes
1 onion, chopped
4oz (100gm) cooked ham
5 eggs, lightly beaten
5 tablespoons cream, milk or water
½ teaspoon salt
¼ teaspoon pepper

1. Melt butter in a large pan. Add diced potatoes and onion and cook slowly for 10 minutes till potatoes are tender.
2. Add ham. Blend together eggs, milk and seasoning.
3. Pour in pan over potatoes and ham. Cover and cook slowly for 6–8 minutes or till eggs are completely set.

SPANISH OMELETTE 1
Serves 4

The first of two versions of a quick and substantial lunch or supper dish.

2 small onions, chopped
2 garlic cloves, finely chopped
4 tablespoons oil
6 eggs
1 teaspoon Tabasco sauce
salt and pepper
6 small potatoes, boiled and chopped
2 tablespoons cooked peas plus a few extra to garnish
thin strips canned pimento (optional)

1. Fry onion and garlic in half the oil till tender.
2. Beat eggs lightly with Tabasco, and season. Add potato, peas and chopped pimento if used.
3. Heat remaining oil in pan. Pour in egg and vegetable mixture.
4. Cook omelette in usual way and serve unfolded, garnished with peas.

SPANISH OMELETTE 2
Serves 6

4oz (100gm) butter
2 large onions, sliced
2 sticks celery, chopped
6 tomatoes, sliced
8 bacon rashers, chopped
12 eggs
salt and pepper
2 tablespoons chopped pimento
1lb (½ kilo) potato, cooked and diced
8oz (200gm) cooked peas
6 tablespoons sweet pickle

1. Melt butter and fry onion, celery, tomato and bacon. Remove from pan.
2. Beat together eggs and season. Fry in same pan and mix with fork while cooking. When nearly set, pile all ingredients in the centre, except pickle. Cook till egg is set.
3. Spoon sweet pickle over ingredients and serve at once.

COUNTRY SUPPER
Serves 4

1lb (½ kilo) potatoes, boiled
8oz (200gm) streaky bacon,
de-rinded
1 medium onion, peeled and
finely chopped
4 large eggs
1oz (25gm) butter
4oz (100gm) cheese, grated

1. Dice potatoes and bacon. Fry
bacon gently, then remove from
pan.
2. Turn potatoes and onions into
a pan and cook until very lightly
brown.
3. Add to the bacon, then turn
into an ovenware dish.
4. Fry eggs in butter and place on
top of mixture.
5. Cover with cheese and brown
under the grill.

DANISH BACON AND EGG CAKE
Serves 3–4

8oz (200gm) bacon rashers
½oz (12gm) flour
6 tablespoons milk
4 eggs
salt and pepper

1. Fry bacon till brown and crisp,
about 3–4 minutes. Keep hot.
2. Mix flour and milk. Beat in
eggs and seasoning.
3. Reheat a little bacon dripping
in pan. Pour in egg mixture and
cook over fairly high heat till set,
lifting edges occasionally.
4. When cooked, about 5–6
minutes, place hot rashers on top
and serve.

BLINI (RUSSIAN PANCAKES)
Serves 4–6

1 level teaspoon dried yeast
1 teaspoon sugar
½ pint (250ml) warm milk
8oz (200gm) plain flour
1 level teaspoon salt
1 egg, separated
2oz (50gm) butter, melted
1 small can evaporated milk
1 can (14oz or 350gm) herrings
in tomato sauce
2 tablespoons soured cream

1. Sprinkle yeast and sugar on
milk. Whisk with a fork and leave
in a warm place for 10–15 minutes
till frothy.
2. Mix with flour and form a
dough. Leave in a warm place to
rise for 1 hour.
3. Mix in salt, egg yolk and
cooled, melted butter.
4. Gradually beat in evaporated
milk. When smooth, leave to rise
for 30 minutes. (The mixture
should be like thick cream.)
5. Heat herrings with soured
cream.
6. Whisk egg white until stiff.
Fold into the pancake mixture.
7. Make a thick pancake with
the batter. Spread herrings on
pancake. Make a second pancake
and lay it on top. Continue piling
pancakes one on top of the other
to form a mound. Serve hot, cut
in wedges.

BREAKFAST PANCAKES
(Illustrated on page 53)
Makes 12

4oz (100gm) self-raising flour
1 level teaspoon baking powder
½ level teaspoon salt
1 egg
2 tablespoons cooking oil
¼ pint (125ml) milk
oil for cooking

1. Sift flour, baking powder and
salt into a bowl. Make a well in
centre.
2. Beat egg and blend in oil and
milk. Add to centre of flour.
Gradually mix in flour and beat
well.
3. Heat a large frying pan and
grease lightly with oil. Put
tablespoons of batter in pan well
apart. Cook till full of bubbles on
top and golden brown underneath.
Turn and cook underside.

Note
These can be served with
breakfast scrambled eggs, eggs
and bacon or for supper with
sliced liver sausage added to the
batter before cooking.

SAVOURY PANCAKES
Serves 4

½ pint (250ml) pancake batter
(see Basic recipes, page 100)
2oz (50gm) margarine
2oz (50gm) flour
1 pint (approximately ½ litre)
milk
3oz (75gm) cheese, grated
4oz (100gm) sliced cooked ham,
cut in strips
1 teaspoon mixed herbs
salt and pepper

1. Fry pancakes in a well greased
frying pan and keep hot over a
saucepan of hot water.
2. Melt margarine in a pan, add
flour, then beat in milk. Bring to
the boil, stirring. Stir in most of
the cheese, all the ham and herbs.
Season well.
3. Spread 1 tablespoon of filling
on each pancake roll and put in
ovenproof dish. Pour rest of sauce
over the pancakes.
4. Sprinkle with remaining cheese
and grill till golden brown.

COUNTRY PANCAKES
Serves 4

oil for cooking
¾ pint (375ml) pancake batter
(see Basic recipes, page 100)
½oz (12gm) margarine
1 small onion, chopped
2 sticks celery, chopped
1 can (14oz or 350gm) peeled
tomatoes
pinch of sugar
salt and pepper
½ pint (250ml) cheese sauce (see
Basic recipes, page 100)
2oz (50gm) cheese, grated

1. Preheat oven to moderate to
moderately hot, 375 deg F or gas 5
(190 deg C).
2. Put a little oil in a frying pan
and pour in enough batter (about
3 tablespoons) to cover pan thinly.
3. Cook until underside is golden
brown, turn and cook other side.
Keep warm. Make 10–12 pancakes.
4. Melt margarine in a pan and
fry onion and celery gently for 5
minutes. Add tomatoes and juice,
sugar and seasoning. Bring to the
boil and simmer for 15–20
minutes.
5. Make cheese sauce. Spread
pancakes alternately with
tomato and cheese sauces, piling
one on top of the other. Repeat
until sauce and pancakes are used
up, finishing with a pancake.
6. Sprinkle with cheese, cover
with foil and bake in centre of
oven for 30–35 minutes.
7. Remove foil and grill till cheese
bubbles.

BEAN SOUFFLETTE
(Illustrated on page 53)
Serves 4

cheese pastry made with 4oz
(100gm) flour (see Basic recipes,
page 100)
½oz (12gm) lard
4 streaky bacon rashers,
chopped
1 medium onion, chopped
1 can (1lb or ½ kilo) baked beans
2 eggs, separated
1 dessertspoon mayonnaise
salt and pepper
1 tablespoon finely grated
Parmesan cheese

1. Preheat oven to moderately
hot, 400 deg F or gas 6 (200 deg C).
2. Line an 8-inch (20-cm) flan ring
with pastry and bake blind for
10–15 minutes.
3. Lower oven setting to
moderate, 350 deg F or gas 4 (180
deg C).
4. Melt lard in a pan. Fry bacon
and onion. Place in flan with
baked beans.
5. Blend egg yolks with
mayonnaise and seasoning.
Whisk egg whites till stiff. Fold
into egg yolk mixture.
6. Pile on baked beans, sprinkle
with cheese and bake in centre of
oven for 25–30 minutes till firm
and golden.

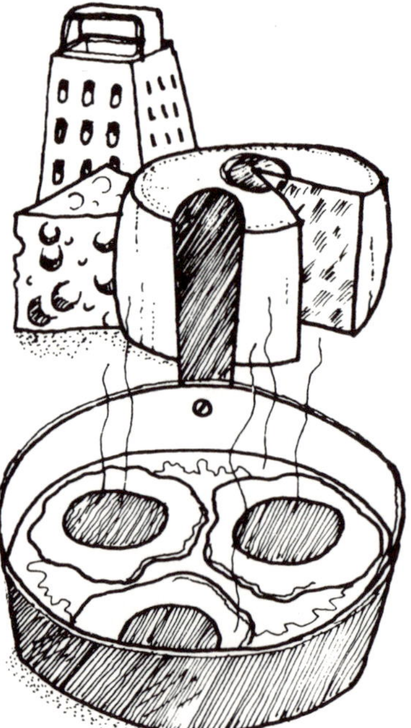

MUSHROOM CRUMB SOUFFLE
Serves 4

4 streaky bacon rashers
1 medium onion, chopped
1oz (25gm) butter
1 can (10½oz or 262gm)
condensed mushroom soup
4oz (100gm) white breadcrumbs
salt and pepper
4 eggs, separated

1. Preheat oven to hot, 425 deg F
or gas 7 (220 deg C).
2. Cut bacon in thin strips, then
cook it with onion gently in
butter for 2–3 minutes.
3. Add mushroom soup,
breadcrumbs and seasoning. Beat
in egg yolks.
4. Whisk egg whites till just stiff
and carefully fold into soup
mixture.
5. Turn into a greased 1½-pint
(approximately ¾-litre) soufflé
dish and bake in centre of oven
for 35–40 minutes.

BOILED EGGS OSTEND STYLE
Serves 4

Hard-boiled eggs can be served
in a variety of ways, as these hot
and cold dishes demonstrate.

4oz (100gm) long-grain rice
½ pint (250ml) water
½ teaspoon salt
1 tablespoon mayonnaise
a little tomato purée
2 hard-boiled eggs, halved
3oz (75gm) shrimps
watercress

1. Put rice, water and salt in a
saucepan. Bring to the boil, stir,
then lower heat to simmer.
2. Cover and cook for 15 minutes
or till rice is tender and liquid
absorbed. Remove from pan and
leave to cool.
3. Mix mayonnaise with tomato
purée.
4. Divide cold rice between four
serving plates. Garnish with
hard-boiled eggs, a little
mayonnaise, shrimps and
watercress.

EGG AND POTATO LAYER
Serves 4

1lb ($\frac{1}{2}$ kilo) potatoes, peeled
$\frac{1}{2}$oz (12gm) margarine
4oz (100gm) cheese, grated
4 hard-boiled eggs
$\frac{1}{2}$ pint (250ml) white sauce (see
Basic recipes, page 100)

1. Preheat oven to moderate to
moderately hot, 375 deg F or gas 5
(190 deg C).
2. Slice potatoes about $\frac{1}{8}$ inch
thick, then parboil.
3. Grease the bottom of an
ovenproof dish with margarine
and sprinkle with half the grated
cheese.
4. Slice eggs, then arrange
alternate layers of potatoes and
eggs, starting with a layer of
potatoes.
5. Cover with white sauce and
sprinkle with remaining cheese.
6. Bake in centre of oven for 35
minutes, or until top is browned.

PICKLED PUFF
Serves 5–6

1lb ($\frac{1}{2}$ kilo) sausagemeat
6 tablespoons sweet pickle
5 hard-boiled eggs
1 packet ($7\frac{1}{2}$oz or 187gm) puff
pastry (or see Basic recipes,
page 100)
1 egg, beaten

1. Preheat oven to hot, 425 deg F
or gas 7 (220 deg C).
2. Combine sausagemeat with
sweet pickle and shape into an
oblong, 10 inches by 6 inches.
3. Place eggs in a line down
centre of sausagemeat. Bring
edges together to form long roll
and seal well.
4. Roll pastry into an oblong, 10
inches by 12 inches. Brush with
beaten egg and roll round the
sausagemeat, sealing the edge and
ends well. Brush with beaten egg.
5. Bake in centre of oven for 45
minutes. Serve hot or cold.

HOT CREAM EGGS
Serves 4

white part of 2 leeks, finely
sliced
2oz (50gm) butter
1 level tablespoon curry powder
1oz (25gm) flour
$\frac{1}{4}$ pint (125ml) milk
juice of 1 lemon
salt
1 heaped tablespoon seedless
raisins
8 hard-boiled eggs, quartered
1lb ($\frac{1}{2}$ kilo) mashed potato

1. Fry leeks in butter with curry
powder for 1–2 minutes. Take care
it does not burn.
2. Stir in flour and cook for 1
minute, stirring all the time.
3. Add milk gradually, still
stirring. Cook till mixture
thickens.
4. Stir in lemon juice, salt, raisins
and then the eggs.
5. Put mashed potato on a serving
dish, make hollows in it and
spoon mixture in.

SPICED EGGS
Serves 4

8 hard-boiled eggs
1oz (25gm) butter
1 dessertspoon curry powder
4 teaspoons chutney
2 teaspoons paprika
salt
1 carton ($2\frac{1}{2}$oz or 62gm) double
cream
1 lettuce
$\frac{1}{2}$ cucumber
1 bunch watercress
8oz (200gm) French beans

1. Cut eggs in half, scoop out
yolks and blend with butter,
curry powder, chutney, paprika,
salt and cream.
2. Spoon back into egg whites.
Set on lettuce and garnish with
sliced cucumber, watercress and
cold, cooked French beans.

SUMMER CASSEROLE
Serves 4–6

9 hard-boiled eggs
9 tomatoes
1 pint (approximately $\frac{1}{2}$ litre)
cheese sauce (see Basic
recipes, page 100)
$2\frac{1}{2}$oz (62gm) breadcrumbs
3oz (75gm) butter

1. Preheat oven to very moderate,
325 deg F or gas 3 (170 deg C).
2. Slice eggs and tomatoes.
3. Place a layer of eggs in a
greased casserole. Add a layer of
tomatoes and pour over $\frac{1}{3}$ cheese
sauce.
4. Add crumbs. Repeat layers till
ingredients are used up and top
with crumbs.
5. Bake in centre of oven for 20
minutes till browned.

DEVILLED EGG BAKE
Serves 4–6

6 hard-boiled eggs
4 tablespoons mayonnaise or
salad dressing
2 teaspoons made mustard
$\frac{1}{4}$ teaspoon salt
1 can (5oz or 125gm) shrimps
1 can shrimp soup
$\frac{1}{4}$ pint (125ml) milk
4oz (100gm) boiled rice (raw
weight)

1. Preheat oven to moderate, 350
deg F or gas 4 (180 deg C).
2. Halve eggs. Remove yolks and
mash them in a bowl with
mayonnaise or salad dressing,
mustard and salt. Pile back into
egg whites.
3. Drain shrimps and rinse them.
Combine with soup and milk in a
pan. Heat slowly, stirring well
till bubbly.
4. Spoon rice into a shallow,
ovenproof dish. Arrange eggs in
it, pushing down into rice.
5. Spoon shrimp sauce over rice
and eggs and bake in centre of
oven for 15 minutes or till
bubbling.

MUSHROOM AND EGG CREAM
Serves 4

1oz (25gm) butter
1 small onion, chopped
pinch of dry mustard
pinch of mixed herbs
1 packet (1 pint or
approximately ½ litre) cream of
mushroom soup
¾ pint (375ml) milk
4oz (100gm) cheese, grated
4 hard-boiled eggs

1. Heat butter and fry onion till golden. Add mustard and herbs.
2. Add soup powder, milk and cheese. Stir over low heat till cheese has melted and mixture is smooth.
3. Slice eggs and stir into sauce.
4. Pour into serving dish and serve with toast fingers.

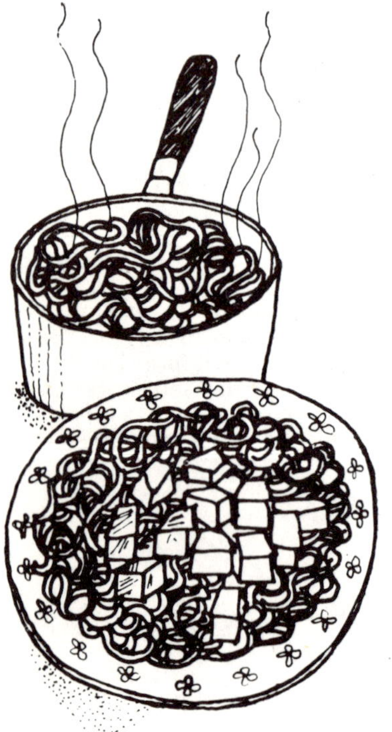

CURRIED EGG CUPS
Serves 4–6

A cheap but effective dish for a buffet party.

12 large thin slices white bread
3oz (75gm) margarine, melted
2oz (50gm) margarine
1 small onion, chopped
1 level teaspoon curry powder
1½oz (37gm) flour
¼ pint (125ml) milk
¼ pint (125ml) chicken stock
1 dessert apple, cored and
chopped
2oz (50gm) sweet pickle
3 hard-boiled eggs, chopped
salt and pepper
1 hard-boiled egg to garnish

1. Preheat oven to moderately hot, 400 deg F or gas 6 (200 deg C).
2. Remove crusts from bread. Cut into 4-inch squares.
3. Grease 12 deep patty tins with margarine. Brush bread with remaining melted margarine and press into tins, greased side up. Bake in centre of oven for 30 minutes. Remove from tins and leave to cool.
4. Melt fat in pan and fry onion and curry powder for 5 minutes.
5. Stir in flour and cook for 1 minute.
6. Remove from heat and stir in milk and stock. Bring to the boil, stirring, and cook for 1 minute.
7. Add apple and pickle and simmer gently for 5 minutes.
8. Stir in chopped egg, season and spoon into bread cases.
9. Serve garnished with slices of hard-boiled egg.

GAELIC EGGS
Serves 4

1 medium onion
3oz (75gm) lamb's liver
5oz (125gm) white breadcrumbs
2 level teaspoons mixed herbs
3oz (75gm) suet
salt and pepper
1 egg, beaten
4 hard-boiled eggs
oil for deep frying
2 cans (15¾oz or 393gm)
spaghetti in tomato and cheese
sauce

1. Chop onion finely and shred liver.
2. Place in a bowl with breadcrumbs, herbs, suet and seasoning. Bind with beaten egg.
3. Divide mixture into four and mould it around the eggs.
4. Fry gently in oil until golden brown. Drain on absorbent paper.
5. Heat spaghetti in a saucepan, then place in a hot dish.
6. Cut eggs into halves and arrange around edge of dish.

CHEESE SOUP
Serves 4

2 large onions, chopped
2 sticks celery, chopped
3oz (75gm) butter
½oz (12gm) flour
1 teaspoon dry mustard
paprika
salt and pepper
1 pint (approximately ½ litre)
milk
8oz (200gm) cheese, grated
3 slices bacon, fried and
crumbled

1. Fry onion and celery in butter for about 5 minutes.
2. Blend in flour and seasonings.
3. Gradually add milk and cook for about 5 minutes on medium heat till smooth and slightly thickened, stirring continuously.
4. Add cheese and stir until melted. Serve at once, garnished with bacon.

CABBAGE, CHEESE AND RAISIN SALAD
Serves 4–6

8oz (200gm) raw cabbage, shredded
8oz (200gm) cheese, grated
2oz (50gm) raisins
3–4 tablespoons mayonnaise
½ level teaspoon salt
pinch of cayenne pepper

1. Toss all ingredients lightly together.
2. Chill, and serve.

GOUDA RICE SALAD
Serves 4

8oz (200gm) Gouda cheese, diced
3oz (75gm) cooked long-grain rice (raw weight)
4oz (100gm) cooked peas
1oz (25gm) walnuts, shelled and halved
2 tablespoons oil
2 tablespoons lemon juice
½ teaspoon salt, pepper and sugar
½ teaspoon made mustard

1. Mix together cheese, rice, peas and walnuts.
2. Make lemon dressing by mixing together rest of ingredients in a screw-topped jar and shaking well.
3. Toss cheese mixture in lemon dressing and serve with lettuce.

EDAM AND APPLE COCKTAIL
(Illustrated on page 53)
Serves 4

A summer hors d'oeuvre idea.

4 lettuce leaves, shredded
1 green apple, cored and sliced
1 red apple, cored and sliced
lemon juice
6oz (150gm) Edam cheese, diced
4 tablespoons mayonnaise
1 teaspoon tomato purée
2–3 drops each Tabasco and Worcestershire sauce
½ teaspoon sherry (optional)

1. Place lettuce in four glass dishes. Dip apple in lemon juice and arrange with cheese on the lettuce.
2. Combine rest of ingredients together to make a sauce and either spoon it over each dish or serve it separately.

BAKED CHEESE OMELETTE
Serves 4

2oz (50gm) butter
2 medium onions, sliced
8 mushrooms, sliced
8 eggs
salt and pepper
12 tablespoons milk
2 heaped tablespoons cooked peas (optional)
6oz (150gm) cheese, grated

1. Preheat oven to moderate, 350 deg F or gas 4 (180 deg C).
2. Grease a deep, ovenproof pie plate with some of the butter.
3. Melt rest of butter and fry onion and mushrooms till tender.
4. Beat together eggs, seasoning and milk. Turn into buttered pie plate.
5. Put onions, mushrooms and peas in egg mixture and top with grated cheese.
6. Bake in centre of oven for 30–35 minutes.

RAPALLO FLAN
Serves 4

shortcrust pastry made with 4oz (100gm) flour (see Basic recipes, page 100)
6oz (150gm) cheese, thinly sliced
12oz (300gm) tomatoes, skinned
8 anchovy fillets

1. Preheat oven to hot, 425 deg F or gas 7 (220 deg C).
2. Roll out pastry and line a 6-inch (18-cm) flan ring. Prick the base, cover with foil and bake blind for 10 minutes. Remove foil and bake for a further 10 minutes. Lower oven setting to moderately hot, 400 deg F or gas 6 (200 deg C).
3. Leave pastry to cool then line the flan case with 1oz (25gm) cheese.
4. Pile cut-up tomatoes on top and cover with rest of cheese.
5. Bake in centre of oven for 15–20 minutes until cheese melts.
6. Garnish with anchovy fillets and serve hot.

VEGETABLE CHEESE FLAN
Serves 4

shortcrust pastry made with 6oz (150gm) flour (see Basic recipes, page 100)
1 level teaspoon cornflour
1 can (10oz or 250gm) vegetable soup
4oz (100gm) cheese, grated
2 hard-boiled eggs

1. Preheat oven to hot, 425 deg F or gas 7 (220 deg C).
2. Line an 8-inch (20-cm) flan ring with pastry. Prick the base, cover with foil and bake blind for 10 minutes. Remove foil and bake for a further 10 minutes.
3. Blend cornflour with 2 tablespoons soup. Bring remaining soup to the boil. Pour over blended cornflour and return to the pan. Reheat to boiling, stirring all the time.
4. Add 3oz (75gm) cheese to the hot soup and stir till melted.
5. Slice eggs and arrange in base of flan case. Pour sauce over.
6. Sprinkle top with rest of cheese and bake for 5–10 minutes until cheese melts and browns.

PLOUGHMAN'S QUICHE
Serves 4

shortcrust pastry made with
4oz (100gm) flour (see Basic
recipes, page 100)
1 large onion, chopped
2oz (50gm) butter or margarine
1oz (25gm) flour
½ pint (250ml) milk
3oz (75gm) Cheddar cheese,
grated

1. Preheat oven to hot, 425 deg F
or gas 7 (220 deg C).
2. Roll out pastry and line a
baking tin.
3. Prick the base and bake in
centre of oven for 15–20 minutes
till golden brown.
4. Meanwhile fry onion in melted
butter or margarine but do not
brown. Blend flour and milk in a
bowl. Add to onions and bring to
boil, stirring.
5. Remove from heat, stir in 2oz
(50gm) cheese and pour into flan
case.
6. Sprinkle with remaining cheese
and brown top either in hot oven
for 5 minutes or under the grill.
Serve hot or cold.

CHEESE AND CORN PUFF
Serves 6

8oz (200gm) stale breadcrumbs
1 pint (approximately ½ litre)
milk
10oz (250gm) cheese, grated
1 can (12oz or 300gm) corn
kernels
2 egg yolks, beaten
salt
1oz (25gm) butter, melted
2 egg whites

1. Preheat oven to very moderate,
325 deg F or gas 3 (170 deg C).
2. Soak breadcrumbs in milk.
3. Add cheese, corn, egg yolks,
salt and butter.
4. Fold in stiffly beaten egg
whites. Pour into a greased,
ovenproof dish and bake in centre
of oven for about 40 minutes.

TIERED CHEESE PANCAKES
Serves 4

½ pint (250ml) pancake batter
(see Basic recipes, page 100)
1½lb (¾ kilo) freshly cooked
spinach, chopped
8oz (200gm) cheese, grated

1. Mix batter ingredients
smoothly and leave to stand at
least 1 hour in a cool place.
2. Cook thin pancakes in a well
greased frying pan and pile on a
warm dish putting a layer of
spinach and grated cheese
between each pancake.
3. Keep pancakes hot and build
them up till all the batter is used.
Top last pancake with grated
cheese and serve hot, cut in
wedges, with vegetables or a
salad.

CHEESE AND ONION ROLY POLY
Serves 4

suet pastry made with 8oz
(200gm) flour (see Basic recipes,
page 100)
4oz (100gm) onions, thinly
sliced
8oz (200gm) cheese, thinly
sliced
pinch of salt, pepper and
nutmeg

1. Preheat oven to moderately
hot, 400 deg F or gas 6 (200 deg C).
2. Knead pastry lightly and roll
out to an oblong.
3. Scatter onions, cheese and
seasonings over surface. Damp
edges and roll up like a Swiss roll.
4. Brush with milk and bake in
centre of oven for 40–45 minutes
until browned.
5. Serve hot with a tomato sauce
or a can of hot tomato soup.

CHEESE CURRY
Serves 4

1oz (25gm) butter
1 onion, chopped
1oz (25gm) flour
1–2 rounded teaspoons curry
powder
½ pint (250ml) stock or water
1oz (25gm) sultanas
8oz (200gm) cheese, cubed
4oz (100gm) long-grain rice

1. Melt butter in a pan and fry
onion till golden brown. Add
flour and curry powder. Stir over
a gentle heat.
2. Add stock or water gradually,
stirring well until sauce thickens.
3. Fold in sultanas and cheese.
4. Cook rice in boiling, salted
water until just soft.
5. Drain and dry rice. Serve with
cheese curry and garnish with
sliced, hard-boiled egg if liked.

BREAD AND CHEESE PUDDING
Serves 4–6

8oz (200gm) fresh white bread
6oz (150gm) cheese, grated
3 eggs
1 pint (approximately ½ litre)
milk
salt and pepper

1. Preheat oven to moderate to
moderately hot, 375 deg F or gas 5
(190 deg C).
2. Remove crusts from bread and
cut into ¼-inch cubes. Place in a
basin and add cheese.
3. Whisk eggs and add to bread
and cheese.
4. Heat milk, pour on to mixture
and season. Mix well together.
5. Grease a 2-pint (approximately
1-litre) soufflé dish and pour in
mixture.
6. Bake in centre of oven for 50
minutes.

POTATO CHEESE PIE
Serves 4

8oz (200gm) cheese, grated
2lb (1 kilo) raw potatoes, thinly
sliced
1oz (25gm) butter
scant ½ pint (250ml) milk
salt and pepper
2 eggs
¼ teaspoon nutmeg (optional)

1. Preheat oven to moderate, 350
deg F or gas 4 (180 deg C).
2. Alternate layers of cheese and
potatoes in a greased, ovenproof
dish finishing with a layer of
cheese.
3. Melt butter in milk, season
well and pour on the well beaten
eggs.
4. Pour this mixture over the
potatoes and cheese and sprinkle
with nutmeg if liked. Bake in
centre of oven for about 1 hour
until potatoes are cooked and top
is browned.

PAN HAGGERTY
Serves 4

A traditional north of England
supper dish.

1lb (½ kilo) potatoes
8oz (200gm) onions
1oz (25gm) butter
6oz (150gm) cheese, grated
salt and pepper

1. Slice potatoes thinly and dry
them in a cloth.
2. Slice onions thinly.
3. Melt butter in frying pan. Put
in a layer of potatoes, the onions,
cheese and finish with another
layer of potatoes, seasoning well
between each layer.
4. Fry gently for about 25 minutes
then place under grill for a further
5 minutes to brown.

CHEESE YORKSHIRE PUDDING
Serves 4

½ pint (250ml) pancake batter
(see Basic recipes, page 100)
1oz (25gm) butter
8oz (200gm) cheese, cut in
¾-inch cubes

1. Leave batter to stand for about
1 hour in a cool place.
2. Preheat oven to hot, 425 deg F
or gas 7 (220 deg C).
3. Melt butter in pudding tin.
4. Toss in cheese cubes and pour
in batter.
5. Bake in centre of oven for
35–40 minutes. Serve at once.

CHEESY BEER AIGRETTES
Makes about 20

2½oz (62gm) plain flour
salt and cayenne pepper
¼ pint (125ml) light ale
2oz (50gm) margarine
2 eggs, beaten
2oz (50gm) cheese, grated
oil for frying

1. Sieve flour, salt and pepper
twice.
2. Heat beer and margarine
together in a pan. Add flour and
stir till mixture forms a soft ball.
3. Remove from heat. Add eggs
gradually, beating hard. Then add
cheese.
4. Drop teaspoonfuls of mixture
into hot oil and fry for about 5
minutes until puffed up and
golden brown. Drain and serve.

SAVOURY SCONES
Makes 5

8oz (200gm) plain flour
1 teaspoon cream of tartar
½ teaspoon bicarbonate of soda
salt and pepper
½ teaspoon dry mustard
2oz (50gm) butter
4oz (100gm) cheese, grated
¼ pint (125ml) milk

1. Preheat oven to moderate to
moderately hot, 375 deg F or gas 5
(190 deg C).
2. Sieve flour, cream of tartar,
bicarbonate of soda, seasoning
and mustard together in a bowl.
3. Rub in butter until mixture
resembles fine breadcrumbs. Add
cheese.
4. Mix in milk to make a soft,
elastic dough.
5. Roll out to about ½ inch thick
and cut out five scones with a
3-inch cutter.
6. Cook on floured baking tray in
centre of oven for about 10–15
minutes until well risen and
browned.
7. To serve, cut in half and spread
with butter.

**FRIED SAVOURY
SANDWICHES**
Serves 4

**8oz (200gm) soft butter
4 tablespoons sweet pickle
8oz (200gm) cheese, grated
freshly ground black pepper
salt
8 slices fresh bread**

1. Mix together 4oz (100gm)
butter, pickle, cheese, pepper and
salt till smooth and creamy.
Spread over 4 slices bread.
2. Place other 4 slices on top and
press together firmly. Trim crusts,
then cut across diagonally.
3. Heat remaining butter in a
heavy frying pan. Fry sandwiches
on both sides till golden brown
and crisp. Drain and serve.

CROQUE MONSIEUR
Serves 4

A more classic fried sandwich
idea than the previous recipe.

**4 thin slices lean ham
8 slices bread and butter
a little French mustard
4 thin slices cheese
butter for frying**

1. Place slices of ham on 4 pieces
of bread and butter. Spread with
mustard.
2. Put cheese on remaining 4
slices of bread and butter.
3. Put 2 slices together, one of
ham, one of cheese, and fry in hot
butter till golden brown. Drain.
Cut in half and keep hot. Repeat
until you have made four
sandwiches.

**CHEESE AND CIDER
FONDUE**
(Illustrated on page 53)
Serves 8

An inexpensive party dish.

**2½ level tablespoons cornflour
3 tablespoons water
1 garlic clove
½ pint (250ml) dry cider
1lb (½ kilo) Cheddar cheese,
grated
1½ level teaspoons vegetable
extract
1–2 French loaves, cut in cubes**

1. Mix cornflour with water to a
smooth cream.
2. Rub the inside of a heavy,
flameproof casserole or fondue
pan with cut garlic clove. Pour in
the cider and put on medium heat.
3. Just before cider comes to the
boil add cheese, a handful at a
time. Stir well till cheese melts.
4. Add cornflour cream and
vegetable extract. Continue to
heat slowly, stirring all the time,
until fondue thickens enough to
coat back of a spoon.
5. Serve on hot plate or
candle-warmers with cubed bread.
Use fondue forks to spear bread
cubes and dip them in the cheese.

ENGLISH APPLE FONDUE
Serves 6

**1 garlic clove
1 level tablespoon cornflour
¼ level teaspoon dry mustard
¼ level teaspoon paprika
¾ pint (375ml) apple juice
1½lb (¾ kilo) Cheddar cheese,
coarsely grated
1–2 French loaves, cut in cubes**

1. Rub inside of a heavy,
flameproof casserole with cut
garlic clove.
2. Blend cornflour, mustard and
paprika with a little apple juice.
3. Warm rest of apple juice in the
casserole, add the cheese and stir
until melted.
4. Stir in blended cornflour, bring
to the boil and simmer gently
10–15 minutes until creamy. Serve
with cubes of French bread.

CHEESE SHELLS
Serves 4

**4oz (100gm) shell-shaped
noodles
1½oz (37gm) butter
1½oz (37gm) flour
¾ pint (375ml) milk
salt and pepper
cayenne pepper
2 sticks celery, chopped
8oz (200gm) cheese, grated**

1. Cook noodles in boiling, salted
water for 10 minutes or until
tender.
2. Melt butter in a pan, and add
the flour. Remove from heat and
gradually add the milk. Return to
heat and cook for a few minutes,
stirring continuously.
3. Beat sauce till smooth and
glossy. Season well, remove from
heat and add celery and cheese.
Stir till cheese has melted.
4. Drain noodles and stir into
sauce. Serve in four scallop shells
or individual dishes.

**CHEESE AND MACARONI
SALAD**
Serves 4–6

**8oz (200gm) Cheddar cheese,
grated
6oz (150gm) cooked macaroni
1 small red pepper, chopped
(optional)
few chopped chives
4 tablespoons chopped celery
4 tablespoons French dressing
(see Basic recipes, page 100)**

1. Mix all ingredients together,
except French dressing, and chill.
2. Toss in French dressing just
before serving.

SALZBURG SUPPER DISH
Serves 4

8oz (200gm) pasta shells
8oz (200gm) cream cheese,
sieved
3oz (150gm) butter
8oz (200gm) cooked ham, diced
salt and cayenne pepper
chopped parsley

1. Cook pasta shells in boiling,
salted water for about 10 minutes.
Drain well and mix with cream
cheese.
2. Melt butter in a large pan. Add
ham and heat through.
3. Add pasta shells and cream
cheese. Mix well and season.
4. Serve sprinkled with parsley
and cayenne pepper.

SAVOURY NOODLES
Serves 4

8oz (200gm) ribbon noodles
1oz (25gm) butter
1 small can mushrooms
1 garlic clove, crushed
1 can condensed chicken soup
2oz (50gm) cheese, grated
2 tablespoons evaporated milk
or cream

1. Cook noodles in boiling, salted
water for 10 minutes, then drain.
2. Melt butter in a pan and add
drained mushrooms and crushed
garlic.
3. Add chicken soup, cheese and
evaporated milk or cream.
4. Toss noodles in this mixture
and serve very hot.

NEAPOLITAN NOODLE PIE
Serves 4

8oz (200gm) noodles
1–2 onions
2–3 tablespoons oil
4oz (100gm) minced pork
4oz (100gm) minced beef
1 glass red wine
1 can (2¼oz or 56gm) tomato
purée
2 sticks celery, chopped
a little Tabasco sauce
salt, thyme and nutmeg
1oz (25gm) bacon, finely
chopped

1. Preheat oven to moderate to
moderately hot, 375 deg F or gas 5
(190 deg C).
2. Cook noodles in boiling, salted
water for 10 minutes, then drain.
3. Chop onion and fry in oil till
soft. Stir in the meat and cook
for a few minutes till browned.
4. Add wine, tomato purée, celery
and mix well. Add Tabasco, salt,
thyme and nutmeg to taste.
5. Alternate layers of meat and
noodles in an ovenproof dish,
finishing with a layer of noodles.
6. Sprinkle with bacon and cook
in centre of oven for about 35
minutes.

BACONAISE
Serves 4–6

10oz (250gm) bacon, diced
2 onions, chopped
2 garlic cloves
1 can (14oz or 350gm) tomatoes
½ teaspoon basil
salt and pepper
1 level tablespoon cornflour
¼ pint (125ml) cider
12oz (300gm) long spaghetti
1oz (25gm) butter

1. Fry bacon, onion and garlic
till tender.
2. Add tomatoes and season with
basil, salt and pepper.
3. Thicken sauce with cornflour
blended with cider. Simmer gently
for about 10 minutes.
4. Cook spaghetti in boiling,
salted water till just tender.
5. Strain, toss in butter and
season well. Serve with sauce
poured over the spaghetti.

SUPPER A LA ROMA
Serves 4

2 cans (16oz or 400gm each)
spaghetti in tomato sauce
1 onion, sliced in rings
4oz (100gm) ham, cut in strips
1 courgette, sliced in rings
2oz (50gm) cheese, grated
4oz (100gm) mushrooms

1. Preheat oven to very moderate,
325 deg F or gas 3 (170 deg C).
2. Mix spaghetti, onion rings,
ham and courgette rings together.
3. Place half spaghetti mix on the
base of a heatproof dish and cover
with grated cheese. Top with rest
of spaghetti mix.
4. Cover with foil and bake in
centre of oven for 35 minutes.
5. While spaghetti is cooking,
grill mushrooms and serve round
edge of dish of spaghetti.

SPAGHETTI SUPPER DISH
(Illustrated on page 54)
Serves 6

2oz (50gm) fresh breadcrumbs
2 eggs
1lb (½ kilo) pork sausages or
sausagemeat
1 medium onion, chopped
1 garlic clove, crushed or
finely chopped (optional)
salt and pepper
1 can (15¾oz or 393gm)
spaghetti with tomato and
cheese sauce
2oz (50gm) cheese, grated

1. Preheat oven to moderately
hot, 400 deg F or gas 6 (200 deg C).
2. Mix breadcrumbs soaked in
half 1 beaten egg with sausages or
sausagemeat, onion, garlic and
seasoning.
3. Line a greased, 8-inch (20-cm)
flan ring with the mixture. Brush
with a little beaten egg and cook
in centre of oven for 20 minutes.
4. Lower oven setting to
moderate, 350 deg F or gas 4 (180
deg C).
5. Turn spaghetti into a pan and
heat gently. Strain off the sauce
and mix it with remaining beaten
egg.
6. Add spaghetti to sauce and
pour into the sausagemeat case.
Cook for a further 20 minutes in
centre of oven.
7. Sprinkle top with cheese and
grill till golden brown.

MARINERS SAUCE SPAGHETTI
Serves 4

8oz (200gm) long spaghetti
2 tablespoons oil
a few bacon rinds
2 garlic cloves
3 medium onions, chopped
1 large can peeled tomatoes
1 teaspoon brown sugar
pepper
pinch of marjoram
3 anchovies, finely chopped
a little grated Parmesan cheese

1. Cook spaghetti in boiling, salted water for 10 minutes. Drain well.
2. Heat oil and fry bacon rinds till crisp. Remove rinds and fry garlic and onion until soft.
3. Stir in tomatoes and simmer for 5 minutes.
4. Remove garlic, then add sugar, pepper, marjoram and anchovies. Simmer for 15 minutes.
5. Pour sauce over spaghetti in serving dish. Serve with Parmesan cheese.

PARTY SPAGHETTI
Serves 4

1 tablespoon oil
1oz (25gm) margarine
2 medium onions, chopped
1 can (14oz or 350gm) tomatoes
1 can (8oz or 200gm) cocktail sausages
$\frac{1}{2}$ teaspoon mixed dried herbs
3oz (75gm) spaghetti
salt and pepper
4 slices cheese

1. Preheat oven to hot, 425 deg F or gas 7 (220 deg C).
2. Heat oil and butter in a frying pan. Add onions and cook gently until soft and transparent.
3. Add tomatoes and mix well. Add drained sausages, mixed herbs and cook gently for 5 minutes.
4. Meanwhile, cook spaghetti in plenty of boiling, salted water till tender. Drain well and chop.
5. Add chopped spaghetti to frying pan and season with salt and pepper.
6. Place mixture in a greased, ovenproof dish and arrange cheese slices on top.
7. Bake in centre of oven for 20 minutes till cheese has melted.
8. Serve with French bread and a green salad.

ANCHOVY SPAGHETTI
Serves 4

8oz (200gm) thin spaghetti
1 garlic clove
2 tablespoons chopped parsley
1 tablespoon oil
4 anchovies
2 level tablespoons tomato purée
4 tablespoons boiling water
grated Parmesan cheese

1. Cook spaghetti in boiling, salted water for 8 minutes. Drain well.
2. Meanwhile, fry chopped garlic and parsley in hot oil till brown.
3. Wash and pound anchovies, add to garlic and parsley and simmer gently for a few minutes.
4. Stir in tomato purée diluted with boiling water. Simmer for a further minute.
5. Place spaghetti in a serving dish and pour sauce over. Serve with Parmesan cheese.

PASTA PIE
Serves 4–6

2 tablespoons olive oil
2 medium onions
1 garlic clove
1 can (14oz or 350gm) tomatoes
1 tablespoon tomato purée
salt and pepper
1 teaspoon sugar
1 teaspoon marjoram
8oz (200gm) macaroni
8oz (200gm) chipolata sausages
12oz (300gm) Bel Paese cheese
pinch of thyme

1. Preheat oven to moderate, 350 deg F or gas 4 (180 deg C).
2. Heat oil and fry peeled, sliced onions and chopped garlic.
3. Add tomatoes, tomato purée, seasoning, sugar and marjoram. Cover and simmer for 20 minutes.
4. Meanwhile, cook macaroni for 12 minutes in boiling, salted water.
5. Brown sausages under grill.
6. Grease a casserole and put 2–3 spoonfuls of tomato mixture at the bottom. Slice sausages and put half the drained macaroni and sausages on the tomato.
7. Cover with a layer of sliced cheese and repeat, ending with a good layer of cheese.
8. Sprinkle with thyme and bake in centre of oven for 30 minutes until golden brown.

Stuffed cabbage leaves (see page 76)

Lemon and cucumber cocktail (see page 81)

Curried cauliflower (see page 78)

Bean and potato open pie (see page 80)

Malted honey nog (see page 98)   Raspberry cider cup (see page 99)

Apricot crunch (see page 89)   Fruity cheese cake (see page 89)

SPICED TOMATO MACARONI
Serves 6

1lb (½ kilo) macaroni
2oz (50gm) margarine
2oz (50gm) flour
1½ pints (approximately ¾ litre) milk
2 teaspoons Tabasco sauce
2 tablespoons tomato purée
10oz (250gm) cheese, grated
salt and pepper
8oz (200gm) bacon, chopped and fried

1. Preheat oven to moderate, 350 deg F or gas 4 (180 deg C).
2. Cook macaroni in boiling, salted water for about 10 minutes.
3. Meanwhile, make a sauce by melting margarine and adding flour. Stir in milk gradually, add Tabasco, tomato purée, 6oz (150gm) cheese, and seasoning.
4. Drain macaroni and add to sauce in pan.
5. Add fried bacon pieces and mix well.
6. Place in an ovenproof dish, sprinkle with remaining grated cheese and bake in centre of oven for about 30 minutes.

MACARONI CHEESE WITH APPLE
Serves 4

6oz (150gm) macaroni
3oz (75gm) margarine
3oz (75gm) flour
¾ pint (375ml) milk
¾ pint (375ml) macaroni liquor
8oz (200gm) cheese, grated
salt and pepper
dry mustard
8oz (200gm) cooked ham, diced
1 red-skinned apple, diced

1. Preheat oven to moderate to moderately hot, 375 deg F or gas 5 (190 deg C).
2. Cook macaroni in boiling, salted water for about 10 minutes, or until tender.
3. Meanwhile, melt margarine in a pan, add flour and gradually stir in milk. Add liquor from the cooked macaroni.
4. Bring to boil, add 6oz (150gm) cheese, seasoning and mustard.
5. Add diced ham and apple. Stir in well.
6. Turn into a greased serving dish and sprinkle with remaining grated cheese. Bake in centre of oven for 20 minutes.

SPAGHETTI ALLA CARBONARA
Serves 4

8oz (200gm) spaghetti
4 small bacon rashers, cut in small pieces
olive oil for frying
2–3 eggs
salt and pepper

1. Cook spaghetti in boiling, salted water for about 10 minutes, or till tender.
2. Place in an ovenproof dish and keep hot in a warm oven.
3. Fry bacon pieces in olive oil till crisp.
4. Place bacon and its fat from the pan on the spaghetti and mix in.
5. Beat eggs lightly and gently turn the spaghetti in the eggs till well mixed. Serve at once very hot.

FRYPAN CASSEROLE
(Illustrated on page 54)
Serves 6

4oz (100gm) onion, chopped
2oz (50gm) fat
2 cans (14oz or 350gm each) tomatoes
1 can (10oz or 250gm) mushrooms
1½ teaspoons salt
shake of pepper
¼ teaspoon basil
1 teaspoon Worcestershire sauce
8oz (200gm) macaroni shells
1 can (12oz or 300gm) luncheon meat, cut in thin strips
2 tablespoons chopped parsley

1. Fry onion in fat for about 5 minutes.
2. Add tomatoes, liquid from mushrooms and seasonings. Bring to boil.
3. Add macaroni, cover and simmer for 10–15 minutes or until tender.
4. Stir in meat and mushrooms. Cover and reheat. Sprinkle parsley on top and serve.

BEETROOT AND NOODLES AU GRATIN
Serves 4

1¼lb (500gm) cooked beetroot (about 3 medium beet)
2oz (50gm) butter
4oz (100gm) noodles
salt and pepper
½ small onion, chopped
1oz (25gm) plain flour
½ pint (250ml) milk
1½oz (37gm) cheese, grated
1½ level tablespoons browned crumbs

1. Preheat oven to hot, 425 deg F or gas 7 (220 deg C).
2. Cut beetroot in ½-inch dice.
3. Melt half the butter in a pan. Toss beetroot in it till heated through.
4. Cook noodles in boiling, salted water for 10 minutes. Drain well. Stir into beetroot and season.
5. Melt remaining butter in a pan and fry onion till tender. Add flour and cook for 1 minute.
6. Gradually stir in milk off the heat. Return to heat and bring to boil. Cook for 1 minute stirring. Season.
7. Put beetroot mixture in an ovenproof dish and pour sauce over.
8. Mix cheese and crumbs together and sprinkle over sauce. Brown in centre of oven for 20 minutes or under a hot grill.

Vegetable dishes

Vegetables can make a meal in themselves, so take advantage of low prices when they come into season or use no-waste frozen vegetables, available throughout the year.

CREAM OF CORN SOUP
(Illustrated on page 54)
Serves 4–6

2 cans (7oz or 175gm) sweetcorn
1 pint (approximately ½ litre) chicken stock
2oz (50gm) butter
2oz (50gm) flour
1 pint (approximately ½ litre) milk
4 tablespoons canned or fresh cream
watercress to garnish

1. Empty sweetcorn into a saucepan with stock and cook for 20 minutes.
2. Melt butter in a pan, add flour and cook for 2 minutes. Remove pan from heat and add milk, stirring continuously. Add the corn mixture and cook for 5 minutes.
3. Sieve the soup or mix in an electric blender.
4. If necessary, add extra milk to give a smooth, creamy consistency.
5. Stir in cream, reheat without boiling and serve, garnished with watercress, or chill and serve.

DUTCH LETTUCE SOUP
Serves 4–6

1 large onion, finely chopped
1 small garlic clove (optional)
2oz (50gm) butter
2–3 heads of lettuce, finely shredded
1½ pints (approximately ¾ litre) chicken stock
1½oz (37gm) flour
½ pint (250ml) single cream
pinch of nutmeg
salt and pepper

1. Fry onion and crushed or chopped garlic (if used) in butter till soft but not brown.
2. Add lettuce and cook, covered, for 10 minutes.
3. Add stock and bring to boil. Reduce heat and simmer for 15–20 minutes.
4. Whisk flour into cream. Add to the soup with the nutmeg, salt and pepper. Stir over gentle heat till soup thickens. Cook, stirring, for a further 2–3 minutes.
5. Sieve or liquidize the soup. Reheat and adjust seasoning if necessary.
6. Serve hot or cold, garnished with chopped chives if available.

CHILLED PEA SOUP
Serves 4–6

1 small onion, finely chopped
8oz (200gm) peas, cooked
1 pint (approximately ½ litre) beef stock
½ teaspoon celery salt
¼ teaspoon pepper
¼ teaspoon salt
4 tablespoons single cream

1. Cook onion and peas in stock for 5 minutes. Add seasonings and allow to cool.
2. Sieve or liquidize the soup.
3. Chill and when ready to serve, stir in cream.

GREEN PEA SOUP WITH EGG
Serves 4–6

2 beef stock cubes
2 pints (approximately 1 litre) hot water
4oz (100gm) cooked peas
2 eggs, lightly beaten

1. Dissolve beef stock cubes in water, bring to boil and cook peas in it for 6 minutes.
2. Remove from heat. Slowly pour in beaten eggs, stirring all the time.
3. Cook, stirring continuously, for 1–2 minutes until the egg is in separated shreds.

MOONSHINE BEAN SOUP
Serves 4–6

**2lb (1 kilo) young broad beans
(weight without pods)
1 small onion, sliced
6 lettuce leaves, shredded
salt and pepper
1 pint (approximately $\frac{1}{2}$ litre)
chicken stock
2oz (50gm) butter, melted
2–3 tablespoons single cream
(optional)**

1. Put broad beans, onion and
lettuce into a pan and add cold
water to cover.
2. Season and cover. Bring to the
boil and simmer for about 20
minutes till beans are tender.
3. Remove from heat. Strain
beans and keep $\frac{1}{2}$ pint (250ml)
cooking liquid. Add this to the
stock.
4. Sieve beans or liquidize them
with a little stock. Add stock to
purée and season well. Stir in
melted butter.
5. Serve hot or cold adding a
little cream, if wished, before
serving.

CREAM OF POTATO SOUP
Serves 4

**1lb ($\frac{1}{2}$ kilo) potatoes
1 onion, sliced
1 stick celery, chopped
1oz (25gm) butter
1 pint (approximately $\frac{1}{2}$ litre)
stock or water
salt and pepper
$\frac{1}{4}$ pint (125ml) milk**

1. Peel and slice potatoes.
2. Fry onion and celery in melted
butter till transparent.
3. Add stock or water, potato,
salt and pepper.
4. Simmer gently for 20 minutes
till vegetables are tender.
5. Sieve or liquidize soup and
adjust seasoning.
6. Add milk and reheat without
boiling.

EMPRESS SOUP
Serves 4–6

**1lb ($\frac{1}{2}$ kilo) potatoes, quartered
1 large onion, sliced
$\frac{3}{4}$oz (18gm) butter
1$\frac{1}{2}$ pints (approximately $\frac{3}{4}$ litre)
chicken stock
1 bayleaf
salt and pepper
1 egg yolk
$\frac{1}{4}$ pint (125ml) cream
1 lettuce heart, shredded**

1. Fry potatoes and onion in hot
fat for 5–10 minutes.
2. Add stock, bayleaf and
seasoning. Simmer for 30–35
minutes.
3. Sieve vegetables and return
them to pan.
4. Combine egg yolk and cream,
stir into soup and reheat gently
without boiling.
5. Cook lettuce in boiling, salted
stock or water for 10 minutes.
Strain and add to the soup just
before serving.

BORSTCH
Serves 4–6

An impressive Russian soup.

**$\frac{1}{2}$ cabbage
2 medium beetroot or 3–4 small
ones
1 onion
2 large potatoes
2 carrots
2 parsnips
2 pints (approximately 1 litre)
meat stock
2 tomatoes
salt and pepper
soured cream**

1. Shred cabbage and grate
beetroot and onion coarsely. Dice
potatoes, carrots and parsnips.
2. Bring stock to the boil. Add
vegetables and simmer gently for
45–50 minutes.
3. Slice tomatoes and add after 30
minutes of cooking.
4. As soup is served, drop 1
teaspoonful soured cream into
each serving.

VEGETABLE AND CHEESE CHOWDER
Serves 4

**2oz (50gm) margarine
2 sticks celery, chopped
4oz (100gm) carrots, chopped
1 medium onion
2oz (50gm) flour
1 pint (approximately $\frac{1}{2}$ litre)
stock
$\frac{1}{2}$ pint (250ml) milk
2 large tomatoes, peeled and
sliced
salt and pepper
4oz (100gm) cheese, grated**

1. Melt margarine and fry celery,
carrot and onion for 4–5 minutes
until soft.
2. Stir in flour, stock and milk.
Simmer for 5 minutes.
3. Add tomatoes and seasoning,
and cook for a further 10
minutes.
4. Stir in cheese just before
serving.

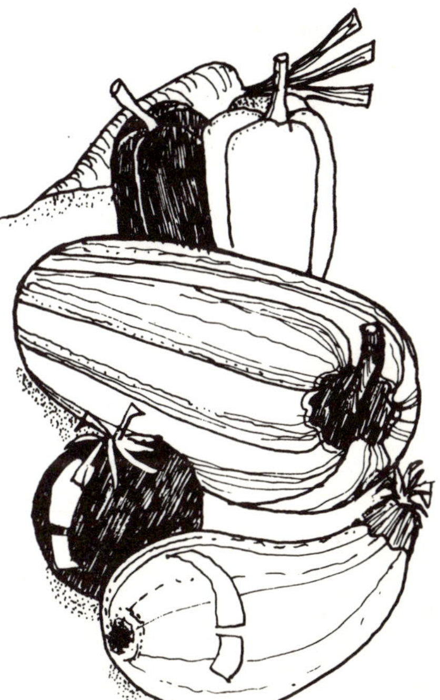

FINNISH SUPPER SOUP
Serves 6–8

6oz (150gm) carrots, sliced
4oz (100gm) peas
8oz (200gm) cauliflower
flowerets
1lb (½ kilo) new potatoes, diced
4oz (100gm) sliced green beans
3 pints (approximately 1½ litres)
water
2 level teaspoons salt
5½oz (137gm) chopped spinach
2oz (50gm) butter
1½oz (37gm) flour
1 egg yolk
¼ pint (125ml) milk
pepper

1. Put carrot, peas, cauliflower,
potatoes, beans, water and salt in
a large pan. Bring to the boil and
simmer, uncovered, for 5 minutes.
2. Add spinach and cook for
another 5 minutes. Remove from
heat and strain vegetable stock
into a basin. Reserve vegetables.
3. Melt butter in a large pan. Add
flour and cook for 1 minute.
Remove from heat and stir in
vegetable stock gradually. Bring
to boil, stirring.
4. Whisk egg yolk into milk.
Gradually whisk ½ pint (250ml)
hot soup into milk mixture. Then
slowly stir milk mixture back into
soup.
5. Add reserved vegetables to
soup and heat through. Do not
boil.
6. Add pepper to taste and extra
salt if necessary.

WINTER VEGETABLE SOUP
Serves 4–6

1 onion
3oz (75gm) mushrooms
1 parsnip
1 medium carrot
1 small turnip
2 sticks celery
4 Brussels sprouts
2½ (approximately 1¼ litres)
chicken stock
bouquet garni
6 peppercorns
salt and pepper

1. Finely slice onion and
mushrooms.
2. Dice parsnip, carrot, turnip
and celery. Shred sprouts finely.
3. Put diced vegetables and onion
into a pan and pour stock over.
Add bouquet garni and
peppercorns and season with salt
and pepper.
4. Cover and simmer for 15
minutes, then add sprouts and
mushrooms.
5. Check seasoning and continue
cooking for 10 more minutes.
6. Remove herbs and turn soup
into a hot tureen to serve.

STUFFED CABBAGE LEAVES
(Illustrated on page 71)
Serves 6

6 large white cabbage leaves
1lb (½ kilo) sausagemeat
1 large cooking apple, peeled,
cored and chopped
1 onion, finely chopped
grated rind of ½ lemon
1 teaspoon powdered sage
salt and pepper
1 can mulligatawny soup

1. Preheat oven to moderate to
to moderately hot, 375 deg F or
gas 5 (190 deg C).
2. Blanch cabbage leaves for 2–3
minutes in boiling water. Drain
and dry carefully. Remove the
thick stem.
3. Mix sausagemeat, apple,
onion, lemon rind, sage and
seasoning. Divide into six
portions, enclose each in a
cabbage leaf and secure with
cocktail sticks.
4. Place in a shallow casserole.
Pour the soup over the cabbage
and bake in centre of oven for
35–40 minutes.

PORK DOLMADES
Serves 4–6

1lb (½ kilo) belly pork, minced
4 lean bacon rashers, minced
2 large onions, minced
2oz (50gm) boiled rice (raw
weight)
garlic salt
pepper
½ teaspoon mixed herbs
8–16 large cabbage leaves
½ pint (250ml) stock
tomato purée
cornflour

1. Mix pork, bacon, onion, rice,
seasoning and herbs.
2. Drop cabbage leaves into
boiling water for 2 minutes, then
plunge in cold water.
3. Divide mixture into equal
portions and roll in sausage
shapes.
4. Wrap each in a cabbage leaf
and pack closely in a small
fireproof dish. Pour stock over
and simmer gently on top of
stove for 1 hour.
5. Drain off stock into a saucepan
and make up to ¼ pint (125ml)
with water if necessary. Add
tomato purée to taste and thicken
with blended cornflour.
6. Heat sauce, pour over cabbage
and serve.

BAKED CABBAGE LEAVES
Serves 4

A diet-conscious dish.

4 large cabbage leaves
3oz (75gm) butter
2 medium onions, chopped
6oz (150gm) calf's liver,
chopped
1 level tablespoon tomato
purée
1 tablespoon water
pinch of nutmeg
salt and pepper

1. Preheat oven to moderate, 350 deg F or gas 4 (180 deg C).
2. Place cabbage leaves in a saucepan, cover with water and bring to the boil. Remove from heat, leave for 5 minutes, drain and dry.
3. Melt 2oz (50gm) butter and fry onion till tender. Add liver and fry lightly for about 5 minutes.
4. Stir in tomato purée, water, nutmeg and seasoning. Leave to cool slightly.
5. Divide filling between cabbage leaves. Fold up tightly and place in an ovenproof dish.
6. Dot with remaining butter and bake in centre of oven for about 1 hour.

CREAMED CABBAGE BEAUMONT
Serves 4

1 medium cabbage
salt
2oz (50gm) chopped nuts
5oz (125gm) cheese, grated
½ pint (250ml) white sauce (see
Basic recipes, page 100)
breadcrumbs

1. Preheat oven to hot, 425 deg F or gas 7 (220 deg C).
2. Remove outer cabbage leaves. Cut into four. Remove core and shred cabbage.
3. Boil ½ inch water in a large pan and add salt and cabbage. Cover and cook over medium heat for 8 minutes until just tender.
4. Drain and place in a greased, ovenproof dish in layers, sprinkling each layer with nuts and cheese. Reserve a little cheese to top dish.
5. Pour white sauce over, cover with remaining grated cheese and a sprinkling of breadcrumbs, and bake in centre of oven until top is golden.

APPLE AND BEAN COLE SLAW
Serves 4

½ white cabbage, finely sliced
1lb (½ kilo) carrots, grated
10oz (250gm) mayonnaise
4 large, green eating apples
juice of ½ lemon
1 can (16oz or ½ kilo) baked
beans
1 can (12oz or 300gm) chopped
ham and pork luncheon meat

1. Mix together cabbage and carrot and bind with mayonnaise.
2. Core apples and make apple balls with a Parisienne cutter. Toss in lemon juice and mix with cabbage.
3. Arrange baked beans round the edge of a serving plate, with cole slaw in the middle and sliced luncheon meat on top.

CHEESE AND CABBAGE CASSEROLE
(Illustrated on page 54)
Serves 4

1lb (½ kilo) white cabbage,
shredded
½ pint (250ml) cheese sauce (see
Basic recipes, page 100)
2oz (50gm) cheese, grated

1. Cook cabbage in boiling, salted water till just tender. Drain and keep vegetable water for cheese sauce, if liked.
2. Make cheese sauce, stir in cooked cabbage and place in a greased, ovenproof dish. Sprinkle with cheese and brown under the grill.

STUFFED CABBAGE AU GRATIN
Serves 4

1 small green cabbage
3 tablespoons breadcrumbs
3 tablespoons sage and onion
stuffing mix
10 tablespoons hot water
2 hard-boiled eggs, chopped
3oz (75gm) luncheon meat,
chopped
2 teaspoons Worcestershire
sauce
2oz (50gm) cheese, thinly
sliced
2 tomatoes, sliced
parsley

1. Preheat oven to moderate to moderately hot, 375 deg F or gas 5 (190 deg C).
2. Hollow out the centre of the cabbage removing most of the stalk. Keep the centre cabbage to use for cole slaw or as a vegetable for another meal.
3. Plunge the hollowed cabbage in a pan of boiling, salted water and cook for 6–8 minutes. Remove and drain on absorbent paper.
4. Mix breadcrumbs and stuffing mix with hot water. Leave to stand for 5 minutes.
5. Add hard-boiled egg, luncheon meat, Worcestershire sauce and mix well.
6. Spoon into centre of cabbage and place in a shallow, ovenproof dish. Cover the filling with cheese and bake in centre of oven for 30 minutes.
7. Garnish with tomato slices and parsley.

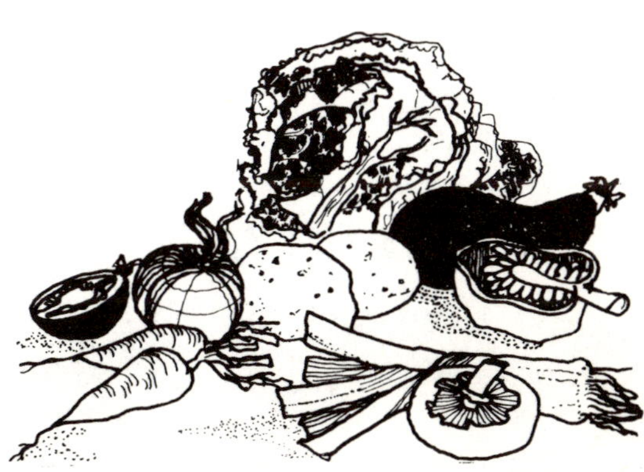

SAUERKRAUT CASSEROLE
Serves 4

2 sticks celery, sliced
2 onions, sliced
2oz (50gm) margarine
2lb (1 kilo) white cabbage,
shredded
1½ pints (approximately ¾ litre)
stock
2oz (50gm) brown sugar
¼ teaspoon cumin seeds
8oz (200gm) long-grain rice
8 large pork sausages

1. Preheat oven to moderately
hot, 400 deg F or gas 6 (200 deg C).
2. Fry celery and onion rings in
margarine.
3. Add cabbage with stock, sugar,
cumin seeds and rice.
4. Pour into casserole, cover and
bake in centre of oven for about
1 hour.
5. Grill or fry sausages and serve
on rice mixture.

SPICED RED CABBAGE
Serves 4

1lb (½ kilo) red cabbage,
shredded
4 tablespoons red wine vinegar
1 teaspoon salt
2oz (50gm) sugar
4 cloves
1oz (25gm) margarine
2 sharp dessert apples, cored
and thinly sliced

1. Combine all ingredients in a
saucepan and add ¼ pint (125ml)
water.
2. Cook, covered, over medium
heat for about 15 minutes or till
cabbage is tender. Stir
occasionally.
3. Serve hot or cold – it is
delicious with cold meats.

CAULIFLOWER BAKE
Serves 4

1 small cauliflower
2 eggs
4oz (100gm) cheese, grated
salt and pepper
2 tomatoes, chopped
½ pint (250ml) milk
4 slices toast, cut in triangles

1. Preheat oven to moderate to
moderately hot, 375 deg F or gas 5
(190 deg C).
2. Cook cauliflower in boiling,
salted water till tender then
drain. Divide into florets.
3. Beat eggs. Add 3oz (75gm)
cheese, seasoning, tomatoes and
milk.
4. Grease a 2-pint (approximately
1-litre) ovenproof dish and line
base and sides with toast
triangles.
5. Place cauliflower inside toast
and pour in egg mixture.
6. Sprinkle with remaining
cheese and bake in centre of oven
for 20–25 minutes.

CURRIED CAULIFLOWER
(Illustrated on page 71)
Serves 4

This can be eaten on its own or
served as an accompaniment to
ham.

1 medium cauliflower
2–3oz (50–75gm) butter
2 tomatoes, chopped
2 sticks celery, chopped
1 large onion, chopped
¼ pint (125ml) chicken or
vegetable stock
1 dessertspoon curry powder
1 tablespoon chutney
2 hard-boiled eggs, chopped

1. Cut washed cauliflower into
small sprigs. Blanch for 2 minutes
in boiling, salted water and drain
well.
2. Melt butter in a large frying
pan. Toss cauliflower in this for a
few minutes. Add tomato, celery
and onion.
3. Mix together rest of
ingredients, except the egg, and
add to pan. Cover and simmer
gently for 10 minutes.
4. Serve sprinkled with chopped
hard-boiled egg.

CAULIFLOWER AND CHEESE FRITTERS
Serves 4

1 medium cauliflower
4oz (100gm) flour
1 teaspoon salt
1 egg yolk
2oz (50gm) butter, melted
½ pint (250ml) warm water
1 egg white
2oz (50gm) cheese, grated
oil for deep frying

1. Divide cauliflower into sprigs.
Blanch in boiling water for 5
minutes, then drain.
2. Sift flour and salt in a bowl.
Make a well in centre and drop in
egg yolk.
3. Stir melted butter into warm
water, then gradually mix into
flour.
4. Beat to a smooth batter and
leave for about 30 minutes.
5. Whisk egg white until stiff, and
fold into batter.
6. Sprinkle in 1½oz (37gm) cheese.
7. Dip cauliflower sprigs in batter
and fry in hot oil till crisp and
golden.
8. Drain on soft paper. Sprinkle
with remaining grated cheese and
serve hot.

CURLY KALE CREAM
Serves 4–6

8oz (200gm) curly kale,
trimmed
1oz (25gm) bacon
1 onion
salt and pepper
2 pints (approximately 1 litre)
ham stock
2oz (50gm) flour
1oz (25gm) butter
¼ pint (125ml) milk
salt and pepper

1. Chop kale, bacon and onion
and cook gently in a soup pot for
about 10–15 minutes.
2. Add seasoning and stock.
Cover and simmer for 1 hour till
tender, then sieve or liquidize
mixture.
3. Return soup to pot and stir in
flour blended with butter and a
little milk to thicken soup. Bring
to the boil, stirring continuously.
4. Remove from heat. Add
remaining milk and reheat but do
not reboil.

KOBI DHALL CURRY
Serves 4

3oz (75gm) lentils
2 medium onions, chopped
oil for frying
1 level tablespoon curry powder
1 medium cauliflower, cut in
sprigs
2oz (50gm) salted peanuts
2 rounded tablespoons coconut
2 tablespoons mango chutney
$\frac{3}{4}$ pint (375ml) stock
juice of 1 lemon

1. Cover lentils with cold water,
bring to the boil and simmer for 5
minutes. Drain.
2. Fry onions in oil, add curry
powder and cook gently for 1
minute.
3. Add cauliflower, nuts, coconut,
chutney, lentils and stock.
4. Bring to the boil and simmer
gently until lentils and
cauliflower are tender but not
mushy.
5. Add lemon juice and check
seasoning.

GREEN BEAN SALAD
Serves 4–6

1lb ($\frac{1}{2}$ kilo) cooked green beans,
cut in 1-inch pieces
4 tablespoons French dressing
(see Basic recipes, page 100)
2 hard-boiled eggs, chopped
2 tablespoons chopped onion
2 tablespoons chopped celery
(optional)
half carton soured cream
$\frac{1}{4}$ teaspoon made mustard
salt and pepper

1. Toss beans in French dressing.
Chill for about 3 hours, turning
occasionally.
2. Mix eggs, onion and celery
together. Toss with soured cream
and seasoning.
3. Combine beans with soured
cream mixture and serve at once.

RUNNER BEAN PIE
Serves 4

1lb ($\frac{1}{2}$ kilo) runner beans
1oz (25gm) butter
$\frac{1}{2}$ bunch salad onions, finely
chopped
8oz (200gm) cooked ham,
chopped
nutmeg
white pepper
2 tablespoons stock
4 large eggs
shortcrust pastry made with
4oz (100gm) flour (see Basic
recipes, page 100)
white pepper

1. Preheat oven to moderate to
moderately hot, 375 deg F or gas 5
(190 deg C).
2. Slice beans and cook in boiling,
salted water until tender.
3. Heat butter in a pan. Add
onion, ham, seasonings and
stock. Cook till onion is tender.
4. Mix onion and ham with beans
and place in a greased pie dish.
5. Carefully drop eggs on top.
6. Cover with pastry and bake in
centre of oven for about 15–20
minutes till pastry is brown and
crisp.

NIÇOISE SALAD
Serves 4

A classic French salad, great on a
hot day.

8oz (200gm) cooked potatoes,
diced
8oz (200gm) cooked French
beans, diced
6 tomatoes, quartered
6 olives, stoned and chopped
8 capers
12 anchovy fillets
$\frac{1}{4}$ pint (125ml) salad dressing
1 lettuce

1. Mix all ingredients together
with the dressing and serve with
lettuce leaves.

**BROAD BEAN AND EGG
SCRAMBLE**
Serves 4

1lb ($\frac{1}{2}$ kilo) broad beans
1lb ($\frac{1}{2}$ kilo) mashed potato
4 bacon rashers
$\frac{1}{2}$oz (12gm) butter
6 eggs
salt and pepper
3oz (75gm) cheese, grated
2 tablespoons cream or top of
the milk

1. Cook beans in boiling, salted
water for 20 minutes till tender.
Drain.
2. Fork potato round edge of a
greased dish. Put beans in the
centre and keep hot.
3. Cook bacon in butter. Beat
eggs well with seasoning. Pour
eggs into bacon, add cheese and
stir over heat till eggs thicken.
4. Stir in cream or top of the milk
and continue stirring till
scrambled.
5. Add eggs to serving dish and
serve at once.

SPICED BEEF AND BEANS
Serves 4

1 dessertspoon oil
1 medium onion, chopped
12oz (300gm) chuck steak,
minced
1 large tomato, chopped
1 can (8oz or 200gm) baked
beans
scant $\frac{1}{4}$ teaspoon chilli powder
salt and pepper

1. Heat oil in pan and fry onion
till soft. Add beef and cook,
stirring, till meat is browned.
2. Add tomato and baked beans.
Stir in chilli powder and salt and
pepper to taste. Bring to the boil.
3. Cover and simmer for 15
minutes over gentle heat.
4. Serve with boiled rice.

PICNIC SALAD
Serves 4–6

1 large can baked beans
1 tablespoon chopped onion
2 tablespoons vinegar
½ teaspoon made mustard
2 tablespoons chopped sweet
pickle
6 Frankfurter sausages, cooked
and sliced
1lb (½ kilo) cabbage, finely
shredded

1. Combine first five ingredients.
2. Chill sausages and cabbage
separately.
3. Just before serving, combine
all ingredients and toss lightly.

BAKED BEAN FRITTERS
Serves 4

4oz (100gm) plain flour
1 level teaspoon baking powder
salt, pepper and cayenne
pepper
garlic salt to taste (optional)
2 eggs, separated
6 tablespoons milk
1 can (16oz or ½ kilo) baked
beans
olive oil for frying
8 eggs
4 bacon chops or thick rashers

1. Sieve flour and baking powder
in a bowl. Season with salt,
pepper, cayenne pepper and
garlic salt.
2. Add egg yolks and milk and
mix to a stiff batter. Add half the
baked beans and mix well.
3. Whisk egg whites till fairly
stiff and combine with batter.
4. Heat ½ inch oil in frying pan.
Drop batter in tablespoonfuls
into oil and fry till golden on
both sides. Drain.
5. Scramble eggs and grill bacon
and serve with fritters topped
with heated remaining baked
beans.

BEAN AND POTATO OPEN PIE
(Illustrated on page 71)
Serves 4–6

1½oz (37gm) butter
2lb (1 kilo) potatoes
a little milk
salt and pepper
¼oz (6gm) lard
1 medium onion, chopped
8oz (200gm) minced beef
2oz (50gm) mushrooms, sliced
1 can (16oz or ½ kilo) baked
beans
2oz (50gm) cheese, grated

1. Preheat oven to very moderate,
325 deg F or gas 3 (170 deg C).
2. Grease an 8-inch (20-cm) pie
plate with ¾oz (18gm) butter.
3. Cook potatoes in salted water
till tender. Drain. Mash and
cream with rest of butter and a
little hot milk.
4. Season. Line pie plate with
potato and bake in centre of oven
for 15–20 minutes.
5. Melt lard in a pan and fry
onion till soft. Add meat and
mushrooms and cook for a further
10 minutes. Fold in baked beans.
6. Pile mixture into pie plate,
sprinkle with cheese and bake for
a further 30 minutes till potato is
crisp.

BEAN BREAKFAST
Serves 4–6

A cold morning deserves this
bean bake booster start.

8oz (200gm) streaky bacon
2 cans (16oz or ½ kilo each)
baked beans
1 hard-boiled egg, sliced
4 slices bread, toasted and cut
in triangles

1. Make small bacon rolls and
place on skewers. Grill till cooked
then remove from skewers.
2. Heat baked beans and arrange
them on a serving dish. Heap
bacon rolls and sliced egg on top.
3. Place toast triangles round
edge of serving dish and serve.

SAUSAGE RATATOUILLE
Serves 4–6

A variation of a French favourite
using marrows and cucumber
instead of more expensive
aubergines.

1lb (½ kilo) pork sausages
1oz (25gm) cooking fat
4oz (100gm) mushrooms
1 medium marrow, peeled and
seeded
½ cucumber, peeled and diced
12oz (300gm) tomatoes, skinned
and chopped

1. Fry sausages in fat quickly for
2–3 minutes until golden brown.
2. Add mushrooms, then marrow
cut in ½-inch cubes, and cucumber,
and fry gently for about 5
minutes.
3. Add tomatoes and simmer
gently, covered, for 30 minutes.
4. Check seasoning and arrange
marrow mixture in serving dish
with sausages on top.

AFTER SCHOOL SAVOURY
Serves 4–5

1 medium marrow
1oz (25gm) butter
2 cans (15oz or 375gm each)
spaghetti bolognese

1. Preheat oven to moderately
hot, 400 deg F or gas 6 (200 deg C).
2. Peel marrow and cut into
even-sized rings. Scoop out the
centres.
3. Place in a buttered ovenware
dish, brush with melted butter,
cover and bake in centre of oven
until just tender.
4. Heat spaghetti bolognese in a
saucepan.
5. Arrange marrow rings on a hot
dish and fill the centre of each
with spaghetti bolognese.

MARROW AND MINCE
Serves 4

1 medium marrow
2oz (50gm) butter
1 large onion, chopped
6oz (150gm) mushrooms,
chopped
1¼lb (600gm) minced beef
pinch of mixed herbs
2 level tablespoons tomato
purée
1 teaspoon Worcestershire
sauce
salt and pepper
butter to grease foil

1. Preheat oven to moderately
hot, 400 deg F or gas 6 (200 deg C).
2. Peel marrow and cut top
section to make a "lid". Scoop out
seeds and discard.
3. Melt butter in a pan and fry
onion and mushrooms for 1–2
minutes.
4. Add meat and fry, stirring, till
browned.
5. Stir in herbs, tomato purée,
Worcestershire sauce and season
well.
6. Butter a large piece of foil, lay
marrow in centre and fill the
hollow with meat mixture.
Replace lid. Fold foil to enclose
marrow.
7. Bake on baking tray in centre
of oven for about 1 hour.

SAVOURY STUFFED MARROW
Serves 4

An economical marrow filling
using breadcrumbs to stretch
meat.

1 marrow (about 3lb or 1½ kilo)
1½oz (37gm) dripping
1 carrot, sliced
1 onion, chopped
8oz (200gm) minced beef
1 teaspoon thyme
1 egg, beaten
3oz (75gm) breadcrumbs
¾ pint (375ml) stock
3oz (75gm) cheese, grated

1. Preheat oven to moderate to
moderately hot, 375 deg F or gas 5
(190 deg C).
2. Peel marrow and cut a slice
from the top. Scoop out and
discard seeds. Season well.
3. Melt dripping in a pan and fry
carrot and onion.
4. Add beef and thyme and fry for
5 minutes.
5. Remove from heat and add egg,
breadcrumbs and stock. Mix well.
Pile stuffing into marrow.
6. Place on a baking sheet and
bake till tender.
7. Sprinkle with cheese and bake
for a further 10 minutes till
brown.

LEMON AND CUCUMBER COCKTAIL
(Illustrated on page 71)
Serves 4

A cool way of making an elegant
meal starter.

1 can (4½oz or 112gm) sardines
2oz (50gm) softened butter
4 lemons
6 teaspoons cucumber spread
freshly ground black pepper
1 egg white

1. Drain oil from sardines. Put
them in a bowl with butter and
mash together till well blended.
2. Remove top quarter of each
lemon and carefully remove flesh
and juice, keeping skins whole.
Add flesh only to sardines and
keep juice in a separate bowl.
3. Add cucumber spread to fish,
then season to taste with pepper
and lemon juice.
4. Whisk egg white till stiff and
fold through sardine mixture.
5. Pile in lemon skins and chill.

CUCUMBER ROLL
Serves 4

1 cucumber
1 tablespoon oil
salt
parsley
1½lb (¾ kilo) mashed potato
6oz (150gm) lean bacon pieces,
minced
3oz (75gm) cheese, grated
1oz (25gm) butter

1. Preheat oven to moderate to
moderately hot, 375 deg F or gas 5
(190 deg C).
2. Place cucumber on sheet of foil
and brush with oil. Sprinkle with
salt and add a sprig of parsley.
3. Seal foil and bake in centre of
oven for 40 minutes, until tender.
Remove from foil.
4. Increase oven setting to
moderately hot, 400 deg F or gas 6
(200 deg C).
5. Place cucumber in an
ovenproof dish. Mix potato,
bacon, 1oz (25gm) cheese and
butter together. Beat well and
spread over cucumber, making a
long hump.
4. Sprinkle with rest of cheese
and bake in centre of oven till roll
is golden.

SPINACH FLUFF
Serves 4

1lb ($\frac{1}{2}$ kilo) cooked spinach,
sieved
$\frac{1}{4}$ pint (125ml) thick white sauce
(see Basic recipes, page 100)
salt and pepper
4 eggs, separated
4 streaky bacon rashers, diced
2 slices of bread, diced

1. Preheat oven to moderately
hot, 400 deg F or gas 6 (200 deg C).
2. Mix spinach with white sauce.
Season to taste.
3. Whisk egg whites till stiff.
4. Stir egg yolks into spinach,
then add egg whites.
5. Pour into a well greased pie or
soufflé dish and bake in centre of
oven for 30–35 minutes until risen
and brown.
6. Meanwhile, render fat out of
bacon, by frying. Add bread and
fry till bacon bits are crisp and
bread browned and crisp.
7. Serve bacon and bread
scattered on spinach fluff.

SARLAT SPINACH
Serves 4

Perfect for invalids and suppers.

1$\frac{1}{2}$–2lb ($\frac{3}{4}$–1 kilo) spinach
salt and pepper
1oz (25gm) butter
4 eggs
4oz (100gm) cream cheese
1 carton (2$\frac{1}{2}$oz or 62gm) double
cream
cayenne pepper

1. Boil spinach till tender in
salted water. Drain well and mash
with seasoning and butter.
2. Divide between four greased
dishes.
3. Meanwhile, poach eggs till just
set and place in centre of spinach.
4. Cream together cheese and
cream and season with cayenne
pepper.
5. Spoon cheese round eggs but
do not cover yolk or all spinach.
6. Place under the grill to melt
cheese and brown the top.

SPINACH SOUFFLE
Serves 4

2oz (50gm) butter
2oz (50gm) flour
8 tablespoons milk
2 cans strained spinach
4 eggs, separated
salt and pepper

1. Preheat oven to hot, 425 deg F
or gas 7 (220 deg C).
2. Prepare soufflé dish securing a
strip of greased paper round the
top.
3. Melt butter in pan, add flour
gradually, then add milk; stirring,
bring to the boil. Add spinach.
4. Off the heat beat in egg yolks
and season.
5. Whisk egg whites till stiff and
fold into the mixture.
6. Put mixture in soufflé dish and
bake in centre of oven for 20–25
minutes.
7. Serve immediately.

CHESTER PIE
Serves 4

Three ideas for using leeks in
main course dishes.

8oz (200gm) cheese, grated
1 level teaspoon mixed herbs
1lb ($\frac{1}{2}$ kilo) potatoes
4 large leeks (white parts only)
salt and pepper
1 dessertspoon Worcestershire
sauce
4oz (100gm) flaky pastry (see
Basic recipes, page 100)
milk

1. Preheat oven to hot, 425 deg F
or gas 7 (220 deg C).
2. Mix cheese with mixed herbs.
3. Slice potatoes. Slice white
parts of leeks thickly. (Keep green
leaves for soups and stews.)
4. Cook leeks in boiling, salted
water for about 2 minutes. Add
potatoes and simmer till just
tender, then drain well.
5. Fill a pie dish with vegetables.
Top with cheese, season and
sprinkle with Worcestershire
sauce.
6. Cover with pastry, brush with
milk and bake in centre of oven
for about 25 minutes.

CAERNARVON EGGS
Serves 4

1lb ($\frac{1}{2}$ kilo) leeks
1oz (25gm) butter
1lb ($\frac{1}{2}$ kilo) mashed potato
salt and pepper
8 hard-boiled eggs
$\frac{1}{2}$ pint (250ml) cheese sauce (see
Basic recipes, page 100)
2oz (50gm) cheese, grated

1. Slice leeks thinly, then cook in
boiling, salted water till just
tender. Strain well.
2. Whisk butter in hot mashed
potato (cream can be added if
wished). Stir in leeks and season.
3. Arrange mixture in a border
round an ovenproof dish.
4. Cut eggs in halves or quarters
and pile in centre of dish. Pour
cheese sauce over, sprinkle with
cheese and grill till lightly
browned.

COTTAGE PANCAKES
Serves 4

1lb ($\frac{1}{2}$ kilo) leeks (white parts
only)
6oz (150gm) cottage cheese,
sieved
2oz (50gm) mushrooms, sliced
salt and pepper
$\frac{1}{2}$ pint (250ml) pancake batter
(see Basic recipes, page 100)

1. Preheat oven to moderate to
moderately hot, 375 deg F or gas 5
(190 deg C).
2. Wash leeks and cut in slices.
Boil in salted water till just
tender and drain well.
3. Mix leeks with cheese and
mushrooms. Season to taste.
4. Make 8 pancakes with batter.
5. Divide cheese mixture between
pancakes and roll pancakes with
filling inside.
6. Place pancakes on ovenproof
dish, cover and bake in centre of
oven for 15 minutes.

SPANISH VEGETABLE FLAN
Serves 4

shortcrust pastry made with
6oz (150gm) plain flour (see
Basic recipes, page 100)
8oz (200gm) leeks
2 large tomatoes, peeled and
sliced
salt and pepper
2oz (50gm) cheese, grated
1 carton (3½oz or 87gm) double
cream
8oz (200gm) cooked potatoes,
sliced

1. Preheat oven to hot, 425 deg F
or gas 7 (220 deg C).
2. Roll out pastry and line a
7-inch (18-cm) flan ring. Fill with
foil and baking beans. Bake
blind for 15 minutes.
3. Remove foil and beans and
bake for a further 7–10 minutes
till pastry is cooked.
4. Slice leeks and cook them in
boiling water for 5–10 minutes
until just tender. Drain well.
5. Arrange all but 6 slices of
tomato in bottom of flan case.
Season.
6. Arrange leeks on top. Sprinkle
with half the cheese and pour
cream over.
7. Arrange potato slices
overlapping slightly with
remaining tomato slices. Season
and sprinkle with remaining
cheese.
8. Bake in centre of oven at same
temperature for 30 minutes till top
is golden brown.

CURRIED VEGETABLES
Serves 4

2lb (1 kilo) leeks
1½lb (¾ kilo) carrots
2oz (50gm) butter
2 level teaspoons curry powder
1 level teaspoon curry paste
2 level teaspoons caster sugar
salt and pepper

1. Trim leeks to 1 inch above
white part. Slice thinly. Slice
carrots thinly.
2. Melt butter in a pan, add
carrots and coat in butter. Cover
and cook gently for 20 minutes.
3. Stir in leeks. Cover and cook
for a further 10 minutes.
4. Stir in curry powder, curry
paste, sugar and seasonings. Mix
well. Cook over high heat for 1
minute.
5. Reduce heat and cook, covered,
for a further 5 minutes.

WINDSOR ARMS LEEKS VINAIGRETTE
Serves 4

2 leeks (white parts only)
chicken stock
1 small onion, finely chopped
1 dill pickle, chopped
1oz (25gm) capers, chopped
1oz (25gm) parsley, chopped
salt and pepper
⅓ pint (170ml) olive oil
3 tablespoons wine vinegar

1. Split leeks in half lengthways.
Cover with chicken stock and
braise for 12 minutes in covered
saucepan.
2. Leave to cool, then cut into
2½-inch lengths. Place in a serving
dish.
3. Make a sauce by mixing
remaining ingredients together
and pour over leeks shortly before
serving.

ICED MUSHROOM AND CUCUMBER SOUP
Serves 4–6

A delicious soup for a hot
summer's day.

1 cucumber
salt
1 shallot
1½ pints (approximately ¾ litre)
chicken stock
3oz (75gm) mushrooms
1 dessertspoon arrowroot or
cornflour
¼ pint (125ml) cream or milk
1 sprig of mint, finely chopped
green food colouring

1. Peel cucumber and cut into
small dice. Sprinkle with salt.
2. Chop shallot and cook gently
in stock for about 15 minutes.
3. Add cucumber and 2oz (50gm)
mushrooms and cook until just
tender. Put through a sieve.
Return to the heat.
4. Blend arrowroot or cornflour
with cream or milk, pour into the
pan and bring to the boil. Boil for
1 minute then turn into a bowl.
Add mint and a little green
colouring, if liked.
5. Chill thoroughly and serve
garnished with remaining
mushrooms, thinly sliced.

MUSHROOM AND COTTAGE CHEESE HORS D'OEUVRE
Serves 4

12oz (300gm) mushrooms
2oz (50gm) butter
1 tablespoon onion, grated
1lb (½ kilo) cottage cheese
2 eggs, separated
salt and pepper
4 thin slices toast

1. Preheat oven to moderate to moderately hot, 375 deg F or gas 5 (190 deg C).
2. Butter four individual ovenproof dishes.
3. Reserve 4 whole mushrooms for garnish, and chop the remainder.
4. Heat butter and lightly cook the 4 whole mushrooms. Put to one side.
5. Fry chopped mushrooms and onion together for 3 minutes. Add cheese and stir in beaten egg yolks. Season well.
6. Whisk egg whites stiffly and fold into this mixture. Pour into individual dishes and bake in centre of oven for about 30 minutes or until mixture is set.
7. Put whole mushrooms in centre of each dish 5 minutes before end of cooking time.
8. Serve with triangles of crisp toast.

PINK CLOUDS
Serves 4

A delicious dinner party hors d'oeuvre.

8oz (200gm) small mushrooms
1 garlic clove
¼ pint (125ml) double cream, canned or fresh
2 tablespoons mayonnaise
4 tablespoons tomato ketchup
¼ teaspoon Worcestershire sauce
1 lettuce, shredded

1. Trim stalks and wipe mushrooms with a damp cloth. Cut larger ones in half. Pour boiling water over them and leave for 1 minute. Drain and leave to cool.
2. Chop garlic finely and squash with the blade of a knife.
3. Whip cream lightly. Stir in mayonnaise, ketchup, Worcestershire sauce and add garlic and mushrooms. Season to taste.
4. Place on a bed of lettuce in four individual glasses and serve chilled.

POTATO PANCAKES
Serves 4–6

Potatoes are the cheapest of vegetables and have infinite variety of serving ways.

1lb (½ kilo) mashed potatoes
3 eggs, well beaten
1oz (25gm) sugar
4oz (100gm) flour
3 teaspoons baking powder
½ teaspoon salt

1. Mix all ingredients into a smooth batter, adding a little milk if necessary.
2. Heat a heavy frying pan and fry spoonfuls of batter turning to brown both sides.
3. Serve hot with fried eggs, bacon etc.

HOLLAND HOTPOT
Serves 4

2lb (1 kilo) potatoes, sliced
2 onions, thinly sliced
14oz (350gm) Gouda cheese, grated
¼ pint (125ml) milk or stock
salt and pepper
2oz (50gm) butter, melted

1. Preheat oven to moderate to moderately hot, 375 deg F or gas 5 (190 deg C).
2. Place potatoes, onions and 12oz (300gm) cheese in layers in an ovenproof dish, topping with a layer of potato.
3. Moisten with milk or stock. Season and pour butter on top.
4. Cover and bake in centre of oven for 1½ hours.
5. Uncover, sprinkle with remaining cheese and bake for a further 30 minutes until golden brown.

POTATO BAKE
Serves 4

1lb ($\frac{1}{2}$ kilo) potatoes, thinly
sliced
8oz (200gm) tomatoes, thinly
sliced
2 medium onions, thinly sliced
1 teaspoon celery salt
salt and pepper
pinch of chopped chives
2oz (50gm) margarine
$\frac{1}{2}$ pint (250ml) cheese sauce (see
Basic recipes, page 100)
2oz (50gm) cheese, grated

1. Preheat oven to moderate to
moderately hot, 375 deg F or gas 5
(190 deg C).
2. Place vegetables in a greased,
ovenproof dish. Season, add chives
and dot top with margarine.
3. Bake in centre of oven for 1
hour.
4. Pour cheese sauce over
vegetables and sprinkle grated
cheese on top. Bake for a further
15 minutes till brown.

RAMEQUINS PARMENTIER
Serves 4

1lb ($\frac{1}{2}$ kilo) potatoes, peeled
salt and pepper
1 packet cheese slices
$\frac{1}{2}$ pint (250ml) pancake batter
(see Basic recipes, page 100)
fat for deep frying

1. Cut potatoes into thick slices
and season.
2. Place a layer of cheese between
two potato slices as if you were
making a sandwich.
3. Dip each sandwich in batter
and fry in deep fat, turning
occasionally, until pale golden
brown. Drain on absorbent paper.

POTATO CHEESE CASSEROLE
Serves 4–6

4oz (100gm) onion, chopped
4oz (100gm) celery, diced
3oz (75gm) butter
1oz (25gm) flour
salt and pepper
$\frac{1}{2}$ teaspoon dry mustard
$\frac{3}{4}$ pint (375ml) milk
4oz (100gm) cheese, grated
1lb ($\frac{1}{2}$ kilo) cooked potatoes,
diced
2 tablespoons buttered
breadcrumbs
6 bacon rashers

1. Preheat oven to moderate, 350
deg F or gas 4 (180 deg C).
2. Fry onion and celery in butter
till soft.
3. Blend in flour and seasonings.
4. Gradually add milk and cook
till smooth and thickened, stirring
continuously.
5. Add cheese and stir till melted.
6. Combine sauce with potatoes.
Place in a greased, ovenproof
dish, sprinkle with crumbs and
bake in centre of oven for about
25–30 minutes.
7. Fry bacon till crisp, arrange on
casserole and serve.

POTATO EGG CUTLETS
Serves 4

1lb ($\frac{1}{2}$ kilo) cooked potatoes,
sieved
4 hard-boiled eggs, chopped
1 tablespoon chopped parsley
salt and pepper
$\frac{1}{8}$ pint (63ml) thick mushroom
or onion sauce or thick soup
beaten egg and breadcrumbs
for coating
fat for shallow frying

1. Beat together potato, eggs,
parsley and salt and pepper to
taste.
2. Add mushroom or onion sauce
or soup to bind mixture.
3. Divide into even rounds and
form into cutlets.
4. Coat with beaten egg and
breadcrumbs and fry in shallow
fat on both sides. Drain on
kitchen paper and serve.

COLCANNON
Serves 4

This is an Irish variant of the
familiar bubble and squeak.

12oz (300gm) carrots
8oz (200gm) swedes
8oz (200gm) parsnips
1 tablespoon sugar
salt and pepper
1$\frac{1}{2}$lb ($\frac{3}{4}$ kilo) potatoes
a little milk
2oz (50gm) butter
2 tablespoons horseradish
cream
2 tablespoons brown
breadcrumbs

1. Preheat oven to moderately
hot, 400 deg F or gas 6 (200 deg C).
2. Prepare the vegetables and cut
into even-sized pieces.
3. Boil carrots, swedes and
parsnips for 25 minutes with
sugar and a little salt.
4. Add potatoes and cook for a
further 20 minutes.
5. Drain well and mash with a
little milk and half the butter.
6. Stir in horseradish cream and
add salt and pepper if necessary.
7. Place mixture in an ovenproof
dish, dot with remaining butter
and sprinkle with breadcrumbs.
8. Bake in centre of oven for 1
hour until crisp and brown on top.

BACON POTATOES
Serves 6

One of many ways of making
baked potatoes into a snack meal.

**6 large potatoes
salt and pepper
paprika
2oz (50gm) butter
2 tablespoons cream
8oz (200gm) bacon rashers
2 tablespoons chopped salad
onions or chives**

1. Preheat oven to moderately
hot, 400 deg F or gas 6 (200 deg C).
2. Scrub and dry potatoes, place
on rack or in tin and bake in
centre of oven for about 1½ hours
till soft.
3. Cut thin slice from top of each
potato. Carefully scoop out soft
potato.
4. Mash with salt, pepper, paprika,
butter and cream.
5. Chop and fry 2 bacon rashers,
then add them, with onions or
chives, to potato. Refill potato
skins and return to oven for 5–10
minutes.
6. Meanwhile, fry rest of bacon
rashers, roll up and serve on each
potato.

GREEN PEA SALAD
Serves 4–6

**1lb (½ kilo) cooked peas
4oz (100gm) green onions,
sliced
a few thinly sliced radishes
4oz (100gm) cucumber, diced
salt and pepper
salad dressing or soured cream
to bind**

1. Mix vegetables and chill.
2. Just before serving, sprinkle
with salt and pepper. Add salad
dressing or soured cream and toss
lightly till well combined.

VEGETABLE RISOTTO
Serves 4

**3oz (75gm) butter
1 large onion, chopped
8oz (200gm) long-grain rice
1 pint (approximately ½ litre)
water or vegetable water
2 packets (8oz or 200gm each)
mixed vegetables
1 dessertspoon Worcestershire
sauce
salt and pepper**

1. Melt butter in a large pan. Fry
onion till tender. Stir in rice.
2. Add water, bring to the boil
and gently simmer for 20 minutes.
3. Cook vegetables as usual.
Drain, add Worcestershire sauce,
and stir into rice.
4. Season, cover and cook for a
further 5 minutes. Serve at once.

PLOUGH BAKE
Serves 4

A casserole based on swedes.

**1lb (½ kilo) swedes, peeled
3oz (75gm) butter
3 medium onions, chopped
1lb (½ kilo) tomatoes, skinned
and sliced
juice of ½ lemon
salt and pepper
pinch of thyme
2 level tablespoons browned
crumbs**

1. Preheat oven to moderate, 350
deg F or gas 4 (180 deg C).
2. Thinly slice swedes and cut
into 1½–2-inch pieces. Boil in
salted water for about 7 minutes
till just soft. Drain.
3. Melt half the butter and fry
onion till tender.
4. Lightly butter a 1½-pint
(approximately ¾-litre) ovenproof
dish. Place half the tomatoes on
base.
5. Sprinkle ⅓ onion on top, a
little lemon juice, seasoning and
thyme.
6. Dot with ½oz (12gm) butter.
7. Put swede on top, repeat other
layers and dot with more butter.
8. Sprinkle with crumbs and dot
with rest of butter. Bake for 25
minutes in centre of oven.

SWEETCORN FLAN
Serves 4–6

**shortcrust pastry made with
8oz (200gm) flour (see Basic
recipes, page 100)
1 onion, finely chopped
1oz (25gm) butter
1 egg
¼ pint (125ml) evaporated milk
1 teaspoon made mustard
pepper
3oz (75gm) Cheddar cheese,
grated
1 can (7oz or 175gm) sweetcorn
4oz (100gm) streaky bacon,
grilled and chopped
1 tomato, thinly sliced**

1. Preheat oven to moderate to
moderately hot, 375 deg F or gas 5
(190 deg C).
2. Roll out pastry and line an
8-inch (20-cm) flan ring.
3. Fry onion in butter for about
10 minutes until soft.
4. Beat the egg, evaporated milk,
mustard and pepper together
until well blended.
5. Add 2½oz (62gm) cheese; drain
sweetcorn and add with bacon
and onion, mixing well.
6. Spoon mixture into pastry case
and spread evenly.
7. Sprinkle remaining cheese on
top.
8. Place slices of tomato in a line
across the top and bake in centre
of oven for 35–40 minutes, until
golden brown.
9. Serve hot or cold.

CHEESE AND CORN
RISOTTO
Serves 4

**1 onion, chopped
2oz (50gm) butter
6oz (150gm) long-grain rice
½ pint (250ml) chicken stock
8oz (200gm) Cheddar cheese,
diced
1 can (11oz or 275gm) sweetcorn
1 can (7oz or 175gm) chopped
ham and pork, diced**

1. Fry onion in butter and stir in
rice.
2. Add stock and simmer for 15–20
minutes.
3. Cut cheese into cubes and add
it to stock with sweetcorn and
chopped meat.
4. Heat through and serve.

STUFFED ONIONS
Serves 4

**4 medium onions
2oz (50gm) fresh breadcrumbs
6oz (150gm) Cheddar cheese,
grated
2oz (50gm) butter
salt and pepper**

1. Preheat oven to moderate to
moderately hot, 375 deg F or gas 5
(190 deg C).
2. Peel and parboil onions for 20
minutes.
3. Remove from pan and leave to
cool slightly. Take centres out
very carefully and chop them.
4. Mix with breadcrumbs and 4oz
(100gm) cheese.
5. Season and stuff the onion
cases. Put in an ovenproof dish,
dot with butter and bake for 45–55
minutes.
6. Sprinkle remaining cheese on
top of onions 15 minutes before
end of cooking time.

STUFFED ONION
DUMPLINGS
Serves 4

**shortcrust pastry made with
12oz (300gm) flour (see Basic
recipes, page 100)
1oz (25gm) long-grain rice
1oz (25gm) fat
4oz (100gm) cooked beef or
chicken
4oz (100gm) cooked ham
2oz (50gm) mushrooms
¼ pint (125ml) stock
salt and pepper
4 large onions
1 egg, beaten**

1. Preheat oven to very moderate,
325 deg F or gas 3 (170 deg C).
2. Divide pastry into four and
roll each piece into an 8-inch
round.
3. Fry rice in fat until well
browned.
4. Stir in finely chopped or
minced meat, ham and mushrooms
with stock, salt and pepper. Cook
gently until stock has been
absorbed.
5. Remove outer skin from
onions and, using a teaspoon,
scoop out the core of onion,
leaving an outer shell and base
about ¼ inch thick.
6. Fill the centres with meat and
rice.
7. Stand onions in centre of each
round of pastry, brush edges with
egg and completely enclose in
pastry.
8. Put onions into an ovenware
dish with seams underneath and
brush with egg.
9. Bake in centre of oven for 20
minutes. Cover with foil and cook
for a further 1 hour 10 minutes.

Desserts and drinks

Here are some eye-appealing and palate-pleasing desserts that cost little, together with some inexpensive ideas for hot and cold punches, ideal for parties.

PEAR AND STRAWBERRY MOULD
Serves 4

Stretch more expensive fruits with jellies and mousses.

½ pint (250ml) water
juice of 2 lemons
grated rind of 1 lemon
¾ level tablespoon gelatine
sugar to taste
vanilla essence to taste
2 tablespoons milk powder
2 ripe pears, peeled, cored and chopped
6oz (150gm) strawberries, halved

1. Place water, lemon juice and rind in a pan. Bring to the boil and remove from heat. Leave to cool.
2. Dissolve gelatine in a little water and add to pan with lemon.
3. Pour into a bowl and allow to become cold. Whisk in sugar, vanilla essence and milk powder. Chill till beginning to set.
4. Whisk till thick and foamy.
5. Add fruit. Pour into mould and allow to set.

RASPBERRY MOUSSE
Serves 4

1 can (8oz or 200gm) raspberries
1 packet raspberry jelly
½ large can evaporated milk

1. Drain raspberries and dissolve jelly in juice over a low heat.
2. Sieve raspberries or put in a blender. Add to jelly and allow to cool.
3. Chill evaporated milk and whisk till thick. Add to jelly.
4. Pour into a 2-pint (approximately 1-litre) mould and chill till set.

CHOCOLATE SAUCE PEARS
Serves 4

Three ideas to present pears in a party dress.

8oz (200gm) sugar
1 pint (approximately ½ litre) water
4 firm pears, peeled and cored
4 tablespoons drinking chocolate
1 teaspoon cornflour
2 tablespoons milk

1. Bring sugar and water to the boil, stirring till sugar dissolves.
2. Stand pears upright in boiling syrup. Cover and simmer for 10–12 minutes till pears are just tender. Drain well and leave to get cold.
3. Measure ¼ pint (125ml) syrup from the pears. Pour into a pan and bring to the boil.
4. Blend drinking chocolate with cornflour and milk. Add to boiling syrup, stirring.
5. Return to pan, bring to the boil stirring continuously. Cook for 1 minute then leave to become cold.
6. Place pears on a serving dish and coat with cold chocolate sauce.

YEOVIL BAKED PEARS
Serves 4

2oz (50gm) sultanas
¼ pint (125ml) cider
4 firm pears, skinned, cored
and halved
½–1oz (12–25gm) demerara
sugar
½oz (12gm) butter

1. Preheat oven to moderate, 350
deg F or gas 4 (180 deg C).
2. Put sultanas and cider in a pan
and bring to the boil. Remove
from heat and allow to stand for
15 minutes.
3. Put pears in a shallow,
ovenproof dish. Pour cider and
sultanas in.
4. Sprinkle with sugar and dot
with butter.
5. Cook and bake in centre of
oven for 35 minutes or till pears
are tender.

RED PEARS
Serves 4

1 jar (1lb or ½ kilo) redcurrant
jelly
juice of 1 lemon
red food colouring
4 large pears

1. Melt redcurrant jelly with
lemon juice in a pan. Add a few
drops of red colouring.
2. Peel pears and cook slowly in
the jelly syrup for 30–40 minutes
until soft.
3. Drain pears and set aside.
4. Boil syrup till reduced to about
¼ pint (125ml) and pour over
pears.

FRUITY CHEESE CAKE
(Illustrated on page 72)
Serves 4–6

shortcrust pastry made with
4oz (100gm) flour (see Basic
recipes, page 100)
1 can (8oz or 200gm) pineapple
pieces
2oz (50gm) sultanas
2oz (50gm) raisins
grated rind and juice of 1
lemon
1 can (6oz or 150gm) cream
1 egg, lightly beaten
1oz (25gm) butter
2oz (50gm) caster sugar

1. Preheat oven to hot, 425 deg F
or gas 7 (220 deg C).
2. Roll out pastry and line a
7-inch (18-cm flan ring. Prick base
and bake blind in centre of oven
for 10 minutes.
3. Lower oven setting to very
moderate, 325 deg F or gas 3 (170
deg C).
4. Drain pineapple. Coarsely chop
pieces and mix with sultanas,
raisins and lemon rind.
5. Spread mixture over base of
baked pastry case.
6. Mix lemon juice, cream and
egg together. Cream butter and
sugar till fluffy. Add to cream
mixture.
7. Blend well together, pour over
fruit and bake in centre of oven
for 30–40 minutes till set. Serve
hot or cold.

APRICOT CRUNCH
(Illustrated on page 72)
Serves 6

8oz (200gm) dried apricots,
washed well and soaked
overnight
2oz (50gm) sugar
½oz (12gm) powdered gelatine
4 tablespoons water
1 small can evaporated milk,
chilled
4 cartons (5oz or 125gm)
natural yogurt
½oz (12gm) butter
2oz (50gm) demerara sugar
2oz (50gm) blanched almonds

1. Poach apricots with sugar for
20–25 minutes covered in water
used for soaking. Cover pan
during cooking.
2. Drain, liquidize or sieve with
4 tablespoons cooking liquor.
3. Dissolve gelatine in 4
tablespoons water over a pan of
hot water.
4. Whisk chilled evaporated milk
till thick. Whisk in apricots and
gelatine. Stir in yogurt. Spoon
into dishes and chill till set.
5. Make topping by heating
butter and sugar gently in a pan
till sugar dissolves. Add chopped
almonds, mix well and leave to
cool. Crush and sprinkle on top.

BAKED APPLE MERINGUE
Serves 4

2oz (50gm) butter
2oz (50gm) sugar
1 teaspoon concentrated
orange juice
4 cooking apples
2 egg whites
3oz (75gm) caster sugar

1. Preheat oven to moderate, 350
deg F or gas 4 (180 deg C).
2. Cream butter and beat in sugar
and orange juice.
3. Core apples and score a line
through skin around the centre.
Place on baking sheet and fill
centres with butter mixture.
4. Bake in centre of oven for
25–35 minutes until almost
cooked. Reduce oven setting to
cool, 300 deg F or gas 2 (150 deg
C).
5. Remove top half of skin.
6. Whisk egg whites until stiff,
then whisk in sugar gently. Pile
over top of apples and cook in
oven for about 30 minutes till
lightly browned.

RAISIN LATTICE PIE
Serves 4–6

**shortcrust pastry made with
8oz (200gm) flour (see Basic
recipes, page 100)
1 egg white
2 medium oranges
1oz (25gm) cornflour
8oz (200gm) stoned raisins
2oz (50gm) brown sugar
2oz (50gm) butter**

1. Preheat oven to moderately
hot, 400 deg F or gas 6 (200 deg
C).
2. Line a 9-inch (23-cm) sandwich
tin with ¾ pastry. Roll rest into
six ½-inch strips.
3. Damp pastry edges with egg
white.
4. Grate rind of oranges, squeeze
juice and make up to ½ pint
(250ml) with water.
5. Blend cornflour with 2
tablespoons orange liquid.
6. Boil remainder with raisins
and sugar.
7. Thicken with cornflour mixture
and reboil.
8. Add butter and orange rind and
leave to cool.
9. Pour into prepared pastry case.
Place pastry strips in a lattice
pattern on top.
10. Brush with egg white and
bake in centre of oven for 30
minutes.

APRICOT TARTLETS
Makes 12

**shortcrust pastry made with
6oz (150gm) flour (see Basic
recipes, page 100)
1 tablespoon custard powder
½ pint (250ml) milk
1oz (25gm) granulated sugar
1 can (15oz or 375gm) apricots
¼ pint (125ml) double cream**

1. Preheat oven to moderately
hot, 400 deg F or gas 6 (200 deg C).
2. Roll out pastry and cut into 12
3-inch rounds.
3. Line 12 patty tins with rounds
and prick with a fork.
4. Bake in centre of oven for
10–15 minutes until cooked, then
leave to cool on a rack.
5. Blend custard with 2
tablespoons milk. Boil remainder
of milk, pour on to blended
custard, return to pan and reboil.
6. Add sugar and stir well. Spoon
into cases and leave to set.
7. Drain fruit and arrange on
custard filling.
8. Decorate with whipped cream
and serve.

LEMON DELIGHT
Serves 4

Oranges and lemons make good
pudding flavourings when fresh
fruit is expensive.

**2oz (50gm) butter
3oz (75gm) caster sugar
grated rind and juice of 1
lemon
2 eggs, separated
2oz (50gm) self-raising flour
scant ½ pint (250ml) milk**

1. Preheat oven to moderate, 350
deg F or gas 4 (180 deg C).
2. Cream butter and sugar with
lemon rind and juice. Beat in egg
yolks.
3. Add sifted flour and milk. Mix
well.
4. Whisk egg white till stiff and
fold gently into mixture.
5. Pour into a greased 2-pint
(approximately 1-litre) pie dish
and bake in centre of oven for
35–40 minutes.
6. Turn out and serve – the top is
sponge and a lemon sauce is
underneath.

APPLE CREAM FLAN
Serves 4–6

**shortcrust pastry made with
4oz (100gm) flour (see Basic
recipes, page 100)
2 eggs
2oz (50gm) sugar
1oz (25gm) plain flour
½ pint (250ml) milk
vanilla essence
8oz (200gm) apples
1oz (25gm) caster sugar
2oz (50gm) apricot jam,
warmed and sieved
½oz (12gm) almonds, flaked
and browned**

1. Preheat oven to moderately
hot, 400 deg F or gas 6 (200 deg C).
2. Roll pastry into a 9-inch circle.
Line a 7-inch (18-cm) flan ring and
prick base.
3. Blend eggs, sugar and flour
together.
4. Bring milk to the boil and add
slowly to egg mixture. Reheat and
boil gently for 1 minute, beating
all the time.
5. Remove from heat and add
vanilla essence. Leave to cool,
stirring from time to time.
6. For topping, peel, core and
thinly slice cooking apples.
7. Spread custard in flan case.
Arrange apple slices in circular
pattern and sprinkle with 1oz
(25gm) sugar.
8. Bake in centre of oven for
about 30 minutes till pastry is
golden and apples tender.
9. Spoon apricot glaze over and
toss on browned almonds.

LEMON PUDDING
Serves 4

2 tablespoons lemon curd
4oz (100gm) butter
4oz (100gm) caster sugar
2 eggs
grated rind of 1 lemon
4oz (100gm) self-raising flour
little milk
extra lemon curd to serve

1. Butter a 1½-pint (approximately ¾-litre) pudding basin and put lemon curd in the base.
2. Cream butter and sugar and beat in eggs.
3. Add lemon rind and fold in sifted flour. Add milk to make a dropping consistency.
4. Put mixture in the basin, cover well with foil or greaseproof paper and steam for 1¾ hours.
5. Turn out and serve with extra heated lemon curd.

ORANGE CASTLES
Serves 4

4oz (100gm) butter
4oz (100gm) sugar
2 eggs
4oz (100gm) self-raising flour
grated rind of 1 orange
3oz (75gm) sultanas (optional)
1–2 tablespoons milk
pinch of salt
¼ pint (125ml) water
1 level dessertspoon arrowroot or cornflour
juice of 1 orange
2 level tablespoons sugar

1. Cream butter and sugar till light and fluffy. Beat in eggs one at a time with a little flour.
2. Stir in orange rind, sultanas (if used) and milk with a little flour.
3. Sieve in remaining flour with salt. Lightly fold into mixture.
4. Turn into eight or nine individual greased castle moulds. Fill to ½ inch from top. Cover tops with foil and steam for 45 minutes.
5. Add 1 dessertspoon water to arrowroot or cornflour in a small basin and blend till smooth.
6. Heat remaining water, orange juice and sugar till boiling. Pour over arrowroot or cornflour, stirring all the time.
7. Return to pan and boil gently, stirring, for 1 minute. Turn out castles and serve with sauce.

MARMALADE ROLY POLY
Serves 4–6

suet crust pastry made with 6oz (150gm) flour (see Basic recipes, page 100)
1 small cooking apple, peeled and chopped
1 tablespoon currants
½oz (12gm) grated orange and lemon peel
pinch of cinnamon
1oz (25gm) marmalade
1oz (25gm) brown sugar

1. Roll out pastry to an oblong 9 inches by 6 inches on a floured board.
2. Mix rest of ingredients together and spread to within 1 inch of pastry edge. Damp edges, roll up firmly (from longer side) and press edges together.
3. Wrap in greased greaseproof paper and pudding cloth and seal well.
4. Boil for 2 hours. Drain, unwrap and serve.

ESSEX PUDDING
Serves 4–6

A fluffy pudding, warming on a cold day.

4oz (100gm) caster sugar
3oz (75gm) butter
2 large eggs, beaten
5oz (125gm) self-raising flour
milk to mix
1–2oz (25–50gm) raspberry jam

1. Beat sugar and butter together to a smooth cream. Gradually add eggs, flour and enough milk to make a thick cream mixture.
2. Grease a pudding basin. Put jam at bottom and spread round sides.
3. Pour in mixture, cover securely and steam for 1½ hours.

DERBY PUDDING
Serves 4

Stale sponge cake with a meringue topping puts this in a 'special treat' class.

strawberry jam
stale sponge cakes
⅛ pint (63ml) apple juice
2 eggs, separated
½ pint (250ml) milk
3oz (75gm) caster sugar
vanilla essence

1. Grease an ovenproof dish. Spread jam liberally over bottom of dish and cover with sliced sponge cake.
2. Continue to layer jam and sponge till dish is nearly full. Pour apple juice over and set aside to soak.
3. Make a custard with egg yolks, milk and 1oz (25gm) sugar.
4. When cooked, flavour custard with vanilla essence. Pour over sponge and put aside to cool for 1 hour at least.
5. Preheat oven to hot, 425 deg F or gas 7 (220 deg C).
6. Whisk egg whites till stiff. Fold in rest of caster sugar and whip till firm.
7. Spread on top of sponge and bake until meringue is golden and set.
8. Serve cold.

CUMBERLAND PUDDING
Serves 6

2oz (50gm) butter
2oz (50gm) caster sugar
3oz (75gm) self-raising flour
pinch of salt
2 eggs
1 pint (approximately ½ litre) milk
4 tablespoons red jam

1. Preheat oven to moderately hot, 400 deg F or gas 6 (200 deg C).
2. Cream butter and sugar. Add flour, salt and beaten egg to make a smooth dropping mixture.
3. Pour into a greased, ovenproof dish and bake in centre of oven for 25–30 minutes.
4. Serve with melted jam.

CREPES NORMANDES
Serves 4–6

A classic recipe for a spiced apple dessert.

½ pint (250ml) pancake batter (see Basic recipes, page 100)
2 cooking apples
4oz (100gm) demerara sugar
cloves or cinnamon
caster sugar

1. Make pancake batter and leave it to stand for 30 minutes.
2. Stew apples with sugar and cloves or cinnamon to taste till tender.
3. Fry pancakes and keep hot over a saucepan of hot water.
4. Roll pancakes with 1 tablespoon apple filling in centre. Dredge with caster sugar and serve hot.

RICE PUDDING WITH RAISINS
Serves 4–6

4oz (100gm) pudding rice
2 pints (approximately 1 l tre) milk
2oz (50gm) seedless raisins
3oz (75gm) margarine
3 eggs
7oz (175gm) sugar
1 teaspoon vanilla essence
¼ teaspoon salt

1. Preheat oven to moderate, 350 deg F or gas 4 (180 deg C).
2. Mix rice with ¾ pint (375ml) milk in a double boiler. Cook till rice is tender, then add raisins and margarine.
3. Mix together eggs, sugar, vanilla essence, salt and rest of milk.
4. Stir into the rice then bake in an ovenproof dish for 20 minutes.

RICE PUDDING
Serves 4–6

1 large can condensed milk
1½ pints (approximately ¾ litre) water
3½oz (87gm) pudding rice
butter
grated nutmeg to flavour

1. Preheat oven to cool, 300 deg F or gas 2 (150 deg C).
2. Well grease a 2-pint (approximately 1-litre) pie dish.
3. Mix milk with water and pour into a dish.
4. Wash rice and stir into milk. Add a knob of butter and sprinkle top with nutmeg.
5. Bake in centre of oven for 2½ hours. Stir the skin in two or three times during the first hour of cooking to increase creaminess.

MAPLE RICE PUDDING
Serves 6–8

6oz (150gm) pudding rice
2 eggs, lightly beaten
8oz (200gm) maple syrup
½ pint (250ml) milk
nutmeg
¼ teaspoon salt
2–3oz (50–75gm) seedless raisins

1. Preheat oven to moderate, 350 deg F or gas 4 (180 deg C).
2. Cook rice in boiling water till tender. Drain well.
3. Mix eggs and maple syrup and blend well.
4. Stir in milk, nutmeg, salt, rice and raisins.
5. Turn into a greased casserole and bake in centre of oven for about 1 hour.

CHOCOLATE MANDARIN RICE
Serves 4

3oz (75gm) grated chocolate
1oz (25gm) butter
1 pint (approximately ½ litre) milk
vanilla essence
2oz (50gm) pudding rice
2oz (50gm) caster sugar
¼ pint (125ml) whipped cream
¼oz (6gm) gelatine, dissolved in 1½ tablespoons water
1 medium can mandarin oranges
2 level teaspoons arrowroot

1. Preheat oven to cool, 300 deg F or gas 2 (150 deg C).
2. Dissolve 2oz (50gm) chocolate and butter in milk. Add vanilla essence to taste.
3. Sprinkle washed rice in a pie dish and cover with sugar and milk. Stir gently.
4. Bake in centre of oven for 2 hours, then leave to cool.
5. Skim and stir in whipped cream and dissolved gelatine. Arrange in serving dishes.
6. Drain oranges, reserving juice, and arrange on top of rice. Dissolve remaining chocolate in ¼ pint (125ml) mandarin orange juice, thicken with arrowroot and pour over as glaze.

MACARONI SURPRISE
Serves 4

Macaroni, usually considered a
savoury ingredient, makes a
substantial sweet.

3oz (75gm) macaroni
1½oz (37gm) butter
1½oz (37gm) flour
¾ pint (375ml) milk
2½oz (62gm) caster sugar
2 eggs, separated
1 medium can apricots

1. Preheat oven to very moderate,
325 deg F or gas 3 (170 deg C).
2. Cook macaroni in boiling
water for 6 minutes. Drain.
3. Make a sweet white sauce with
butter, flour, milk and ½oz (12gm)
sugar.
4. Leave to cool, then add egg
yolks and macaroni.
5. Put into a 1-pint
(approximately ½-litre) ovenproof
dish. Add drained apricots.
6. Whisk egg whites till stiff.
Whisk in remaining sugar lightly.
Arrange meringue on top and
bake in centre of oven for 45
minutes till brown.

MINCEMEAT CUSTARD FLAN
Serves 4–6

3oz (75gm) butter
12oz (300gm) digestive biscuits
2oz (50gm) golden syrup
1lb (½ kilo) mincemeat
2 eating apples
2 tablespoons thick cream
½ pint (250ml) thick custard

1. Melt butter in saucepan. Stir
in finely crumbled digestive
biscuits and golden syrup.
2. Cook for a few minutes then
leave to cool. Mould into a flan
dish.
3. Heat mincemeat in a pan for a
few minutes. Grate apples into
the mincemeat, then remove from
heat.
4. When cool, spread over base of
flan, reserving 2 or 3 tablespoons
for decoration.
5. Beat cream into custard and
spread over mincemeat.
6. With the point of a knife, make
grooves in a 'spoke' design on the
custard. Fill grooves with rest of
mincemeat.

MINCEMEAT MARSHMALLOW FLAN
Serves 4

shortcrust pastry made with
4oz (100gm) flour (see Basic
recipes, page 100)
1½ tablespoons Guinness
12oz (300gm) mincemeat
8 marshmallows

1. Preheat oven to moderately
hot, 400 deg F or gas 6 (200 deg C).
2. Roll out pastry and line a
7-inch (18-cm) flan ring.
3. Prick base, line with foil and
bake blind in centre of oven for
10 minutes. Remove baking beans
and bake for a further 5 minutes.
4. Reduce oven temperature to
moderate, 350 deg F or gas 4 (180
deg C).
5. Mix Guinness with mincemeat
and spread evenly in flan case.
6. Heat through in the centre of
oven then arrange marshmallows
on top.
7. Grill until lightly browned on
top.

RHUBARB BETTY
Serves 6

2½oz (62gm) butter, melted
8oz (200gm) ¼-inch bread cubes
2oz (50gm) brown sugar
½ teaspoon nutmeg
1½lb (¾ kilo) rhubarb, chopped
8oz (200gm) sugar
1 tablespoon grated orange
rind
8 tablespoons desiccated
coconut

1. Preheat oven to moderate, 350
deg F or gas 4 (180 deg C).
2. Melt butter, add bread and stir
till crisp and golden.
3. Remove from heat. Stir in
sugar and nutmeg and cook,
stirring continuously, till cubes
are coated with sugar.
4. Put half the bread in a large
ovenproof dish and add half the
rhubarb. Sprinkle with half the
sugar and orange rind. Repeat
layers.
5. Mix remaining bread cubes
and coconut and sprinkle over
top.
6. Cover and bake in centre of
oven for 30 minutes. Uncover and
continue cooking till top is
golden.

SUMMER PUDDING
Serves 4–6

5 large thin slices white bread
2 packets frozen raspberries,
thawed

1. Remove crusts and line sides
and bottom of a 5–6-inch (13–15-cm)
pudding basin with bread.
2. Fill with raspberries and cover
with rest of bread.
3. Place a tightly fitting plate or
saucer on top, weight it and leave
preferably in a fridge overnight.
4. Turn out and decorate with
cream if wished.

FRIARS' FINGERS
Serves 3–4

6 slices bread and butter
2oz (50gm) jam
1 egg
1 small can evaporated milk
1 teaspoon sugar
2oz (50gm) lard or cooking oil
caster sugar

1. Make bread and butter into
sandwiches with jam. Trim crusts
and cut into fingers.
2. Beat egg, milk and sugar
together. Melt lard or oil in frying
pan. Dip fingers in milk mixture
and fry till golden. Drain.
3. Sprinkle with caster sugar and
serve hot.

BREAD AND BUTTER
PUDDING
Serves 4–6

8 slices bread and butter
3oz (75gm) marmalade
2 eggs
2oz (50gm) sugar
1 small can evaporated milk
made up to ¾ pint (375ml) with
water

1. Preheat oven to moderate, 350
deg F or gas 4 (180 deg C).
2. Spread 6 slices bread with
marmalade. Sandwich them
together and cut in triangles.
Arrange in layers in a greased
1½-pint (approximately ¾-litre) pie
dish.
3. Beat eggs with sugar and milk.
Strain mixture over bread and
leave to soak for 1 hour.
4. Cut 2 remaining slices of bread
and butter into triangles. Arrange
on top, butter side up.
5. Bake in centre of oven for
30–40 minutes till pudding is set
and top toasted and brown.

BRAPPLES
Serves 4

2–3 good-sized apples
few drops lemon juice
6oz (150gm) brown sugar
4oz (100gm) walnuts, chopped
4 thin slices white bread
and butter
butter

1. Peel, core and slice apples.
2. Mix with lemon juice, sugar
and walnuts. Arrange bread on
baking sheet. Pile apple mixture
on each slice.
3. Dot well with butter.
4. Grill slowly till sugar and
butter run together.

APRICOT BREAD AND
BUTTER PUDDING
Serves 4

4 thin slices bread
2oz (50gm) butter
4oz (100gm) dried apricots,
soaked for 24 hours, drained
and chopped
2 eggs
3oz (75gm) sugar
¾ pint (375ml) hot milk

1. Preheat oven to moderate, 350
deg F or gas 4 (180 deg C).
2. Butter bread and cut in 1-inch
squares.
3. Arrange in layers with apricots
in a greased 1½-pint
(approximately ¾-litre) pie dish.
4. Beat eggs, then stir in all but 1
level tablespoon sugar. Stir in
milk until well mixed. Pour over
bread and apricots.
5. Sprinkle rest of sugar over top
and bake in centre of oven for ¾–1
hour.

APPLE CHARLOTTE 1
Serves 6

One of 3 ways of making this
traditional bread-based dessert.

2lb (1 kilo) cooking apples,
peeled, cored and sliced
juice and grated rind of 1 lemon
6oz (150gm) demerara sugar
4oz (100gm) fresh, white
breadcrumbs
1½oz (37gm) butter, melted

1. Preheat oven to moderate to
moderately hot, 375 deg F or gas 5
(190 deg C).
2. Toss apples with lemon juice
and 2oz (50gm) sugar.
3. Mix lemon rind with rest of
sugar and the crumbs.
4. Place apple and crumbs in
alternate layers in an ovenproof
dish, finishing with breadcrumbs.
5. Pour melted butter over top
and bake in centre of oven for
40–45 minutes till golden brown
on top.

APPLE CHARLOTTE 2
Serves 4

8oz (200gm) cooking apples,
peeled and sliced
4–5 slices stale white bread, ½
inch thick
4oz (100gm) butter, melted
grated rind and juice of ¼
lemon
2oz (50gm) caster sugar
¼ teaspoon cinnamon
1 egg yolk

1. Preheat oven to moderate, 350
deg F or gas 4 (180 deg C).
2. Cook and mash apples.
3. Cut 2 bread circles, one to fit
base and the other to fit top of
1-pint (approximately ½-litre)
pudding basin.
4. Cut rest of bread into 1½-inch
fingers and dip in melted butter.
Line base of basin with smaller
bread circle and sides with bread
fingers.
5. Mix rind and lemon juice,
sugar and cinnamon with apples.
Beat in egg yolk.
6. Pour into basin and cover with
top circle of bread.
7. Cover with foil or greaseproof
paper, press down well and bake
in centre of oven for 1½ hours.

SPICED APPLE CHARLOTTE
Serves 4–6

6oz (150gm) white breadcrumbs
4oz (100gm) chopped suet
2oz (50gm) sugar
1oz (25gm) butter
2 tablespoons water
1½lb (¾ kilo) cooking apples,
peeled, cored and diced
2oz (50gm) brown sugar
1oz (25gm) sultanas or seedless
raisins
¼ level teaspoon cinnamon or
spice

1. Preheat oven to moderate, 350
deg F or gas 4 (180 deg C).
2. Grease a 2-pint (approximately
1-litre) pie dish. Mix breadcrumbs,
suet and sugar together. Press
three-quarters of it to bottom and
sides of pie dish.
3. Melt butter and add water,
apples and brown sugar. Heat
gently, stirring till apples are well
glazed but not too soft. Stir in
sultanas or raisins and cinnamon
or spice.
4. Pour into pie dish, top with
rest of crumb mixture and press
down neatly.
5. Sprinkle with a layer of brown
sugar and dot with butter. Bake
in centre of oven for 50–60
minutes till golden brown.

WALNUT BREAD PUDDING
Serves 4–6

4 large slices bread and butter
2oz (50gm) walnuts, chopped
3oz (75gm) sultanas
2 eggs
1½oz (37gm) caster sugar
¾ pint (375ml) hot milk

1. Preheat oven to moderate, 350
deg F or gas 4 (180 deg C).
2. Cut slices of bread and butter
in half and arrange in a 1½-pint
(approximately ¾-litre) pie dish.
3. Sprinkle on half the nuts and
sultanas. Beat eggs and sugar and
add hot milk. Pour over bread.
4. Add remaining nuts and
sultanas and bake in centre of
oven for 45 minutes.

**JAMAICAN BREAD
PUDDING**
Serves 4–6

3oz (75gm) butter
9 thin slices bread, crusts
removed
3 bananas, sliced
3oz (75gm) raisins
3½oz (87gm) demerara sugar
1 pint (approximately ½ litre)
milk
2 eggs, beaten

1. Preheat oven to moderate, 350
deg F or gas 4 (180 deg C).
2. Butter bread. Arrange 2 slices
in the bottom of a greased, 2½-pint
(approximately 1¼-litre) ovenproof
dish. Top with 1 sliced banana,
1oz (25gm) raisins and 1oz (25gm)
demerara sugar. Repeat layers
twice more, reserving ½oz (12gm)
sugar.
3. Cut remaining bread slices into
triangles and arrange, butter side
up, on top.
4. Mix milk and eggs and pour
over pudding. Sprinkle with rest
of sugar and bake in centre of
oven for 50 minutes till pudding is
set and top golden.

STAR PUDDING
Serves 4–5

4oz (100gm) butter
2oz (50gm) soft brown sugar
6oz (150gm) fresh breadcrumbs
1½lb (¾ kilo) gooseberries,
cooked and drained

1. Put butter and 1oz (25gm)
sugar into a pan and heat till
melted. Add breadcrumbs and fry
till crisp and golden.
2. Leave to cool and stir in rest of
sugar.
3. Place alternate layers of
crumbs and gooseberries in a
serving dish, beginning and
ending with a layer of crumbs.
4. Chill well and serve with
cream.

QUEEN OF PUDDINGS
Serves 4

1½oz (37gm) butter
1 small can evaporated milk
made up to ¾ pint (375ml) with
water
3oz (75gm) white breadcrumbs
1½oz (37gm) sugar
grated rind of 1 lemon
2 eggs, separated
2 tablespoons redcurrant jelly
2oz (50gm) caster sugar

1. Preheat oven to very moderate,
325 deg F or gas 3 (170 deg C).
2. Melt butter in milk and bring
to the boil. Pour over
breadcrumbs, sugar and lemon
rind, stir and leave to cool.
3. Add egg yolks and mix well.
4. Pour into a greased, 1½-pint
(approximately ¾-litre) pie dish
and bake in centre of oven for
15–20 minutes till set.
5. Reduce oven temperature to
cool, 275 deg F or gas 1 (140 deg
C).
6. Melt redcurrant jelly and
spread on top of pudding. Whisk
egg whites stiffly and fold in the
sugar.
7. Spoon meringue on top of
pudding and bake in centre of
oven for 30 minutes till set.

BROWN BREAD MOUSSE
Serves 4

½ pint (250ml) milk
2 eggs, separated
2oz (50gm) caster sugar
vanilla essence
4oz (100gm) brown
breadcrumbs
2 level teaspoons gelatine
2 tablespoons water

1. Heat milk and whisk into egg
yolks and sugar. Cook gently (do
not boil) till it thickens, stirring
continuously.
2. Add vanilla essence to taste,
then leave to cool and stir in
breadcrumbs.
3. Dissolve gelatine in water over
a pan of hot water and stir into
mixture.
4. Whisk egg whites till stiff.
Fold into mixture and pour into a
wetted, 1-pint (approximately
½-litre) mould. Leave to set.

BAKED HONEY PEARS
Serves 4

1oz (25gm) seedless raisins
2oz (50gm) honey
1oz (25gm) white breadcrumbs
2oz (50gm) walnuts, chopped
4 large pears
2oz (50gm) apricot jam
1 tablespoon water
juice of ½ lemon

1. Preheat oven to moderate to
moderately hot, 375 deg F or gas 5
(190 deg C).
2. Mix together raisins, honey,
crumbs and half the walnuts.
3. Core pears, keeping base of the
pears intact.
4. Fill pears with honey mixture
and bake in centre of oven for 30
minutes till pears are tender.
6. Prepare glaze by heating jam,
water and lemon juice together.
Bring to the boil and simmer for 3
minutes.
7. Remove from heat and sieve.
8. Brush glaze on cooked pears
and coat sides with rest of
chopped walnuts.

SEVILLE PUDDING
Serves 6

4oz (100gm) plain flour
1½ level teaspoons baking
powder
¼ level teaspoon salt
4oz (100gm) white breadcrumbs
3oz (75gm) shredded suet
3oz (75gm) caster sugar
3 oranges
1 egg, beaten
8 tablespoons milk
2 level teaspoons cornflour
¼ pint (125ml) water
4oz (100gm) marmalade
2 teaspoons lemon juice

1. Sift flour, baking powder and
salt into a bowl. Stir in crumbs,
suet and caster sugar.
2. Grate rind from two oranges
and add, with beaten egg and
milk. Mix to a soft batter.
3. Grease a 3-pint (approximately
1½-litre) pudding basin. Peel all
oranges, cut in ¼-inch thick slices
and arrange some slices on base
of basin.
4. Cover with a layer of pudding
mixture, then a layer of oranges.
Repeat layers, ending with a
layer of pudding mixture.
5. Cover with greased foil or
greaseproof paper and steam for
2¾–3 hours.
6. To make sauce, blend cornflour
and water in a pan. Stir in
marmalade and lemon juice.
Bring to boil, stirring and simmer
for 5 minutes.
7. Serve separately with the
pudding.

CRUNCHY APRICOT PUDDING
Serves 5–6

1 can (30oz or 750gm) apricot
halves
4oz (100gm) butter
pinch of salt
1 level teaspoon cinnamon
¼ level teaspoon nutmeg
6oz (150gm) clear honey
6oz (150gm) bread, crusts
removed, toasted and cut in
¼-inch cubes
2oz (50gm) cornflakes

1. Preheat oven to moderate, 350
deg F or gas 4 (180 deg C).
2. Drain apricots, keeping ¼ pint
(125ml) of the syrup.
3. Put butter, salt, cinnamon,
nutmeg and honey in a large pan.
Heat gently and mix well
together.
4. Stir in syrup. Remove from
heat.
5. Add apricots, bread and
cornflakes. Toss all ingredients
together lightly.
6. Put in 2½–3-pint (approximately
1½-litre) ovenproof dish and bake
in centre of oven for about 30
minutes. Serve hot or cold.

APPLE AND RAISIN CRISPY
Serves 4

4oz (100gm) butter
4oz (100gm) brown sugar
4oz (100gm) rolled oats
1–2oz (25–50gm) raisins
1 can apple pie filling

1. Preheat oven to moderate, 350
deg F or gas 4 (180 deg C).
2. Cream butter and sugar. Add
rolled oats and raisins.
3. Place apple pie filling in an
ovenproof dish and put rolled oats
mixture on top.
4. Bake in centre of oven for
30–40 minutes.

PEAR AND GINGER CRUNCH
Serves 4

2 tablespoons custard powder
4oz (100gm) sugar
1 pint (approximately ½ litre)
milk
grated rind and juice of 2 small
lemons
6 pears, peeled, cored and diced
24 or 10oz (250gm) ginger
biscuits, crushed finely

1. Blend custard powder and
sugar with a little milk.
2. Heat rest of milk till steaming.
Pour over custard blend, stirring.
Return to pan and bring to the
boil. Boil for a few minutes then
remove from heat.
3. Add lemon rind and juice. Fold
in diced pear and allow to cool.
4. When cold, spoon some mixture
into base of tall glasses. Sprinkle
layer of biscuit crumbs over.
5. Repeat layers till glasses are
filled. Serve chilled.

LEMON CRUNCH
Serves 4-6

4oz (100gm) caster sugar
2oz (50gm) cornflour
2 small cans (5½oz or 137gm)
evaporated milk
4 eggs, separated
grated rind and juice of 2
lemons
6oz (150gm) ginger biscuits,
crushed
flaked chocolate to decorate

1. Mix sugar with cornflour and
blend with evaporated milk.
2. Gradually stir in ¼ pint (125ml)
boiling water. Pour into saucepan
and bring to boil, stirring.
3. Beat egg yolks, add to pan and
return it to heat. Cook for 2–3
minutes, stirring, but do not boil.
4. Add lemon juice and rind, and
leave to cool.
5. Beat egg whites to soft peaks
and fold into mixture, blending
well.
6. Spoon into sundae glasses with
alternate layers of biscuit crumbs.
7. Top with curls of flaked
chocolate.

DANISH APPLE CAKE
Serves 4–5

2lb (1 kilo) cooking apples,
peeled, cored and sliced
3 tablespoons water
sugar
4oz (100gm) margarine
4oz (100gm) dry brown
breadcrumbs or crushed rusks
2oz (50gm) sugar

1. Cook apples with water over
low heat. Add sugar to taste and
leave to cool.
2. Melt margarine in a frying pan
and add breadcrumbs or crushed
rusks and sugar. Cook, stirring
all the time, till crumbs are
browned. Stir off heat while
crumbs cool.
3. When cool, place alternate
layers of crumbs and apple in a
serving dish. Top with crumbs.
4. Decorate with cream and
redcurrant jelly if wished.

TOFFEE CRUNCH APRICOT SUNDAE
Serves 4

1 large can apricot halves
2oz (50gm) butter
1oz (25gm) golden syrup
1oz (25gm) sugar
2oz (50gm) rice krispies

1. Purée or sieve apricots.
2. Heat butter, syrup and sugar
till melted. Cook quickly until a
little will set if dropped in a cup
of cold water.
3. Mix with rice krispies. Place
layers of apricot purée and rice
krispies in serving glasses,
finishing with a layer of rice
krispies.

CHOCOLATE LIME WHIPPED SUNDAE
Serves 4

1 packet lime jelly
1 small can evaporated milk
½ packet chocolate biscuits

1. Dissolve jelly in a little boiling
water and make up to ¾ pint
(375ml) with cold water.
2. Cool and leave until almost
setting.
3. Chill evaporated milk and
whisk until thick.
4. Slowly add jelly, whisking
continuously until mixture is
thick and almost set.
5. Crush the chocolate biscuits in
a polythene bag and layer crumbs
and jelly mixture in tall glasses.
6. Chill and serve.

HOT CIDER TODDY
Serves 4

4–8 tablespoons whisky or rum
4 teaspoons sugar (optional)
2 pints (approximately 1 litre)
cider

1. Put whisky in a heatproof jug
and add sugar if wished.
2. Heat cider almost to boiling
point and pour over whisky.

ROYAL CINNAMON
Serves 4

1½ pints (approximately ¾ litre) milk
4 tablespoons drinking chocolate
a little cinnamon or pieces of cinnamon stick

1. Heat milk and stir in chocolate and cinnamon. Whisk well.
2. Pour into mugs. Sprinkle cinnamon on top or add a piece of cinnamon stick.

SPICY WHIP
Serves 4

This and the following are fine for late night winter drinks.

1½ pints (approximately ¾ litre) milk
2oz (50gm) golden syrup
grated nutmeg

1. Bring milk almost to the boil.
2. Stir in syrup.
3. Pour into mugs and sprinkle lightly with nutmeg.

MALTED HONEY NOG
(Illustrated on page 72)
Serves 4

1½ pints (approximately ¾ litre) milk
2 tablespoons honey
2 eggs
2 tablespoons malted milk beverage

1. Put all ingredients in a bowl. Beat well until frothing.
2. Pour into glasses and serve.

Note
The addition of a tot of brandy to each glass makes this drink a real luxury.

GLÜHWEIN
Serves about 8

An Austrian mulled wine and one of the cheapest drinks for a winter party.

1 bottle red wine
4 cloves
½ stick cinnamon
3oz (75gm) brown sugar
rind of ½ lemon

1. Place all ingredients in a pan. Heat gently but do not allow to boil.
2. Another budget idea is to add 1 pint (approximately ½ litre) strong black tea or water to make the brew go further.

HEATWAVE CUP
Serves 4–6

An apple wine type of mulled Glühwein recipe suitable to serve to welcome guests on a cold day.

2 tablespoons clear honey
1 bottle dry apple wine
small stick cinnamon
juice and rind of 1 lemon

1. Put honey in a saucepan.
2. Add apple wine and heat gently without boiling. Add cinnamon and lemon juice and rind.
3. Pour into jug or bowl and serve very hot.

EGG NOG
Serves 4

4 eggs, well beaten
2oz (50gm) sugar
1½ pints (approximately ¾ litre) milk, chilled
3 teaspoons vanilla essence
nutmeg

1. Beat eggs and sugar together.
2. Beat in milk and vanilla.
3. Serve in tall glasses sprinkled with nutmeg.

RASPBERRY MARSHMALLOW NOG
Serves 4

8 marshmallows
4 tablespoons raspberry jam or purée
1 pint (approximately ½ litre) milk, chilled

1. Melt marshmallows in a basin over hot water.
2. Add raspberry jam or purée, then pour in the milk and whisk well. Serve at once.

HONEY ICED CHOCOLATE
Serves 4

1 pint (approximately ½ litre) milk
4oz (100gm) plain chocolate, grated
6 tablespoons honey
4 tablespoons crushed ice
4 tablespoons whipped cream, fresh or canned

1. Heat milk to boiling point.
2. Blend grated chocolate with honey and add it to milk.
3. Pour into a jug, add crushed ice, then pour into glasses and top each glass with 1 tablespoon whipped cream.

BEERY FRUIT CUP
Serves 4

Beer and fruit together make an unusual inexpensive summer punch or party cup.

1 small can brown ale
2 small cans light ale
1 can (11oz or 275gm) apple juice
1 can (6oz or 150gm) grapefruit juice
juice of ½ lemon

1. Mix all ingredients in a bowl.
2. Chill and serve decorated with thin slices of lemon.

HAPPY PINEAPPLE
Serves 4

1 pint (approximately ½ litre) cider
½ pint (250ml) pineapple juice
½ pint (250ml) soda water
small pieces pineapple, mint leaves and pieces of red, soft fruit to decorate

1. Chill all the liquids.
2. Pour carefully into a large jug and leave froth to subside.
3. Add small pieces of pineapple, washed mint leaves and red fruit. If liked, thread pieces of the fruit on cocktail sticks and serve one on each glass.

RASPBERRY CIDER CUP
(Illustrated on page 72)
Serves about 8

1 lemon
½ pint (250ml) bottled raspberry syrup or juice from can raspberries
8oz (200gm) raspberries
1 bottle cider (2 pints or approximately 1 litre)
1 pint (½ litre) soda water
sprigs of mint
slices of unpeeled apple

1. Wipe lemon and slice thinly.
2. Place in a large jug or bowl and pour on raspberry syrup or juice.
3. Add raspberries. Soak for at least 1 hour before serving.
4. Pour on cider, soda water and add mint and apple slices. Stir well, add ice and serve.

CIDER LADY'S FINGER
Serves about 8

1 pint (approximately ½ litre) cider, chilled
½ pint (250ml) pineapple juice, chilled
¼ pint (125ml) grapefruit juice, chilled
maraschino cherries
1 tablespoon maraschino-flavoured syrup
½ unpeeled rosy apple, thinly sliced
2 pineapple rings, cut into small chunks
2 strips orange peel

1. Pour cider and fruit juices into a large bowl.
2. Add remaining ingredients, stir and serve.

TEA ORCHARD PUNCH
Serves about 8

Everyday tea makes a surprisingly good and refreshing hot or cold party or picnic drink.

1oz (25gm) tea
1 pint (approximately ½ litre) water
4oz (100gm) caster sugar
1 pint (approximately ½ litre) pure apple juice
2 pints (approximately 1 litre) sweet cider
1 bottle (4oz or 100gm) cocktail cherries
1 dessert apple, cored and sliced

1. Steep tea in water for 12 hours then strain liquid.
2. Stir tea with sugar till dissolved. Add apple juice.
3. When ready to serve, add ice, cider, cherries, cherry liquor and sliced apple.

PEPPY TEA CUP
Serves 4

4 measures tea liquor (see previous recipe)
4 measures Pimms No 1 cup
ice
lemonade
orange
cherries
apple
cucumber
mint

1. Pour tea and Pimms over ice in glass mugs. Top up with lemonade to taste.
2. Decorate with long cocktail stick with orange wedges, cherries, apple slices and cucumber rings arranged on it.
3. Add sprig of mint to serve.

ORANGE TEA
Serves 4

crushed ice
juice of 4 oranges
1 pint (approximately ½ litre) tea liquor (see Tea orchard punch, this page)
lemonade

1. Put ice in glasses.
2. Pour in strained orange juice and tea.
3. Top up with lemonade and decorate with orange slices.

ICED MINT TEA
Serves 4

2 pints (approximately 1 litre) tea liquor (see Tea orchard punch, this page)
ice
thin slices of orange
thin slices of lemon
crushed mint leaves

1. Pour tea over ice in glasses or a bowl.
2. Add slices of orange and lemon and 5–6 crushed mint leaves per glass.
3. Sweeten if wished and mix well.

Basic recipes

FRENCH DRESSING

4 tablespoons olive oil
½ level teaspoon salt
¼ level teaspoon caster sugar
½ level teaspoon freshly
ground pepper
2 tablespoons white wine
vinegar

1. Put oil into a basin and add salt, sugar and pepper.
2. Whisk in the vinegar drop by drop and continue beating until mixture thickens slightly.

Variations
Add a few chopped fresh herbs, a little crushed garlic or a dash of mustard etc.

ASPIC JELLY
Makes ½ pint or 250ml

½oz (12gm) gelatine
½ pint (250ml) boiling water
¼oz (6gm) caster sugar
¼ level teaspoon salt
2 tablespoons tarragon vinegar
2 tablespoons lemon juice

1. Dissolve gelatine in boiling water. Add all other ingredients.
2. Leave to cool and thicken.
3. Use as required either before or after it has set as the recipe demands.

Note
Alternatively, thicken a can of consommé with approximately 2 teaspoons gelatine. Or dilute clear meat extract or a bouillon cube with ½ pint (250ml) water and add approximately 2 teaspoons gelatine.

WHITE SAUCE
Makes ½ pint or 250ml

½oz (12gm) butter or margarine
½oz (12gm) flour
½ pint (250ml) cold milk (or
milk and stock or water mixed)
salt and pepper

1. Melt the butter or margarine in a pan over a gentle heat.
2. Stir in flour and cook without browning for 2 minutes, stirring all the time.
3. Remove pan from heat and gradually beat in the liquid. Alternatively, add all the liquid and whisk thoroughly.
4. Return to heat and bring to boil, stirring well. Simmer gently for 2–3 minutes and add seasoning. If sauce is to be kept, cover it with greaseproof paper or foil to prevent a skin forming.

THICK WHITE SAUCE
Makes ½ pint or 250ml

Make exactly as for white sauce, above, but double the quantities of butter or margarine and flour used.

CHEESE SAUCE
Makes ½ pint or 250ml

Make up ½ pint (250ml) white sauce (see this page). After sauce has come to the boil and thickened, add 2–4oz (50–100gm) grated cheese and ½ level teaspoon mustard. Stir sauce over low heat until cheese melts.

SHORTCRUST PASTRY
Makes 8oz or 200gm pastry

8oz (200gm) plain flour
1 level teaspoon salt
2oz (50gm) lard
2oz (50gm) butter or margarine
cold water to mix

1. Sift flour and salt into a bowl.
2. Cut fats into flour with a knife.
3. Rub fats into flour with fingertips until mixture resembles fine breadcrumbs.
4. Add water little by little, stirring with a knife until mixture forms large lumps.
5. Bring mixture together with fingertips and knead lightly into a ball.
6. Roll out briskly on a floured board. Avoid stretching the pastry.

Note
Baking temperature: moderately hot, 400 deg F or gas 6 (200 deg C).

RICH SHORTCRUST PASTRY

Make as for shortcrust pastry, above, but sift the flour with ½oz (12gm) icing sugar and mix in 1 egg before adding the water.

Note
Baking temperature: moderate to moderately hot, 375 deg F or gas 5 (190 deg C).

CHEESE PASTRY
Makes 8oz or 200gm pastry

Use for savoury pies, canapé
bases, cheese straws and savoury
flans.

8oz (200gm) self-raising flour
1 level teaspoon salt
pinch of cayenne pepper
2oz (50gm) lard
2oz (50gm) butter or margarine
5oz (125gm) cheese, grated
1–2 egg yolks
cold water to mix

1. Sift flour, salt and pepper into
a bowl.
2. Cut fats into flour with a knife.
3. Rub fats into flour with
fingertips until mixture resembles
fine breadcrumbs. Add cheese.
4. Mix in egg, then add water
little by little, stirring with a
knife until mixture forms large
lumps.
5. Bring mixture together with
fingertips and knead lightly into a
ball.
6. Roll out briskly on a floured
board. Avoid stretching the
pastry.

Note
Baking temperature: moderate,
350 deg F or gas 4 (180 deg C).

SUET CRUST PASTRY
Makes 8oz or 200gm pastry

Use for steak and kidney
puddings, sweet puddings and
roly polies.

8oz (200gm) self-raising flour or
8oz (200gm) plain flour plus 2
teaspoons baking powder
1 level teaspoon salt
4oz (100gm) beef or mutton
suet, shredded or grated
¼ pint (125ml) cold water

1. Sift self-raising flour (or plain
flour and baking powder) into a
bowl with salt.
2. Add suet then mix in water
with a knife until lumps begin to
form.
3. Gather mixture lightly
together and knead until smooth.
4. Turn out on a floured board
and shape into a ball. Leave to
stand 10 minutes before using.

Note
Baking temperature: moderately
hot, 400 deg F or gas 6 (200 deg C).
Alternatively, steam.

FLAKY PASTRY
Makes 8oz or 200gm pastry

Use for pies, vanilla slices,
sausage rolls.

8oz (200gm) plain flour
1 level teaspoon salt
3oz (75gm) lard
3oz (75gm) butter or margarine
1 teaspoon lemon juice
water to mix

1. Sift flour and salt into a bowl.
Blend the fats on a plate and
mark into four portions.
2. Rub one portion into the flour
until it resembles fine
breadcrumbs.
3. Mix to a smooth dough with
lemon juice and water.
4. Knead dough lightly and roll it
out on a floured surface into an
oblong.
5. Dot two-thirds of the pastry
with second portion of fat.
6. Fold the bottom third up and
the top third over into an
envelope shape.
7. Allow pastry to relax for 10
minutes in a cold place. This is
especially important in warm
weather.
8. Repeat the whole process until
all the fat is used up.
9. Fold pastry in two, roll out to
¼–½ inch thick and use as
required.

Note
Baking temperature: hot, 425 deg
F or gas 7 (220 deg C).

Note
When using metric measures for
your pastry it will be necessary
to increase the amount of flour
to 225gm and other ingredients
proportionately, as 1oz is equal
to 28·35gm.

PUFF PASTRY
Makes 8oz or 200gm pastry

Use for vol au vents, bouchée
cases, patties, mille feuilles,
palmiers. It is essential to keep
everything including hands very
cold for this pastry.

8oz (200gm) plain flour
½ level teaspoon salt
8oz (200gm) unsalted butter in
a block or 4oz (100gm) cooking
fat and 4oz (100gm) margarine
mashed and formed into a
block
2 teaspoons lemon juice
6–8 tablespoons very cold water

1. Sift flour and salt into a bowl.
2. Chill the fat if soft. Rub ½oz
(12gm) fat into flour.
3. Mix to a dough with lemon
juice and water.
4. Roll out dough to twice the
length of the block of fat. Place
fat on dough and fold dough down
over it, sealing edges well with a
rolling pin.
5. Give pastry one half turn and
roll gently out into a long strip.
6. Fold dough in three, envelope
style, and leave, covered, in a
cold place for 30 minutes.
7. Repeat turning, rolling and
folding six times.
8. Leave pastry to relax for 30
minutes between rollings and
before use.

Note
Baking temperature: hot, 450 deg
F or gas 8 (230 deg C).

PANCAKE BATTER
Makes ½ pint or 250ml

4oz (100gm) plain flour
pinch of salt
1 egg
½ pint (250ml) cold milk
1 tablespoon oil

1. Sift flour and salt into a bowl.
2. Make a well in the centre and
break egg into it.
3. Gradually beat in half the milk
and continue beating until batter
is smooth.
4. Fold in rest of milk with oil.

Index